PRAISE FOR *HOW TO BE BOLD*

"Engaging and meaningful, *How to Be Bold* will keep readers turning the pages for more of its wonderful stories of courage, cowardice, and learning. Packed with insight about human psychology and organizational behavior, this exciting new book offers readers a path forward to become better leaders or simply to lead fuller lives."
—Amy C. Edmondson, Novartis Professor of Leadership at Harvard Business School, and author of *Right Kind of Wrong*

"In today's fractured world, leadership demands more than skill—it demands courage. Not the performative kind, but the steady conviction to do what's right when it's hardest. In *How to Be Bold*, Gulati offers a clear-eyed reminder that bold leadership is not reckless; it is principled, grounded, and deeply needed. For leaders committed to long-term value and societal impact, this is a timely and substantive guide."
—Paul Polman, business leader, investor, and philanthropist

"Some of the best decisions I made in my career were also the bravest. This is also true of many of the leaders, in many fields, that I have met over the years. This book gives the reader a pathway to becoming a better, bolder leader."
—Sir Alex Ferguson, former manager of Manchester United Football Club

"Courage is the hidden engine behind every meaningful innovation, every act of justice, and every human breakthrough. This remarkable book reveals that courage isn't some rare trait possessed by a lucky few—it's a muscle we can all strengthen. *How to Be Bold* is both a timely guide and a timeless call to action. In a world that needs more moral leadership and compassionate risk-takers, this book could not have come at a better time."

—Anand Mahindra, chairman, Mahindra Group

"In *How to Be Bold*, we're reminded that real courage isn't limited to the battlefield; it's found in the quiet, often unseen choices that define our character. This book offers a thoughtful, research-based look at how everyday acts of bravery can shape lives, teams, and communities. Its message resonates as powerfully in the context of military service as it does in everyday life."

—General James F. Amos, USMC (Ret.), 35th Commandant of the United States Marine Corps

HOW
TO BE
BOLD

ALSO BY RANJAY GULATI

*Deep Purpose: The Heart and Soul of
High-Performance Companies*

HOW
TO BE
BOLD

The Surprising Science of Everyday Courage

RANJAY GULATI

HARPER
BUSINESS

An Imprint of HarperCollinsPublishers

Without limiting the exclusive rights of any author, contributor or the publisher of this publication, any unauthorized use of this publication to train generative artificial intelligence (AI) technologies is expressly prohibited. HarperCollins also exercise their rights under Article 4(3) of the Digital Single Market Directive 2019/790 and expressly reserve this publication from the text and data mining exception.

HOW TO BE BOLD. Copyright © 2025 by Ranjay Gulati. All rights reserved. Printed in the United States of America. No part of this book may be used or reproduced in any manner whatsoever without written permission except in the case of brief quotations embodied in critical articles and reviews. For information, address HarperCollins Publishers, 195 Broadway, New York, NY 10007. In Europe, HarperCollins Publishers, Macken House, 39/40 Mayor Street Upper, Dublin 1, D01 C9W8, Ireland.

HarperCollins books may be purchased for educational, business, or sales promotional use. For information, please email the Special Markets Department at SPsales@harpercollins.com.

harpercollins.com

FIRST EDITION

Library of Congress Cataloging-in-Publication Data has been applied for.

ISBN 978-0-06-339481-0

25 26 27 28 29 LBC 5 4 3 2 1

To my parents, Satya Paul and Sushma Gulati,
who were my first role models of courage.
And to my wife, Anuradha, and my children, Varoun and Shivani,
who inspire me every day with their quiet acts of boldness.

All things are ready, if our minds be so.

— WILLIAM SHAKESPEARE, *Henry V*, ACT 4, SCENE 3

CONTENTS

FOREWORD BY HIS HOLINESS THE DALAI LAMA   xv
INTRODUCTION   xvii
ON COWARDICE   xxix

PART I: BUILDING YOUR COURAGE MUSCLES

Chapter 1: Coping   3

It's scary enough taking risks, but grappling with situations that are fundamentally uncertain is even more frightening. We can cope by building reassuring narratives about the world that make chaos seem more bearable.

Chapter 2: Confidence   29

Science shows that we behave more courageously when we truly believe that we're well equipped to accomplish our goals. To boost your confidence and in turn your boldness, don't just bolster your skills—take additional action to shift the situation in your favor.

Chapter 3: Commitment   50

The stories we tell about ourselves galvanize our courage, fueling our commitment and motivating us to sacrifice ourselves for a noble cause. The most inspiring stories of all are anchored in deep purpose and take the form of a hero's journey.

Chapter 4: Connection   67

Behind every Great Hero stands a team of helpful supporters. To build your courage muscles, work on fostering your connections with others, building a squad that can provide you with the emotional support, tangible resources, and feedback you need to excel.

Chapter 5: Comprehension   89

Radical uncertainty destabilizes us, to which our natural response is to freeze up. By learning to act our way toward more comprehension and clarity, we can prevent ourselves from becoming stuck and behave more courageously in the moment despite our fears.

Chapter 6: Calm   111

Dangerous situations can cause our fears to run wild. Some simple mental strategies can preempt this natural response, calming us and allowing us to behave more boldly.

PART II: LEADING FOR COURAGE

Chapter 7: Clan   129

To unleash collective courage, leaders can take team-building to a new level, creating far deeper connection and commitment. They can help people see the group as a close-knit clan or tribe that is a powerful extension of themselves.

Chapter 8: Charisma   154

We often think that heroic leaders have some mysterious, inborn charisma that the rest of us don't. In fact, any of us can learn to project charisma through our actions, harnessing it to inspire more collective courage.

Chapter 9: Culture   175

Most large organizations are designed for cowardice. You can remake your organization's culture to instill a courageous mindset and enable your people to behave boldly.

Epilogue   201

ACKNOWLEDGMENTS   209
THE COURAGE PLAYBOOK   213
NOTES   225
INDEX   277

FOREWORD

Courage is not the absence of fear but the ability to act with wisdom and compassion despite uncertainty. It arises from inner strength, patience, and a sincere concern for others. I believe courage is not limited to acts of physical bravery but is reflected in our willingness to stand for truth, practice forgiveness, and act selflessly for the well-being of all.

Fear and uncertainty often hold us back from making the right decisions. Yet, when we develop a calm mind and a compassionate heart, we can face challenges with clarity and confidence. Each one of us can nurture courage through compassion, reasoning, ethical action, and service to others.

This book explores how we can cultivate everyday courage—not through aggression, but through wisdom, resilience, and a deep understanding of our shared humanity. When we recognize our interdependence, our courage naturally expands beyond personal ambition toward the greater good.

May this book help readers to develop true courage in fostering the oneness of humanity.

The Dalai Lama
February 11, 2025

INTRODUCTION

One of the most courageous people I know wasn't a legendary explorer, activist, or soldier. She wasn't a Hollywood stuntperson or an astronaut or a firefighter. She was my mother. In India during the 1960s and 1970s, when I grew up, society was staunchly traditional. Men served as the breadwinners and heads of households, while women were expected to prioritize domestic roles, placing their husbands' goals and happiness above their own. Few women back then would have dared to separate from their husbands, forge their own careers, and use their life savings to start a business. But that's precisely what my mother did.

I was too young then to understand all the risks she took, but some were obvious to me—and quite stunning. I'll never forget a dramatic moment that occurred when I was a teenager. Having achieved a level of prosperity thanks to her business, my mother bought five acres of land in what was then a rural area outside of New Delhi, planning to use it as a weekend retreat. No sooner had she acquired the property than authorities announced plans to turn the area into a new township and build residences on it. Overnight, her farmland became much more valuable. A real estate developer approached her, asking if she would sell for an attractive price. She refused, telling him she didn't care about the money—she felt drawn to this particular property on account of its location close to her home. The developer became aggressive, threatening her with consequences if she didn't sell. Repeatedly, she declined.

One day, a stranger showed up at our home, introducing himself as a representative of the developer and asking to speak with my mother. He was a big, stocky guy dressed in a cheap, ill-fitting blazer. My mother initially refused to see him, but he pleaded that he only wanted five minutes of her time, and that afterward she'd never see him again. I showed him into our living room, and he took a seat on the sofa across from her. I watched from a nearby doorway as he took out a document from his pocket, placed it on the table in front of my mother, and glared at her. "I'm here to get you to sign this."

My mother glanced at the document and saw that it was a bill of sale. She pushed it back toward him. "I've already told your boss that I won't sell. Why do you folks keep wasting my time? I won't change my mind."

"I know," the man said. "I'm here to get you to change your mind. I have brought a check with me. We just need to agree on the amount. I'm not leaving until that contract is signed."

"Look, you can say anything you want. The land isn't for sale."

The man stared long and hard at my mother. Slowly, he reached his hand down and pushed back the flap of his jacket, revealing a revolver tucked into his belt.

I froze in terror. I thought of running over and tackling the man, but I did nothing of the sort. Instead, I played out the scene in my head, pondering the risk. How long would it take him to react? Would he fight back? If he did, would I be strong enough to take him? Could I wrestle the gun away from him without endangering my mother?

She, meanwhile, did something incredible. She stood up, walked over to the man, and slapped him—hard—across the face. "You think you can scare me with a gun? Get out of my house right now!" The man sat frozen in his seat, utterly shocked. She pointed toward the front door. "I want you out of my house this minute. And don't you come back. I don't ever want to see your face. Get up!"

Incredibly, the man did as she demanded. We never saw him again.

Later that day, I asked my mother about this experience and whether she was scared. "Scared of what?" she asked.

"The man had a gun."

"You know what?" she said. "No one pushes me around. This is my land. I earned it."

Knowing my mother, I'm sure that she experienced at least some trepidation in this particular moment. Still, she wasn't about to let it determine her behavior. Fearful or not, she made a deliberate choice to stand up to a bully. Having fought hard against traditional Indian gender roles, she regarded herself as a tough, decisive person who took charge of her own destiny. That understanding no doubt informed her actions.

As I'll argue in this book, what ultimately allows courageous people to take action isn't their lack of fear but their ability to make sense of situations in helpful ways, and also see themselves as strong, capable people who can control their destinies. Most courageous people experience fear just like any of us do. But they come to understand the world and themselves in ways that incline them to take action when it really counts. Courage is a learned behavior, not an innate one, and it hinges on our development of what we might call a *courageous mindset*. Any of us can become braver and more action-oriented at work and at home, but we must spend time understanding, analyzing, and modifying the mental frames we're using to make sense of our lives and the dangers we face.

I came to such insights through a circuitous route, beginning with my childhood observations of my mother and my reactions to them.

I felt awed by her boldness—I still do. But I also felt ashamed by my own, relative fearfulness. What was wrong with me? Why didn't I jump up and tackle that man with the gun? Why did I tend to shrink from making other bold decisions, like raising my hand with a creative idea in class or challenging authority figures when they seemed to be behaving unjustly? As an avid athlete, I tended to hesitate or freeze up during clutch moments, fearful of disappointing my teammates. Why did that keep happening? My mother managed to conquer her fears, yet it seemed that I couldn't.

I struggled with fear for decades, although I did try my best to rid myself of it. During my twenties and thirties, I forced myself to take risks in hopes of proving to myself that I was more courageous than I knew myself deep down to be. I signed up for hiking expeditions in the Himalayas. I learned to fly an airplane and earned a pilot's license. I took up windsurfing. These activities were fun and enriching, and they helped me overcome fears I had in other areas of my life. As I achieved difficult goals, I realized that many challenges I'd feared were actually quite attainable, fueling my confidence to take on new risks. In my professional life as well, I found myself gradually feeling stronger and more capable of stepping up into situations that required moral courage. Ringing in my head was always my mother's exhortation: be bold!

Over decades, then, I sort of stumbled my way toward becoming bolder—still not as courageous as I aspired to be, but much better. I also wondered if there might have been a quicker, more efficient way of getting to boldness. As I discovered, the answer was yes.

In the wake of the financial crisis of 2008, my colleagues Nitin Nohria and Franz Wohlgezogen and I undertook a study that explored how companies operated during difficult economic times. Our goal: to figure out which approaches to managing through a crisis worked best. Examining 4,700 public companies during three previous recessions, we were intrigued to find that a small group—about

9 percent of companies—emerged from each recession in stronger shape than they had been before it.

You might think that these companies were more careful and conservative in their approach than others, but that wasn't the case. As our statistical analysis showed, these companies thrived because they behaved *more* boldly than their peers. They resisted the urge, usually triggered by a fear of failure, to retrench when faced with adversity—a response that in the business world often translates into slashing budgets and workforces. These firms cut costs, surely—but at the same time, they took risks and invested in growth despite the challenging circumstances. Without intending to per se, we had wound up documenting the significant difference that courage makes in business.

Following this study, I began to consider more seriously why some companies and people managed to transcend their fears while others didn't. For people, this question might seem to have a simple answer: character or temperament? Philosophers as far back as Socrates, Plato, Aristotle, and Mencius perceived courage as an innate virtue, an outgrowth of the hero's "courageous disposition." Scholars as well as the general public have long recognized individuals like Napoleon, General Patton, Joan of Arc, or Florence Nightingale as quintessential examples of courage. They have tended to celebrate the valor of military men in particular; consider the strategist Carl von Clausewitz, who remarked in his 1832 tome, *On War,* that "[w]ar is the province of danger, and therefore courage above all things is the first quality of a warrior."

Yet I suspected that personality couldn't be the whole answer for why some people behave more courageously than others. Trained as a sociologist, I had learned to explain human behavior by studying not only individuals per se—their talents and personalities—but the social situations in which they're placed, and in particular, how those situations shape our perceptions of ourselves and others. Although we do have some ability to choose our environment and at times transcend it, popular notions of a courageous temperament seemed overly simple. Was it *really* just innate disposition that prompted certain people to overcome their fears and take bold action, or was it perhaps some more complex interaction between themselves and the specific situations they faced? Recognizing that some heroes have no track record of bravery, I wondered if courageous acts reflected how people made sense of their particular situation and their role in the moment. It seemed that something about those two factors might best explain their actions.

I spent a decade researching cases in which people in diverse settings felt energized to hang in there, act, and succeed in the face of fear. Some of these individuals had jobs or careers that were inherently dangerous, but many were everyday people like my mother who had found a need to behave boldly and rose to the challenge. My research assistants and I sometimes looked at extreme situations that had a large impact, recognizing that even if most of us won't find ourselves in similar circumstances, the lessons we could learn would apply in more mundane settings too. Thus we interviewed leaders and employees who worked during Japan's 2011 Fukushima nuclear disaster to prevent nearby reactors from melting down. We probed the secrets of coach Nick Saban's massively successful football team at the University of Alabama. We spoke to a foot soldier on the front lines of the war in Ukraine. And we considered many business-related examples, interviewing over three hundred corporate leaders and entrepreneurs. Most of these examples eventually became Harvard Business School case studies that I taught in my classes.

Based on all this work, I concluded that courageous people are *those who willfully take bold, risky action to serve a purpose that they perceive to be worthy, usually in the face of an abiding fear.* Fear isn't an absolute requirement; after all, we might regard bodyguards willing to take bullets for their bosses as courageous even if these bodyguards weren't especially anxious in the moment. But much of the time, courageous people *are* afraid, yet they are undaunted, managing to find the strength to take action anyway, becoming everyday heroes.

This definition has the virtue, I think, of being quite broad. Courageous action can be deliberate, but it can also be something we do spontaneously in the moment. It can involve taking physical risks, but it also can entail making ourselves emotionally vulnerable to others; risking our social or economic standing for our moral beliefs; or publicly championing new and unorthodox ideas. Importantly, this definition also is value-neutral. A nuclear plant employee can behave courageously in saving her community from a nuclear meltdown, but so can extremists, gang members, or others who commit atrocious acts following a warped moral compass. They *think* they're serving a worthy cause, even if the rest of us don't. We can and must condemn their deeds in the strongest terms, but because these individuals might be fighting their fears and taking bold action, we technically can characterize their behavior—again, recognizing its depravity—as courageous.

In addition to helping me better understand the concept of courage, the case studies I examined shed light on the forces that helped to produce bold behavior. As I repeatedly saw, acts of courage were enabled by specific *stories* that individuals crafted about both themselves and the world, narratives that allowed them to assign meaning to uncertain, extraordinary, or otherwise bewildering situations. These stories often had to do with each individual's sense of identity, including the roles they played in life, the expectations they felt they had to live up to, and the ideals they set for themselves.

In both everyday and extraordinary situations, mental stories acted like mantras that allowed people to embolden themselves to take action. By crafting narratives, people could convince themselves that they had sufficiently reduced the uncertainty they faced to manageable levels; that they were adequately trained and equipped to face obstacles; that their risk-taking and self-sacrifice were legitimate given the higher cause they were serving; that they owed it to friends and colleagues around them to take risks; and more. Like all of us, the individuals I studied lived in a social realm of symbols, language, and culture. Their perception of the world, shaped by both their individual psychology and social context, helped to determine their choice to act.

For a good example of how the meanings we devise through stories can enable action, consider frontline doctors. During the COVID pandemic, Dr. Suma Jain, a pulmonary critical care specialist at Ochsner Medical Center in New Orleans, put her life on the line helping to manage an ICU overloaded by throngs of sick patients. Grappling with uncertainty about how bad the COVID pandemic would get, how long it would last, and how her team would manage, she soldiered on, focusing on the tasks at hand and serving as a resource and sounding board for anxious colleagues. "We had a lot of uncertainty, fear, and anxiety," she wrote of the pandemic's early days. "We had no idea what was coming for us."

Jain likened the experience to living through a devastating hurricane, which she had done during Katrina in 2005 and Maria in 2017. There was perhaps a tingle of anticipation at first, but then the proverbial storm bore down, and the uncertainty took hold. Later, as the pandemic dragged on, the fear of COVID led her and her colleagues to bargain with the virus. "If we stay home, maybe we can be protected. If we wear a mask, maybe we can be protected. If we get vaccinated, maybe we can be protected."

Although Jain's temperament might have inclined her to step up and face danger, her perception of her circumstances and her role within them also mattered. When I interviewed her during the summer of 2023, she cited the close relationships she had built with her fellow team members as a force for helping her act. It seemed unthinkable to her to walk away from her colleagues, many of whom she had known for years, just because she felt afraid. "We were a team," she said. "And there's something about this that I think does sustain you. We were all working together. It never even occurred to me to let people down. I just felt that responsibility."

Jain's identity as a doctor also inclined her to step up. She felt deeply committed to taking care of patients in their time of need—it was the very reason she had gotten into health care in the first place. "This is who we are," she said. "This is what we do." She took comfort in the technical training she had received, which prepared her to remain resilient in unpredictable situations, as well as her past experiences dealing with hurricanes and other crises. For these and other reasons, Jain didn't cave as colleagues became ill with the virus. She didn't hang up her white coat as the hospital struggled with shortages of supplies or rising death tolls. She overcame her fears and *acted*.

Having guts seems to be an instinctive expression of our character, but when you really look at it, it's more than that. Our conscious minds play a role as we, in dialogue with our social environment, shape and create what the world means to us and how we see ourselves in relation to others. The everyday people I studied managed feats of bravery not solely or even primarily because their gut instinct told them to. Indeed, their brains in many cases urged them to flee, not fight. Fortunately, these individuals had developed certain patterned ways of framing meaning that made fear seem less palpable or even largely irrelevant. Sometimes my research subjects weren't aware of how their meaning-making contributed to their gutsiness. Other times, they purposely shaped reality to support their boldness.

Observing their behavior, I became convinced that understanding their patterns of meaning-making had practical value. By nurturing specific patterns and adopting them as mindsets, I could prime myself to step up in moments of crisis and to sustain bravery for extended periods. I didn't need to take up risky hobbies to prove to myself that I had a courageous temperament, nor did I have to hang my head in shame and presume that I didn't inherit the courage gene from my mother. I could *train* myself to step up and behave bravely. By modeling my thought patterns after those that courageous people like my mother tend to adapt, I could become just as bold as they are.

The more I understood these ways of thinking, the more I realized that I couldn't keep them to myself. Many people feel inhibited by their fears and wish they could behave more boldly. They feel shame and regret as they look around and see others making gutsy decisions but feel incapable of doing so themselves. Without courage, as the organizational psychologist Adam Grant has taught us, we struggle to realize our full human potential. I suspected that a wide readership would feel reassured, as I did, at knowing that courage is accessible to us *all*—that it's an action rather than an innate virtue. Wouldn't it be amazing, I thought, if I could give people the tools they needed to speak up more at work, accept more stretch assignments, take more creative risks, express themselves more in their personal relationships, or fight harder for their beliefs?

—

How to Be Bold shares everything I've learned about courage, offering a science-based playbook for becoming bolder at work and throughout your life. Its premise is simple: when we take steps to prepare in advance for courageous action, and know how to maximize boldness in the moment, we position ourselves to take bold action when it really counts, despite our fears.

Before delving into my formula for becoming more courageous, what I call the 9 C's, I first offer some reflections on the enemy: cowardice. Exploring the powerful forces that all too often prevent us from behaving boldly, I suggest that you shouldn't feel bad, as I did, if you recoil in fear when facing danger. It's natural. And fortunately, it's also surmountable.

With this background in place, Part I of this book provides six strategies that we as individuals can use to develop a courageous mindset. The first four C's help us to build our courage "muscles" *in advance*, shaping meaning and our sense of identity in ways that will leave us better able to step up when situations that call for bravery arise. Describing the conditions that trigger our fears, I explore how we might preempt that emotional response so that we can take action. In particular, I discuss how we can work to navigate uncertainty, build up our self-confidence, frame our goals as heroic quests, and create a small group of supporters.

The next two C's help us to stay poised and courageous *in the moment*. Fear can be overwhelming and cause us to freeze when we confront danger face-to-face, no matter how prepared we may be. By learning how to make sense of chaotic situations through our actions, and by taking steps to regulate our emotions as they arise, we can fight our instincts and take action *despite* our fear.

In Part II of the book, I turn to what I call collective courage, examining how leaders can inspire entire teams and organizations to engage in bold action. Those of us who don't lead others should also pay attention to the three C's in this part, since they can help us to choose leaders, teams, and organizations that will help inspire and enable our courage rather than squelch it. The epilogue rounds out the book by reflecting on what it truly takes in terms of time and commitment to cultivate everyday courage.

Courage is a universal virtue, valued and celebrated across time periods and cultures. But if there was ever a time to enhance our ability to control or manage fear and show more everyday courage, this is it. As the leadership scholar Warren Bennis once reportedly remarked, "Courage is the 'X' factor that can make or break corporate America." Today that X factor can make or break all of us in our personal and professional lives, and it can make or break society. To make progress on big problems like climate change, economic inequality, or political polarization, we need people to coalesce at every level, fired up to achieve unimaginable feats. That's not to say that we should take any and all risks: left unchecked, courage can verge into a recklessness that causes problems of its own. But most of us tend to be too cowardly, not too reckless. A bit more boldness can do a lot of good, both for us individually and in the wider world.

Most of us have at least some mental habits in place that prime us for gutsiness. But we seldom lean into them, nor do we recognize the full range of strategies available to us. We don't acknowledge, examine, or control the meanings we create as we move through the world. Imagine if we did. By consciously shaping how we perceive ourselves and the world, we can steel ourselves in the face of everyday challenges and behave more boldly. We can become the heroes of our own lives.

ON COWARDICE

If you haven't lived through a natural disaster, you might wonder how you would respond if an earthquake struck or a tsunami blasted through your neighborhood. Would you put yourself in danger to help others around you, or would you panic and try only to save yourself?

Fan Meizhong, a high school language teacher in the Chinese province of Sichuan, knows how he handles such moments of acute crisis—and it isn't pretty. On the afternoon of May 12, 2008, Fan was at his school, doing his best amid hot and sticky weather to keep his teenage students engaged in a discussion of an eighteenth-century Chinese literary text. Without warning, a desk in the room began to shake, startling everyone. Fan thought it was an earthquake, probably just a minor tremor. He began to comfort the students, telling them to stay calm and that everything would be fine. But then the entire school began shaking violently. This wasn't a tremor—it was a massive quake!

Fan didn't hesitate. This valiant, committed teacher jumped into action—to save himself. Forgetting all about his students, he raced "as fast as possible" outside the building and then began crawling to safety at a nearby soccer field. When he arrived, he realized that he was the first person to make it out. As a few others began to appear, "the ground shook violently again. . . . I just felt that the end of the world was coming." The shaking was so severe that a nearby wall bordering the field "collapsed in a few seconds."

Miraculously, Fan's school building stayed intact. Sometime afterward, his students began to migrate outside, stunned. Fan asked them why they had delayed their exit, and they told him that they had been too scared to move and had taken refuge under their desks. They turned the question around: Why hadn't he stayed and helped them to evacuate?

Fan might have evaded the question or offered up excuses, but instead he leveled with them, explaining that where his own personal safety was concerned, he was a fundamentally selfish person. "I have never been a person who has the courage to sacrifice," he said. "I only care about my own life."

Fan later reflected that his decision to exit quickly had been an instinctive one. When danger strikes, his gut response is to get the heck out of the way. If his own mother's life were in jeopardy, he says, he wouldn't sacrifice his own well-being to help her. The only other person he would ever think to save in a moment of crisis might be his daughter. His attitude: "There's no point in me dying with you." Fan wasn't necessarily proud of his behavior, but he wasn't mired in shame either. He felt that all of us have limitations, and we might as well own up to them.

Although all of Fan's students survived that day, many others in the area weren't so lucky. Registering 7.9 on the Richter scale, the earthquake resulted in almost 90,000 people reported or presumed dead. Many children died across the region when their school buildings crumbled on top of them. At one middle school near Fan's, hundreds of students and teachers perished.

In the weeks after the quake, as China processed the tragedy, Fan became infamous on social media. Learning of his cowardice and selfishness, observers roundly denounced him, with one remarking, "I can't see any 'person' here, I just see a big 'me.'" A news report called him "the most hated man in China," with some bestowing the ignominious nickname "Runner Fan." A government official denounced him as "shameless." After Fan went on TV to defend himself, he was fired from his teaching job.

It is tempting to condemn Fan. Certainly *we* would have behaved more valiantly in similarly dangerous circumstances—or would we have? Despite whatever moral precepts we purport to follow, many of us are notable for our utter *lack* of courage in moments of crisis.

The concept of cowardice originated in the context of military conflict, referring to soldiers who panicked and fled their posts when facing mortal peril. The word *coward* derives from the Latin and Old French words for "tail"—as in a frightened animal "turning tail" and fleeing. Examples of cowards in this classic sense include knights who abandoned the crusading armies during the Middle Ages, the American Revolutionary War officer who was court-martialed for cowardice in 1775, deserters who hobbled the efforts of Allied forces in World War II during the North African campaign, and the American soldier who served prison time for deserting his fellow soldiers during the Vietnam War. European governments executed thousands of soldiers for cowardice during World War I. To this day, the US military considers "cowardly conduct"—defined as dereliction of duty while "before or in the presence of the enemy" —to be a serious offense for which a soldier might be court-martialed.

During the nineteenth and twentieth centuries, observers began to speak of cowardice more broadly, expanding it to include civilian life as well as the military. Applying a moral lens, observers condemned terrorists and criminals as cowards—a practice that continues to this day. Following the 9/11 attacks, George W. Bush and Hillary Clinton described the perpetrators as cowardly, while after the 2013 Boston Marathon bombings a billboard went up in the city that simply read, "Cowards." Observers also applied the concept of cowardice to civilians like Fan Meizhong who were duty bound to take risks for others' benefit but who failed to do so. These individuals gave in to their fears and behaved selfishly when they should have surmounted them and perhaps made a noble sacrifice. Cowardice, in short, came to designate not merely the act of fleeing the battlefield but a general moral bankruptcy.

Examples of cowards like Fan Meizhong appear frequently in the media. There was the captain of the cruise ship *Costa Concordia*, who in 2012 abandoned his sinking vessel before hundreds of passengers had been evacuated. Dozens of passengers and crew died, and the captain later did prison time for manslaughter. More recently, we've seen a number of instances in which police failed to respond during school shootings and other terrorist acts. In February 2018, an assailant attacked students and staff at Marjory Stoneman Douglas High School in Parkland, Florida. As surveillance video later showed, the school resource officer and several other sheriff's deputies failed to go inside the building to confront the gunman. In May 2022, a former student at Robb Elementary School in Uvalde, Texas, killed twenty-one people and injured seventeen others. According to public records, police officers waited for over an hour to engage the shooter out of concern for their own safety—a timid response that outraged everyone.

If we look beyond professional duties and think of our values and the moral responsibilities we have to society and our fellow humans, we find that cowardice is pervasive throughout daily life. On so many occasions, we shrink from making risky career or life choices that align with our values and sense of higher purpose. Surveys have found, for instance, that three in five Americans dream of becoming entrepreneurs, a career move that, depending on the business, can create jobs, fulfill important consumer needs, and deliver other important economic and social benefits. But how many Americans actually take their chances and start a new venture? Fewer than 15 percent in 2023.

Another way in which we can fail to show courage in daily life is by declining to speak up at key moments when we have something important to say. The research professor and bestselling author Brené Brown has described courage as a willingness to show vulnerability and express ourselves honestly around others, including by acknowledging our failures, opening ourselves up to criticism from others, and admitting limits to our knowledge. But we so seldom manage to make ourselves vulnerable. We've all sat in meetings and watched colleagues refrain from sharing new ideas or alerting higher-ups to serious problems. We've seen people decline to share bad news or unpleasant opinions with friends, family members, or acquaintances out of a desire to please or a fear of angering or alienating them.

Research confirms that this behavior is endemic. Over 40 percent of respondents in one study told researchers that they hadn't spoken up to raise the alarm about unsafe working conditions. When asked why, some claimed that they didn't think the concern was serious enough, but some of those who declined to speak up did so out of fear. Either they didn't think it was their place, didn't think it was worth the risk or effort, or they anticipated negative consequences.

We can also find any number of instances of corporate cowardice in which companies take the easier route, choosing profits over doing the right thing. Think of health insurance companies that deny coverage to customers who need lifesaving procedures with an eye toward the bottom line, or mortgage firms that engage in predatory lending. Even when leaders believe that, say, retooling their food portfolio could reduce obesity, or that changing investment strategies could mitigate the climate crisis, they choose silence over courageous action to protect their jobs or the company's stock prices.

The inability of many people to face their fears and take worthy risks, and the presence of people like Fan Meizhong who are comfortable seeing cowardice as part of their identities, suggests that timidity might be a profound, even fundamental human tendency. A glance at the science confirms this. When we find ourselves under threat, forces arise within our bodies and psyches to prevent us from behaving bravely. Elements of our social environments further inhibit us from showing courage, both by magnifying the fear we feel and by making it easier for us to give in to fear and shrink back from taking action. In large organizations, cultural norms add to the mix, making bravery even more difficult and unlikely. The more we understand the origins of cowardice, the more compassion and understanding we can have for people like Fan—and all too often, ourselves—who don't behave as boldly as they might. Given everything in our lives pushing us *not* to be bold, it would seem almost miraculous that anyone would behave courageously at all.

BORN TO BE TIMID

I have no idea if Fan Meizhong has read Aristotle, but he might feel comforted to hear the great philosopher opine on how natural it is to experience fear. "He would be a madman or insensitive to pain," Aristotle has been thought to have said, "if he feared nothing, neither earthquakes nor the waves." Modern science bears out Aristotle's intuition about the universality of the fear response, particularly when we lack a sense of certainty and control. Neuroscience teaches us that when we confront danger or come under stress in everyday settings, our amygdala, the primal portion of the brain involved in regulating our emotions, activates a survival response by signaling other brain regions to initiate fight, flight, or freeze reactions. This response evolved over time thanks to our forebears' ongoing efforts to adapt to their surroundings. Natural selection favored those among our ancestors who could pass on their genes to the next generation. Most of the time, these were the more fearful, risk-averse types who avoided putting themselves in harm's way.

As the sociologist Allan V. Horwitz suggests, the phenomenon of courage is puzzling when you think about it. From an evolutionary standpoint, it's not clear why people would ever choose to disregard their fear instincts and rush *toward* danger on behalf of a worthy cause. "All organisms, even the simplest biological creatures, strive to avoid dangers that threaten to kill or cause serious harm to them," Horwitz observes. In some situations, taking on personal risk could help us to pass our genes on to the next generation, but only if we're contributing to the welfare of people whose genetic makeup comes close to our own or if we think the person who benefits from our risk-taking will save *our* backs in the future. Our genetic survival—the ultimate goal of evolutionary processes—would stand to gain little if we were to sacrifice ourselves for our moral beliefs or for the welfare of strangers, without any clear indication of reciprocity.

According to popular beliefs about courage, cowardice reflects one's underlying character. Although psychologists haven't firmly tied courage and cowardice to temperament, some recent research would seem to support this connection. Scholars have linked courage, particularly when it comes to speaking up, to elevated levels of traits such as risk-taking, selflessness, openness to experience, and emotional stability. In contrast, cowardly people appear to possess comparatively low levels of these traits.

Even if we're not predisposed temperamentally to behave in cowardly ways, the fleeting emotions we experience can nudge us away from taking bold action by affecting how we make sense of the world. In one study, researchers found that the experience of fear tended to lead research subjects to shrink away from taking risks and to feel pessimistic about future outcomes, while feeling angry tended to make them take more risks and feel more optimistic. This makes sense: anger, especially about things like a perceived injustice, often motivates people to step up and act, even if that means taking on a certain amount of risk. When we're angry, dangers appear smaller in our eyes, the world looks simpler, and we feel hungrier to see a change in our circumstances. As we'll see, rousing emotions such as anger can be an effective way of fostering boldness in ourselves and others despite strong fears we might be experiencing.

CONFORMING OUR WAY TO COWARDICE

The innate, biologically rooted forces that prompt us to play it safe are strong enough on their own, but social factors also contribute. One of these is peer pressure. Depending on the context, we might feel a subtle—or not so subtle—push to stay quiet or refrain from intervening, lest we be excluded, shamed, or marginalized. A teenager might feel bad that a fellow student is being bullied but refrain from stepping in because they fear antagonizing the bullies and looking "uncool" in front of their friends. At a police department, officers might refrain from reporting instances of misconduct because they fear violating an unwritten code of silence and alienating their colleagues. We're wired to value our relationships; we have a basic need for belonging, acceptance, and group affiliation. Taking action that might jeopardize our social relationships feels scary and dangerous, which is why we frequently opt to stay quiet and passive.

The impulse to conform to the dictates of a social group is powerful indeed. In a famous experiment, the psychologist Solomon E. Asch asked participants to announce whether lines drawn on a series of cards matched one of three lines shown on other cards. Though one member of the group went in "cold," the others were actually working in league with the researchers, who had previously arranged for them to unanimously choose wrong answers for a certain number of the cards. The idea was to put research subjects in situations where everyone else around them was touting blatantly incorrect answers. Would they in turn modify their judgments because of the peer pressure? Many of them did. A full third of responses that research subjects made were mistakes similar to those that the majority had made. Peer pressure had influenced subjects to come forward with answers they believed to be wrong.

Other classic experiments have demonstrated how willing people are to give up their free will in social contexts, whether by respecting the commands of authority figures or hewing to the social roles that have been assigned to them. In Stanley Milgram's obedience experiments, research subjects who thought they were participating in a scientific study were perfectly willing to zap others with seemingly painful electric shocks because an authority figure—the important-looking scientist ostensibly running the experiment—told them to. As these studies suggest, social pressures often don't inspire us to face our fears and take bold action. They intensify fears, shaping our interpretations of the world in ways that heighten and lock in our cowardly instincts.

A second aspect of social life that squelches our courage has to do with the lesser sense of ownership we can feel in group settings. In January 2023, Adam Klotz, a meteorologist living in New York City, was on the subway when he noticed a group of young people harassing an older man. Defying the biological programming that might have told him not to intervene, he spoke up, boldly telling the bullies to stop in response. The group turned from their initial target and instead focused on him, issuing verbal taunts. When Klotz moved to a different subway car in an attempt to get away, the group pursued him. What followed was a brutal beating, with Klotz on the ground attempting to shield his head as the young people hit and kicked him.

New Yorkers are known to be aggressive and tough-minded,

willing to stand up for what's right. Klotz lived up to that image, but he was the exception that day. As the young people were attacking him, not a *single* bystander came to his aid. "No one else spoke up," Klotz says. "A lot of people just [watched] me get beat down. They were quick to help me [. . . as] soon as the beat down was over, but no one wanted to step in and stop me from getting stomped on."

People tend to feel less duty bound to take action if they are members of a group—what psychologists call the "bystander effect." With others around, we reason that it's not necessarily *our* responsibility to stick our neck out and help. We assume that others will take action, rationalizing that anything we do will just repeat their efforts. We also sense that we won't receive all the blame if nobody takes action—it will be spread among members of the group too. Why risk bodily harm if it's not even necessary? In each of these ways, our sense of moral obligation becomes watered down.

CULTURES OF COWARDICE

We often find a similar erosion of personal responsibility in large organizations, not just because of the bystander effect but the broader cultures that reign there. As you may know from your own work experiences, some companies put a great deal of emphasis on mitigating business risks. Organizations that have experienced past success can appear especially risk-averse, afraid to make changes of any kind because they might jeopardize what they've built. In such organizations, old ways of doing things are built into core operational routines and become a defining part of the culture. People adhere slavishly to the status quo and resist change. They fail to acknowledge their own mistakes, however slight, for fear of the consequences, and they may even provide cover for their colleagues when they mess up. Although their consciences might beckon them to speak up about shortcomings or questionable activity, the lack of what my colleague Amy Edmondson calls psychological safety leads them to stay silent. They perpetuate what scholars have called institutional cowardice.

In a medical setting, a surgeon who makes a mistake during a procedure might refrain from ever taking responsibility and giving their potentially traumatized patient a sense of closure. For the surgeon, apologizing is risky on multiple levels. The surgeon's reputation might become tarnished, and the surgeon could face professional or even legal sanction. But of course, there's another risk: lawsuits, targeting not just the individual surgeon but also the institution in which they're operating. The surgeon's duty to safeguard their organization from legal exposure piles on top of their own self-preservation instinct, preventing them from boldly stepping up and offering a meaningful apology.

Institutional cowardice runs rampant inside companies, and it appears in other kinds of large organizations, such as political parties or governments. One of the most notorious instances concerns the behavior of members of the Nazi regime during World War II. At the Nuremberg trials held in 1946, Nazi officials and military leaders claimed that they had taken part in atrocities not out of malicious intent but because their superiors had commanded them to do so. Rudolf Höss, who oversaw the notorious Auschwitz death camp, related that he and other members of the Nazis' elite corps of protectors, the SS, "were not supposed to think about these things; it never even occurred to us.... We were all so trained to obey orders without even thinking that the thought of disobeying an order would simply never have occurred to anybody." The orders Höss references were given in the context of a larger organizational system whose interests Höss was serving. He and other Nazis could hide behind the institution and its norms, using it as a pretext for giving in to their fears and declining to take action.

Interestingly, some of the cultural norms we might think would support effective, high-performing organizations can backfire, discouraging courageous behavior. Several years ago, I was leading a continuing education class for seasoned CEOs. One of them confidently remarked that in his opinion, the CEO's most important job was to create accountability. To ensure this, he made a point of finding "one throat to choke" whenever something went wrong. That hardline approach might seem smart to some leaders, but as other students in the class pointed out, it has a serious downside: it creates a culture of fear. Although fear might encourage people to be fastidious about their work and stick to established protocols, it can also have the nasty side effect of discouraging people from taking risks. Knowing that management would seek them out and "choke their throat" were they to fail, employees would fear failure so much that they would take the safer route. Over time, that would mean less experimentation, innovation, dynamism, and growth. The company would languish as excessive accountability gave rise to a pervasive cowardliness. Even worse, the company might become vulnerable to strategic missteps or scandals as fearful employees became reluctant to deliver bad news to senior management.

GOOD COWARDS—AND BETTER ONES

Understanding the biological, social, and cultural origins of cowardice has important implications for how we judge this behavior and the people who display it, including ourselves. Across the world and through the centuries, societies and individuals have not only repudiated cowardice but used it as a moniker to tar "others" of various kinds, including enemies, adversaries, and social inferiors. In our own day, cowardice remains one of the most potent insults someone can throw at us.

Our glance at the science complicates such moralistic views of cowardice. Everyday cowards aren't by definition morally reprehensible. They're people like you and me—imperfect beings born with inherent impulses and left to grapple with them as best they can. If we look closely, we can even find that some apparent cowards turn out to be more inspiring than they might seem at first glance. In his book *The Mystery of Courage,* the legal scholar William Ian Miller presents an account of a so-called "good coward" from a Civil War veteran named Robert J. Burdette. While fighting on the front line, Burdette encountered a fellow soldier who was quite virtuous in many respects but simply couldn't manage to overcome the impulse to shrink from danger. This good coward, Burdette said, was "a good soldier. A pleasant looking man . . . A manly voice; an intelligent mind." He was tidy, conscientious, and generous toward his fellow soldiers. He prepared for battle and had every intention of staring death in the face alongside his comrades. But just as his unit was about to charge forward, he seized up and ran away.

To his credit, this good coward wasn't cowed by his initial failure. Again and again, he went to battle intending to be brave, yearning for it. Yet each time, he flinched when the moment of truth arrived. This determination to push hard to be more courageous led Burdette to develop a grudging respect for the man. Other, "true" cowards fled before they even reached the battlefield. This good coward fought his impulses as fully as he could. In a sense, he might have been braver than soldiers who didn't run away but, for whatever reason, didn't experience fear quite so intensely. It must have taken incredible strength of character to come up repeatedly against one's limitations and yet remain undaunted. "What is a coward anyhow?" Burdette asked. "Cravens, and dastards, and poltroons, we know at sight. But who are the cowards? And how do we distinguish them from the heroes? How does God tell?"

We might say that Fan Meizhong was a good coward, although in a slightly different way. Yes, he ran in terror when the earthquake struck, leaving the students under his charge to fend for themselves. But there's a twist: the world only knows about his fearful response because Fan himself courageously blogged about it ten days after the earthquake, openly admitting his weakness and holding it up for others to see. His posting went viral, eliciting a great deal of criticism from online readers but also some support.

Fan came clean about his cowardice in this way because he wanted to positively influence public discussion in his country of the earthquake and its meaning. The Chinese media, in his view, was making propaganda out of the earthquake, valorizing the self-sacrificial acts of a few and trying to guilt others into donating to relief efforts—which Fan regarded as moral blackmail. Journalists were failing to scrutinize the real problem: poor building construction that contributed to the mass deaths the country experienced. "I just wanted to leave a true account of what happened during this extraordinary experience in my life," Fan says. "I was very dissatisfied with the narrative of sacrifice and emotional upheaval in the mass media. I felt this was a false construct, which obscured what really happened."

Courage comes in various forms: physical, moral, intellectual, relational. Fan behaved in a cowardly way when confronted with physical danger, but he showed unusual moral courage in blogging about it, especially in a country like China with significant restrictions on public discourse. Fan was well aware that he would be exposing himself to public ridicule and perhaps worse by describing his impulse to flee. He had a history of being punished for speaking his mind, having previously lost his job on several occasions for broaching forbidden topics during class discussions. But he felt compelled to raise his voice anyway. "I couldn't give up my freedom of speech and expression because of the possible consequences of my actions."

You can be a good coward by pushing hard to make worthy sacrifices, even if you never quite manage to surmount your fears. And you can be a good coward by continuing to behave boldly in certain areas of your life, even if you shrink back fearfully in others. But you need not content yourself with being a good coward. You can also become a *better* one, a person who over time becomes less shackled by your primal fears and more capable of sacrificing on behalf of your ideals. That's not to say you will *always* behave courageously. Your willingness to take risks will of course still depend on the specific situations you're in. For instance, you might risk your life for certain people and causes but not for others. But you can boost your *general* inclination toward courage by taking steps that shift your interpretations of the world, reducing the forces that magnify or support your fear response.

A logical place to start is with the risks that trigger your fears. In many situations, the dangers we face are all too real. By taking the time not just to anticipate the dangers we know about, but also to make sense of and contain our uncertainty about what might happen, you can make risk-taking seem more manageable and surmountable.

PART I

Building Your Courage Muscles

Chapter 1

COPING

> It's scary enough taking risks, but grappling with situations that are fundamentally uncertain is even more frightening. We can cope by building reassuring narratives about the world that make chaos seem more bearable.

It was, in all likelihood, a Sunday night, sometime during the 1850s. The abolitionist Harriet Tubman was leading a band of enslaved people north through hostile Maryland backwoods to freedom. This wasn't a relaxing jaunt through nature, but rather a perilous trek lasting days or even weeks over perhaps one hundred miles or more of rough terrain. Traveling at night to avoid detection, the group battled exhaustion and sore feet, not to mention nerves. If discovered, the group risked torture or death. Hundreds of professional and amateur bounty hunters were on the lookout, eager to claim a reward for returning someone who had escaped slavery. As of 1850, thanks to the second Fugitive Slave Act, police had to help capture runaways, even in northern states. Most of the thousands of people who tried to escape from slavery each year never reached freedom.

On this night, just the second of the journey, another danger arose unexpectedly. One of the men who had been walking shoeless protested that he couldn't continue, even if it meant death—his feet hurt too much. What would Tubman do? If he were discovered, the slave catchers might torture him, forcing him to give up the group's whereabouts. They might squeeze out of him the names of sympathizers who had helped them along the way, jeopardizing future missions. Even if they didn't, this man's lack of fortitude might cause others in the group to lose heart.

Tubman was a deeply religious person who often prayed to her god for guidance. In this case, though, it appears that she didn't hesitate. Knowing that some of the party were armed with guns, she told them to prepare their weapons and shoot the man if he tried to leave. As Tubman later explained, she intended to kill the man rather than let him return to his plantation. "If [a man] was weak enough to give out, he'd be weak enough to betray us all, and all who had helped us; and do you think I'd let so many die just for one coward man?" As it turned out, the threat of violence did the trick—the man continued walking.

This episode is but one, rather extreme, example of Tubman's proficiency at managing or mitigating risk. We often think of courage in terms of split-second decisions, but brave people often work shrewdly and thoughtfully in advance to mitigate danger. They take action not just to avoid a risk, which might be impossible to do, but to *optimize* for it. They might catalog and categorize potential dangers; quantify their chances of occurring; compare risks to potential rewards; implement measures to prevent negative outcomes from materializing; and work to cap each risk's consequences.

Tubman appears to have been quite adept at anticipating and mitigating risks. Rarely did she visit plantations herself in search of enslaved people to rescue, she used an underground network to get the word out about departure times and locations, throwing her enemies off the scent by sometimes giving false information. When meeting strangers, she tested them by showing them cards she carried that were printed with pictures of fellow antislavery activists she knew. If the strangers could identify them, she could feel more comfortable that they were fellow believers in the cause. When bringing small children up north, she gave them opium to prevent them from drawing unwanted attention from their crying. Critically, she lowered the risk that she and her party would be discovered by having them leave on Saturday nights. Since Sunday was a day of rest, owners of enslaved people wouldn't notice anyone missing until Monday morning. Leaving Saturday night gave Tubman and her party a critical head start.

Tubman took still other measures to minimize the risk of being discovered. She planned her trips for the colder months of the year. Not only would the longer nights allow more time to travel; the cold weather would be more likely to keep slave catchers and unfriendly locals indoors. She and other members of the Underground Railroad, the network of sympathizers that helped enslaved people escape to the North, also developed a system of code words to prevent others from learning of their plans. "Baggage" referred to the enslaved people themselves; "Canaan" or "Promised Land" meant Canada, the final destination of many freedom seekers; and "Gospel train" signified the Underground Railroad itself. Such language appeared in spirituals or "signal" songs that Tubman used to communicate in ways that unsympathetic white people wouldn't understand. Singing a phrase like "bound for the land of Canaan" might have indicated to other enslaved people an intention to escape the United States and cross into Canada. White people would only have interpreted it as meaning being ready to face death and enter the afterlife.

Tubman is a lofty example, one of the bravest figures in US history, but her story still offers lessons that we can apply to our everyday lives. Certainly her emphasis on mitigating risk conforms with modern thinking about how we can best position ourselves to take bold action. Focusing on workplace settings, courage experts encourage us to identify risk and carefully manage it, in particular by performing a risk-benefit analysis. As management professor Kathleen K. Reardon has written, "courageous action is really a special kind of calculated risk-taking." Strong leaders operate "through careful deliberation and preparation," taking an "intelligent gamble" by, among other tasks, "weighing risks and benefits."

Many of us heed such advice, knowing we'll feel more confident and less fearful once we've spent at least some time reducing the odds of negative outcomes, capping their potential consequences, and in general optimizing our decision-making. We might know we can't lower our risk to zero, but common sense tells us that we must at least try to reduce the risk to levels we perceive as tolerable relative to the potential benefits, especially when it concerns weighty decisions like whether to switch jobs, invest in a new business, undertake a merger or acquisition, or speak out on a controversial topic.

And yet, mitigating risk usually isn't enough to help us behave boldly, for the simple reason that we often can't identify all of the dangers we face, nor can we pin down their chances of occurring. Lacking such relevant knowledge, we can't optimize risk-taking through our usual risk-benefit calculations. Consider President Barack Obama's 2011 decision to confront Osama bin Laden at his secret hideaway in Abbottabad, Pakistan. Some of Obama's advisors felt that there was a 95 percent chance that bin Laden was at the location, but others judged the chances to be as low as 30 percent. That's a big difference! Without sufficient clarity on this critical question, Obama couldn't perform a proper risk-benefit analysis to conclude on balance whether it was worth it to risk the lives of the U.S. Navy SEALS he would be putting in harm's way. "In this situation," he later said, "what you started getting was probabilities that disguised uncertainty as opposed to actually providing you with more useful information." What Obama was dealing with wasn't risk—it was *uncertainty*, which is a more nuanced form of the "unknown." Let's disentangle the two.

FROM RISK TO UNCERTAINTY

Economists have posited a basic distinction between risk on the one hand and uncertainty on the other. Risks, they suggest, are dangers whose nature we can identify and whose likelihood of occurring we can pin down in advance, whether by mobilizing past experience as our guide or by using statistics or probabilistic reasoning. Using weather models, for instance, we might find that there is a 30 percent chance of rain today. Epidemiological studies might reveal that given our particular health profile, we have a 60 percent chance of developing cancer within ten years. These are known risks. We don't know for sure if they'll happen, but we can gaze into the future, understand the range of possible outcomes, and ascertain with at least some ballpark accuracy *the chances* that they will. That in turn can allow us to protect against risks or otherwise optimize our decision-making. We may not deem it necessary to carry an umbrella today, but we may start exercising more and eating healthier foods to lower the chances of serious illness in the next decade.

Uncertainty is more like the question of bin Laden's presence at his compound: no amount of analysis on our part will help us pin down its likelihood of occurring. We can take some guesses, but in the end we simply don't know, and that prevents us from protecting or optimizing our way around it. In some situations, we might not even be able to *imagine* some of the specific dangers we'll face in advance, much less calculate their odds of occurring—what the late US secretary of defense Donald Rumsfeld memorably called "unknown unknowns."

In leading people to freedom, Harriet Tubman confronted a *mix* of quantifiable risks as well as uncertainties. Sure, she could catalog and mitigate the risks that were known to her, but she couldn't predict every last obstacle she'd encounter. Perhaps the weather would suddenly turn bad, or someone in her party would become sick or gravely injured, or police in a given town would become alerted prematurely to her presence. Most everyday situations are like this too: we can understand risks, but only to a point. And that's a problem.

Faced with the prospect of unexpected and unquantifiable dangers, our situation can feel ambiguous, unknowable, unfamiliar—beyond our control. It can seem as if the situations are controlling *us*, rather than the other way around, and that to an important extent we lack agency and are at the mercy of outside forces. This one-two punch of uncertainty and loss of control in turn arouses an emotional response that can make courage much more difficult, sparking doubt and, perhaps more profoundly, fear. As psychologists have observed, uncertainty and loss of control are two basic features of lived experience that tend to underlie the fears we feel. I like to think of it as the "fear equation": uncertainty + loss of control = fear. That fear in turn can prevent us from acting, even if we're normally quite brave.

To bolster our courage muscles, we can take steps not only to mitigate risk, but also to cope better with uncertainty and the loss of control that comes with it so that we can overcome fear. We can equip ourselves to stare uncertainty in the face and not feel quite so vulnerable and out of control. Humans have an innate need, as scholars have written, "to see the world as structured, orderly, and nonrandom"—in other words, as more certain. When we lack a sense of personal control, our overall perception of certainty and orderliness declines. We compensate by seeking *external* sources of structure, which may include religious beliefs, membership in a community, social hierarchies, or political leaders that "impose structure." If we're unsettled by a death or some other trauma that leaves us feeling out of control, for instance, we might find ourselves leaning into a belief that God or some spiritual force is in control and that there is a higher plan for us after all. Such a belief reaffirms our sense of the world as an orderly, comprehensible place. Our sense of certainty is restored, as is our perception of our own agency. We feel once again that we're in a position to make things happen, rather than simply letting life happen to us.

The courageous individuals I've studied tend to follow one of two basic strategies to compensate for uncertainty and a loss of control, depending on their beliefs and outlook on life. Some put their faith in external, nonrational forces that would intervene and protect them against unforeseen threats. By believing in such forces, people could tell themselves stories—often taking the form of logical arguments—about the future that comforted them and allowed them to exercise more personal agency as threats arose. Others took a different, more rational tack. They mobilized traditional risk mitigation strategies, but they did so in extreme ways that, as a kind of happy side effect, allowed them to address uncertainty, not merely known risks. By obsessing over risk, they too told themselves comforting stories about the future, convincing themselves that they had accounted for the potential dangers so thoroughly that they had essentially reduced uncertainty to near zero. Risk mitigation, in other words, came to serve a psychological function for them, not simply the practical one of optimizing their decision-making.

These two strategies obscured the reality of uncertainty in different ways, but they had the benefit of enabling these individuals to keep fear at bay and act when they might otherwise hold back. Acknowledging our imperfect grasp of the future, you too can become bolder by convincing yourself of your ability to address any danger you might face, even if it's utterly unexpected.

UNCERTAINTY MITIGATOR #1: THE POWER OF FAITH

In 2021, Joe Ybarra and his team of firefighters from the US Forest Service arrived at Scarface Mountain in Idaho to contain a small fire. At first the fire wasn't especially dangerous: it seemed to be waning thanks to water that another crew had dumped on it from the air. The next day, however, the situation changed drastically as winds blew through, giving the fire a second life. Soon it was roaring so high that they had to retreat to their base camp. And soon that location too was threatened. When Ybarra's team leader told them to prepare the portable fire shelters they carried with them, Ybarra knew it was bad, as firefighters typically deployed them only in truly dire situations when they had exhausted other options.

In these desperate moments, Ybarra and his colleagues faced extreme uncertainty. They didn't know where the fires blazing around them would move, nor how quickly. They didn't know if other teams operating nearby would be able to help them in time. In this terrifying situation, Ybarra might have panicked and become paralyzed. Instead he fell back on his religious faith to comfort him and give him a sense of control, allowing him to stay in the game. As he told a reporter, "I remember asking myself what I was doing out there, 26 hours away from family and everything I know. As my mind began racing, I grabbed my radio, a water bottle, my fire shelter and my rosary as we got to our safe spot and waited to see what the fire was going to do next. When I found my rosary, it was then when my racing mind stopped."

In this moment of crisis, Ybarra's rosary eased the uncertainty just a little bit. As an expression of his faith, it affirmed for him that whatever might happen, the same God that was present in his life prior to the crisis was still there and would continue to be in the future. "During the fires," he said, "you definitely felt God was there." Relatedly, Ybarra's rosary also calmed him and gave him a sense of agency. It allowed him to summon a powerful force, one that knew him personally, would hear him, and quite possibly would take action to see him through. And as Ybarra saw it, his gesture of faith did in fact work. Seconds later, a helicopter crew dropped a load of water from above, saving Ybarra and his team. "I felt God had answered my prayers," Ybarra said. Despite this harrowing experience, Ybarra would continue working as a firefighter, carrying a rosary to bolster his courage.

Like Ybarra, many of us not only feel the presence of the divine, but we perceive that God or some other supernatural force can jump in to influence events on our behalf. Scientists have described such perceptions using an umbrella term: *magical thinking*.

While the word *magic* sometimes holds negative connotations, I use *magical thinking* in a nonjudgmental way to describe interpretations of everyday phenomena that aren't strictly rational, logical, or scientific—in short, that appear to run counter to the physical laws of nature. By this definition, magical thinking includes a range of phenomena, including religious beliefs, new-age spirituality, superstitions, and beliefs in our own luck or fate.

Such thinking can serve us as we interpret past events, but we also can use it to cope with a future that seems uncertain and beyond our control. If we are about to leave on a long trip and aren't sure if we'll make it back safely, we might cross our fingers or say a prayer. If we're about to give a big speech and we're uncertain about how it will go, we might wear our lucky sweater. Performing such actions frames reality for us in a way that reduces our perceptions of uncertainty while also enhancing our sense of control. The world might still be disorienting and unintelligible, but it's not entirely so: we at least can glimpse *some* underlying principle at work, one that is familiar to us and that often tilts events more favorably in our direction. Further, by actively summoning this benevolent, outside force, we affirm that we're capable of positively influencing our situation. We create a mini-narrative in our minds that says, *I have encountered adversity, but I'm not entirely powerless. I can appeal to God (or fate, or luck, or the universe), and I will probably emerge victorious.* We might even build our identities around such narratives, perceiving ourselves as inherently lucky or faithful people who do God's work.

Some people disparage magical thinking, regarding it as childish or silly, but researchers have tended to see it as healthy and adaptive, an important way of coping with the world's chaos. Magical thinking might have played an evolutionary role in our history: by calming us down in dangerous situations, it could have allowed us to take action, increasing our odds of surviving and passing on our genes. Magical thinking certainly seems to have been prevalent enough as a spur to courage. From the ancient Hebrews to the Christian crusaders to the samurai, we can find many examples of groups or individuals who relied on faith-based beliefs in battle or who even fought on behalf of these beliefs. In his classic study of religious life, the French sociologist Émile Durkheim observed that a personal belief in God enabled brave deeds by fueling confidence in the face of adversity. As he put it, "This confidence of an individual in the efficacy of his protector is so great that he braves the greatest dangers and accomplishes the most disconcerting feats with an intrepid serenity: faith gives him the necessary courage and strength."

Research confirms that magical thinking is good for us, precisely because it lends us "a helpful hand in circumstances that are beyond rational control." Studies have shown that invoking common superstitions—for instance, crossing your fingers for good luck—increases performance in sports, because people feel more self-confident and capable of persisting in the face of obstacles. Likewise, a belief that we have good luck in general increases our sense of agency, which can lead us to want to embrace more difficult challenges.

In dangerous situations, religious or superstitious rituals can serve as a tangible means of accessing magical thinking. We can think of rituals—grasping rosary beads, saying prayers, crossing our fingers, wearing a religious symbol, donning our lucky sweater, and so on—as actions that have no practical impact of their own but that enact our beliefs. The structured and predictable nature of these actions can calm us, providing us, as one scholar observes, with "a sense of control" that helps us "soothe anxiety." Ultimately, rituals and magical thinking serve as a form of mental future-proofing. We remind ourselves that whatever dangers we encounter, the divine or the supernatural will somehow show us what to do or intercede personally to see us through.

What rituals and beliefs have you or others around you mustered to help normalize uncomfortable situations in your life? Might you turn to them more regularly or fully to help you cope with uncertainty?

My research turned up many instances of people who relied on magical thinking. Athletes do it all the time: The Olympic skater Eileen Gu draws a "lucky cat" on her hand before competing, while John Henderson, a former defensive tackle in the NFL, had someone slap his face as part of his pregame ritual. Tennis superstar Serena Williams ties her shoes in a specific way before her matches and bounces the tennis ball a certain number of times before she serves. "It's like I have to do it and if I don't then I'll lose," she says.

Soldiers have their rituals too: As *The New York Times* reported in 2023, members of a tank crew on the front lines in Ukraine prepared for battle by reciting the Lord's Prayer, circling the tank, and uttering phrases like "Please, don't let us down in battle." Even entrepreneurs rely on magical thinking. As research has shown, they seem to be more devout than the public at large, feeling "closer to God than the rest of us do." They pray more often and are more inclined to perceive that God sees them individually and cares about them.

Of course, you need not *only* mobilize magical thinking to cope with uncertainty. You also take steps to mitigate the dangers that you can predict and quantify. Managing risk and limiting our fear response in the face of uncertainty go hand in hand. Take Harriet Tubman. Even as she went to extraordinary lengths to prepare for identifiable risks, she also mobilized magical thinking to help keep her fears in check amid tremendous uncertainty. Her answer was to craft a narrative about herself, the universe, and her identity that incorporated her deeply held Christian beliefs.

Following her survival from severe head trauma at a young age, Tubman developed an especially intense and personal relationship with God. As she said later in life, "Pears like, I prayed all de time, about my work, everywhere; I was always talking to the Lord." Tubman's subsequent efforts to liberate the enslaved arose, she said, because the Lord asked her three times to embark on this holy mission. And if the Lord had called her on this mission, Tubman believed that He also was looking after her, interceding when necessary to protect her and show her the way. Regardless of the circumstances she encountered, she remained convinced that God was there with her as a tangible resource she could access as needed.

While on the run, Tubman often asked God to guide her in dangerous situations and to keep her safe. As another abolitionist, Thomas Garrett, recounted, Tubman said that she "never ventured [except] where God sent her." In one situation Tubman described, she listened to God and bypassed one of her usual resting places, eventually arriving at a stream. Unsure whether to brave the stream's waters, which rose to shoulder-height and were life-threateningly cold, or to waste precious time finding a way around the stream, she "consulted" God, who told her to pass through the stream. She and her group made it to safety. In another instance, when Tubman was rescuing a young girl named Tilly and the two were in imminent danger of being discovered, she prayed to God, exclaiming, "Oh, Lord! You've been wid me in six troubles, *don't* desert me in the seventh!" A moment later, the danger passed, a resolution that an outside observer might regard as lucky but that Tubman attributed to divine intervention.

A nonbeliever might protest that Tubman was mistaking instinct or gut feeling for divine intervention. But what is most important is the effect of the story Tubman believed—the meaning she was creating that gave her courage. In her worldview, the divine presence was a tangible force and source of knowledge—in fact, the ultimate one. By consulting the same deity who had sent her on her mission to begin with, and by acting accordingly, Tubman could feel calmer, less fearful, and more confident that she would keep herself and her group of travelers as safe as possible, even if she couldn't prepare for many of the dangers in advance. As she told Thomas Garrett, "she felt no more fear of being arrested by her former master, or any other person, when in his immediate neighborhood, than she did in the State of New York, or Canada, for . . . her faith in the Supreme Power truly was great."

Tubman's personal relationship with God and ability to communicate with the divine made her perceive her situation as less uncertain. Although she still didn't know what would happen, she at least could know that a divine logic was always at work. Her personal relationship with God also gave her a renewed sense of personal control, paradoxically because she had given herself wholly over to God's will. In her mind, she didn't have to figure everything out; a benevolent and friendly God was watching over her and would protect her when summoned, providing for what she couldn't foresee. If she failed, that too would be okay, because her God would have ordained it. As she once remarked, "Jes' so long as he wanted to use me, he would take keer of me, an' when he didn't want me no longer, I was ready to go; I always tole him, I'm gwine to hole stiddy on to you, an' you've got to see me trou."

Leading people to freedom put Tubman in great peril—that was unavoidable. By tackling the reality of risk head-on, she could lower the odds of being caught. But by focusing on her religious mission and personal relationship with the divine, she could shift the *meaning* of the situations she encountered, crafting a narrative that made the world seem less unsettling.

UNCERTAINTY MITIGATOR #2: HUNTING DOWN RISK

You too can deploy the power of magical thinking to boost your courage muscles, interpreting the world in ways that keep you feeling more in control and less fearful in the face of uncertainty. But what if you don't believe in God, aren't superstitious, or don't put much store in luck? Is there another way you might craft a narrative that mentally future-proofs you and enables you to feel more confident?

There is—it's an approach characterized by a kind of hyper-rationality. We've seen that we can build our confidence by engaging in risk mitigation: identifying dangers, quantifying them, comparing them to potential benefits of taking action, and taking steps to lower our risk or minimize the impact of bad outcomes. But some courageous people I studied took risk mitigation further, using these very same tactics not just to take smarter risks, but also to prepare psychologically to confront uncertainty. They enabled themselves to feel a greater sense of control amid the chaos by engaging in a heightened form of risk identification and mitigation that I call *risk-hunting*. The point of risk-hunting isn't just to reduce known, quantifiable risks as we make decisions. It's also to subtly shift how we perceive reality so that all of those nasty unknown unknowns *also* appear less threatening, allowing us to feel more in control. Although courageous people I studied didn't necessarily realize it, the process of chasing down risks enabled them to build a narrative about themselves and the world, one that often took the form of a logical argument and centered on the notion that they had conquered the world's chaos.

With risk-hunting, you take the mitigation of hazards to an extreme. You don't just make reasonable efforts to minimize danger. You become utterly obsessed with identifying every conceivable danger and finding ways to protect against them. You become a risk *expert*, dedicating yourself to conquering risk entirely. By hunting risk so exhaustively, you can convince yourself—truthfully or not—that you've gone further than merely mitigating risk and also reduced uncertainty to negligible levels. The very arduousness of the effort gives you an *illusion* of certainty; you convince yourself that for all intents and purposes you now only face known, quantifiable risks that you can manage. Risk-hunting domesticates the world, allowing us to spin a narrative that frames it as orderly, comprehensible, and predictable. We regain a sense of control and our fears diminish, leaving us with more capacity to behave courageously.

One of the best examples of risk-hunting I've encountered is that of the French tightrope walker Philippe Petit, who astonished New Yorkers in 1974 by walking unassisted on a wire between the World Trade Center's twin towers, some 1,350 feet above the earth. A practitioner of his craft since the age of sixteen, Petit has claimed that he doesn't actually take risks during his tightrope walks because he has already identified and addressed every conceivable danger that he might face. "I do not put myself in a state of question mark on the wire," he told National Public Radio. "I have composed my text in my head and I'm just now writing."

When Petit prepared for his 1999 walk 1,200 feet across the Grand Canyon, at an incredible 1,600 feet off the ground, he spent *eleven years* collecting data about the site—everything from weather records, to surveys of the area's geology, to technical specifications about the many pieces of equipment he planned to use, to the customs and culture of the area's Native Americans. He practiced the walk on a cable raised only twelve feet off the ground and set up near the location of the actual walk, doing so under stormy conditions, under blinding sun, in the dark, with others purposely jarring the wire, when he was fatigued, and so on. In setting up the cable, which he had specially made, he closely mapped out the surrounding terrain and brought in a team of rock-climbing veterans to set up nearly two dozen stabilizing lines. Reflecting on these preparations, he notes that he aims at "reducing the unknown to nothing. . . . If I think I am a hero who is invincible, I will pay for it with my life."

While surely Petit was infinitely more prepared than we would be in the circumstances, one would not likely agree that walking on those wires so high in the air without a harness (or parachute) was safe no matter how much preparation was done. Still, Petit had the confidence to perform this feat. As he remarked, the way to "destroy fear" is to "[s]tart by reacting to fright not by burying your head in the sand but by burying your mind in knowledge; then follow with specifics."

Risk-hunting is also quite common in the business world. One of my favorite stories about risk, and one that I often recount to my students, turns out to be a story about coping with uncertainty too. Its protagonist is a bright, ambitious young man who lived in New York City during the mid-1980s and worked at a large investment bank. Within a few years, he became a hot ticket inside the bank; the team he led brought in big profits by buying up mortgages, credit card loans, and other kinds of consumer debt, combining them together, and reselling them as a bundle to investors. But then disaster struck. Within a few days in 1986, his group lost $100 million—about $287 million in 2024 dollars. As he would later tell my colleagues and me, it took all of about four minutes for him to go "from a star to a jerk."

How could he have lost so much money so quickly? Analyzing what had happened, the man realized that it had to do with his failure to properly comprehend risk. "We built this giant machine," he said, "and it was making a lot of money—until it didn't. We didn't know why we were making so much money. We didn't have the . . . tools to understand [the risk involved]." His team had earned profits because they were willing to assume a certain amount of risk. But since they had no reliable way of quantifying the danger they were taking on, they had been taking on excessive risk all along without even realizing it. It was only a matter of time before that risk would catch up with him.

This man didn't lose his job, but as you might imagine, his career prospects at the firm declined. So, two years later, he struck out on his own, teaming with some partners to open a new firm dedicated to managing the assets of investors. Unlike other asset management firms, this one had a unique business model that emphasized risk quantification for fixed-income products that can be difficult to quantify. The company would build complex computer algorithms that would allow it to quantify reliably how much risk it was taking on when making investments on behalf of clients. In essence, they performed an exercise similar to what Philippe Petit did, using the power of modern computing to quantify risk. With exhaustive knowledge about risk in hand, the company would be able to price these products more accurately so investors could make decisions in a more informed way.

This concept of an asset management firm focused around quantifying risk revolutionized the industry. The firm grew dramatically since, expanding into a whole array of products. Today it is the largest asset manager globally, managing over $11 *trillion* of assets. As you might have guessed if you're familiar with the financial markets, I'm talking about BlackRock. The person who turned a $100 million mistake into a Fortune 500 company is none other than Larry Fink, who today serves as BlackRock's CEO.

BlackRock and its peers in the asset management industry go to extraordinary lengths to quantify risk. Their algorithms are so complex, and the underlying datasets so vast, that even reasonably smart, well-informed people can't begin to understand them. Their Aladdin system has played a significant role in advancing sophisticated risk mitigation across the economy. The system, which is available to be licensed to all, helps companies and government agencies identify, quantify, and mitigate risks.

You could argue that these algorithms enable bold action solely by quantifying risk so that investments are safer and smarter. That is indeed true. But in reality, finance executives also use their algorithms to frame *meaning* for investors, helping to create the narrative of a predictable and orderly world. Algorithms are never perfect representations of the real world—they can't account for every last risk. But they certainly seem to give us some comfort in knowing that we have done our very best to cover the risks that are under our control.

As finance professionals speak about the sophistication of their algorithms, while also of course acknowledging their limitations, investors can sometimes misconstrue what they hear as affording them a sense of certainty. Not understanding the inner workings of the algorithms, some investors might feel calmer and more in control knowing that they have such mathematical brilliance on their side. Algorithms seem powerful and mysterious to them—mathematical black boxes that protect them just like a God might. Even if the models haven't *truly* conquered uncertainty, investors can believe they've done so to such an extent that they're practically immune to uncertainty and only face known, manageable risk. They can then feel more comfortable taking on greater amounts of risk to meet their goals. Similarly, corporate risk management, which has become a burgeoning field in recent years, serves as a form of risk-hunting. It shifts the sense of reality that business leaders and investors have, enhancing a sense of control, preempting the fear response, and facilitating bold action.

Risk-Hunting in Everyday Life

You might not have proprietary algorithms at your disposal in everyday situations, nor do you likely have the time and energy to plan your risk-taking the way Philippe Petit did. A smarter strategy might be to practice a more muted but still useful form of risk-hunting adapted for everyday life. As the Nobel Prize winner Herbert Simon observed, we typically make cognitive compromises in our daily lives, contenting ourselves with solutions that are "good enough" simply because our knowledge, time, and cognitive abilities are limited. Such practical considerations limit our reasoning, causing us to practice what he termed "bounded rationality." Instead of aiming for optimal solutions, we engage in so-called satisficing—coming up with answers that suffice to let us operate productively in the world.

You can take a similarly imperfect approach to risk-hunting. You can feel somewhat calmer and more in control of your destiny if you become just *a bit* more fastidious about future-proofing yourself than you normally would be, aggressively identifying new risks you hadn't previously thought of and planning for them. In other words, by pushing traditional risk mitigation tools further, you can use them to cope with uncertainty, creating an internal narrative about your own ability to shrink uncertainty to negligible proportions. You can tell yourself a (technically incorrect) story about how you've gone to so much trouble mitigating risks that you've actually covered *all* your bases—your known risks *and* the unknown unknowns. You can cajole yourself into feeling calmer and more in control of your destiny amid your chaotic circumstances.

Let's say you've always wanted to live in another country. While you probably would research many aspects of your intended destination in any case, risk-hunting could include more than one visit to the exact neighborhood where you will be living and creating safety net plans for yourself should any conceivable issue arise. You would likely make a solid effort to learn at least the basics of the local language in the country where you'll be living, even if you were participating in an English-speaking program. While you most certainly are bound to find out that there are more risks involved than you thought at the beginning, now they are known, not unknown, and you're more likely to find that your courage to follow through on your plan will increase.

To support the narrative in our minds that we're taming uncertainty, while at the same time taking care that we don't drive ourselves crazy by taking risk mitigation too far, we can make a few tactical adjustments. First, we can *limit our assessment of risk*, deciding at the outset to seek out and aggressively mitigate only those risks that, if they materialize, would cause us serious harm. In other words, we can aim to cap but not necessarily eliminate our downside risk. As you identify potential new risks that you might face, ask yourself: How likely is a given risk to materialize, and how consequential might it be if it does? If you find risks that are both likely and consequential, taking action in advance to mitigate them will help you to feel more comfortable, increasing the odds you'll take action. If a risk isn't all that likely but could prove devastating if it happens, mitigating it too will also provide peace of mind, making the overall situation seem safer and more manageable. Knowing that you've cataloged the most consequential risks in a meaningful way can give you a sense that you're reducing your exposure to uncertainty, not exhaustively but enough to make the situation feel safer.

Returning to our hypothetical example of an overseas adventure, you might consider whether not knowing how to swim all that well constitutes an important risk. If you're going to the desert, for example, you may not need to consider this issue seriously. On the other hand, if you're planning to live on a sailboat, you would want to focus on becoming a stronger swimmer as part of your risk mitigation strategy.

A second tactical adjustment that can make risk-hunting easier in everyday situations is to *narrow the scope* of the bold action you plan to take. Courage researchers have suggested that we approach risk-taking incrementally, starting with relatively low-risk actions and laddering up boldness from there. By deciding in advance which actions you will and won't take, you can place upper limits on the actual uncertainty you face, thereby reducing the amount of risk-hunting you'll need.

Members of the US Air Force (USAF) and the National Aeronautics and Space Administration (NASA) routinely limit uncertainty by maintaining what they call "flight discipline." They hold briefings before conducting individual missions, and they then conduct the mission *only* according to what was discussed during the briefings. As NASA astronaut and former USAF fighter pilot Terry Virts told me, flight discipline "is just doing what you briefed and staying within the rules. If you do these two things, it'll probably work out for you. And if you don't do those two things, you're going off a risk cliff. A lot of the fatalities I know are guys doing things that they shouldn't have been doing."

Before a highly dangerous spacewalk Virts undertook in 2015 at the International Space Station, he agreed with mission control that if he finished his planned tasks earlier than expected, he would come back inside straightaway and not conduct any extra tasks, which carried extra risk, required significant advance planning, and opened him up to extra uncertainty. Virts did finish early, but mission control surprised him by asking him to perform an additional task: finding a bag that an astronaut had left outside the station years earlier and bringing it back inside. That sounded like an easy request, but as Virts will tell you, nothing in space is easy. When he came back in twenty minutes later, he was so tired that he struggled to close the airlock. "Doing that task at the behest of Houston caused me to spend precious minutes at risk while solo in the vacuum of space and also dipped into my already depleted reservoir of strength. Not good."

Looking back on it, Virts blames himself; he should have had the discipline to refuse mission control's request. "If you're going to do a dangerous and complicated task, you plan it, brief it, and execute it. If something extraordinary happens you flex as required, but in general you don't fly by the seat of your pants." Under a disciplined approach we might still face uncertainty, but potentially much less of it than if we leave our scope of action open-ended.

Let's go back to our example of moving to another country. If you think you might wish to make a side trip someday to a country that borders your new home but that holds extra risks, you might decide in advance that those risks aren't worth taking and that you'll stay put in the safer country. By narrowing the scope of your adventure in this way, you can limit the uncertainty you face, saving yourself the trouble of some extra risk-hunting.

A third way to make risk-hunting easier in everyday situations is to limit your need for it by *equipping yourself to improvise*, or handle unpredictable threats as they arise. Recognizing that you can arrive at solutions in real time, you'll feel more comfortable facing some measure of uncertainty. Intriguingly, studies have found that cultivating an ability to improvise on the spot—for instance, by training in improvisational theater—can lower stress, reduce anxiety, and allow people to tolerate uncertainty better.

To increase improvisational ability in the face of uncertainty, you can *adopt shortcuts that you can use in the moment to simplify reality and solve problems*. We know from behavioral economics that our brains use common heuristics or mental shortcuts as a way of dealing with the world's manifold complexity. Heuristics reduce large amounts of information into a manageable amount by identifying a small number of criteria that can be used to arrive at a decision.

For example, we often quickly assess situations, objects, or people by bucketing them into preexisting categories. Scholars call this the "representativeness" heuristic, in that we make sense of something by seeing it as representative of a category. These types of snap judgments, while beneficial in situations like smelling smoke and immediately thinking "fire," can be problematic in other contexts, so it's important to remain aware of their limitations. We might meet a person who is outgoing, chatty, and persuasive and intuitively file them in our brains as a "salesman type." Our assessment might be wrong: it's based, after all, on a stereotype, not an in-depth understanding of this particular person. We also risk falling prey to our own biases. Fortunately, simply being aware of the biases drastically curtails their impact. And what we might lose in accuracy we make up for in speed and ease.

Consciously adopting shortcuts for handling unknown events can help in dangerous, uncertain situations, allowing us to feel more comfortable with uncertainty and in turn enabling more bold action. The point isn't to be able to reason our way through adversity in an ironclad way; we simply want to know that we can react in a way that is good enough. Evidence suggests that those who are practiced in taking bold action do precisely this.

One study of experienced firefighters found that they tended to make quick, consequential decisions in high-pressure, crisis situations by reverting to something akin to the representativeness heuristic. Upon entering a burning building, they decided how best to proceed by noticing patterns and on that basis comparing the particular fire they faced to a category of fires they had dealt with in the past. That analysis in turn informed the action they took—they deployed what had worked previously in those similar fires.

It turns out that another breed of risk-taker—seasoned entrepreneurs—operates in a similar way when deciding whether to strike off on a new venture. They look for patterns in the idea before them, considering elements like what kind of product or service the proposed company will sell, how it will go about that, the market conditions, and so on, comparing what they see to a prototypical category of a "good idea" for a business opportunity based on their own past experience or what they have learned observing others. This quick analysis allows them to assess a potential deal and come to a gut decision on whether it's worth pursuing.

In our example of moving to a new country, you might learn from people who live there what parts of the city to avoid late at night, or what kinds of scams are commonly used against foreigners. While you don't want to make too many judgments preemptively that will keep you from seeing the place with your own eyes, you also don't want to fall into traps that you might have avoided with some basic knowledge. When you have some idea of what to look for in an area that is dangerous for foreigners, you can improvise decisions when you go to another city in the same country to help you stay safe.

A second way to become more comfortable improvising solutions to unknown risks that pop up is to *always try to take actions that keep your options open*. As research has shown, the best chess players rely on such tactics to proceed boldly through their matches. We tend to think of great chess players as strategic visionaries who can plan dozens of moves ahead, but in fact that doesn't work very well: the uncertainty of the chess match is too great. To handle this uncertainty, great chess players make their moves with an eye toward being able to adapt as needed. They ask themselves: "Will a move I'm considering limit me in important ways going forward, as compared with other moves I might make?" If the answer is yes, they factor that into their final decision. Research has shown that bold innovators in the arts and in business also try to behave in ways that keep their options open. Thomas Edison made the electric light a success by designing it in ways that seemed to adhere to the established gas-lighting technology of his day, while at the same time "not constraining the potential evolution of understanding and action that follows use." Edison couldn't predict how people would use electric lights, so he designed the bulb in ways that didn't preclude future innovation.

Consider again our example of relocating to a foreign country. You might have been inclined to buy a home right away in which to live. Another option might be to rent a place first. That way, if it turns out that you don't like the city in which you're living, or the particular neighborhood within that city, you can always move to a new locale you like better. If it turns out that you've lost your job or are running too quickly through your savings, you can move to a cheaper place.

Knowing that you haven't locked yourself in can give you the confidence to move ahead despite the uncertainty.

These three basic tactics—limiting the scope of risk mitigation, reducing the scope of your planned action, and improvising better to handle unforeseen threats—can make risk-hunting more manageable in the real world, in turn making it easier to convince yourself of your prowess at taming uncertainty. You don't need a supercomputer or to have the commitment of a Philippe Petit. You just need to be a bit more obsessive about mitigating risk than you ordinarily would be. Not only will your actual decision-making be smarter and more optimized; the world around you will seem less disorienting. You'll have embedded a story in your mind that says, "Yes, the world is a scary place, but I've done what's needed to shrink the uncertainty so that it won't hurt me." You'll be more psychologically equipped to face a chaotic landscape than you were before—and to take bold action.

WORKING WITH WHAT YOU ALREADY KNOW

In both our careers and personal lives, many of us might feel somewhat like innovators, forced to experiment our way through a shifting, uncertain landscape. It's true that in some areas scientific advances have shed new light, transforming uncertainties into known risks that we can quantify. In medicine, for instance, we now understand the molecular foundation of diseases, allowing us to better gauge our risk of contracting them. Yet uncertainty abounds and even seems to be intensifying. With climate change advancing, geopolitical order in flux, and advances in AI accelerating, will social and economic relationships fundamentally change? How will these and other changes interact with one another to change life as we know it in the coming years?

It's comforting to think that technology will finally solve the problem of uncertainty once and for all. In truth, uncertainty will continue to intrude upon our lives, much more than we might wish. We're left to cope with it, just as Harriet Tubman did during the mid-nineteenth century. In the presence of uncertainty, our fears can grow so intense that bold action seems impossible. But it isn't. Just as we can take steps to mitigate known risks, we also can take action to cope with our basic lack of clarity about the future, regaining a sense of control.

Most of us will have some natural inclination toward mobilizing either the power of faith or the more rational approach of risk-hunting, and we can use either to help us behave more courageously. We don't have to learn some strange, new formula to embolden ourselves—we can rely on strategies we're already using to make sense of the world. If you're religious or superstitious, lean into magical thinking more. If you're more rationally inclined, turn up the volume on traditional risk mitigation efforts. Your capacity for bold action will increase in turn.

In the chapters that follow, we'll consider a range of other mental strategies that can help you to feel more confident and also more inspired to behave boldly.

Chapter 2

CONFIDENCE

Science shows that we behave more courageously when we truly believe that we're well equipped to accomplish our goals. To boost your confidence and in turn your boldness, don't just bolster your skills—take additional steps to shift the situation in your favor.

Adult corn snakes, which can grow up to six feet long, are fairly innocuous as far as humans are concerned. They're not aggressive, and their bites are ultimately harmless. Farmers tend to look upon them as helpmates, since these creatures subsist on rodents, among other animals, and thus help keep infestations under control. Nonetheless, if you're afraid of snakes, to the point where you obsessively worry about them, have nightmares about encountering them, and refrain from enjoying outdoor activities to avoid them, then a lecture on the virtue of corn snakes won't sway your opinion very much. The last thing you'll want to do is approach a glass box containing a wriggly corn snake. Did I mention they grow up to six feet long?

In a 1982 study, Stanford social psychologists Albert Bandura, Linda Reese, and Nancy E. Adams recruited ten people with severe snake phobias to do just that. These people agreed to Bandura's study in order to seek help because their "phobic dread" was getting in the way of enjoying everyday life. To help them face their fears, Bandura and his colleagues asked these people to perform a series of tasks, each scarier than the previous one. First the participants had to come up to the snake. Then they had to gaze at it. Then they had to feel it with a gloved hand. Then they had to feel it with a bare hand. Then they had to let the snake roam freely around the room. Then they had to hold it up close to their noses. Then—worst of all—they had to let the snake make itself comfortable on their laps, while they did nothing to impede it.

This activity was just the beginning of the experiment. The point of these initial tasks was to judge how terrified these participants really were of snakes. Pretty terrified, it turned out: none of the participants managed to pick up the snake, and six couldn't even bring themselves to come near the box. From there, researchers provided our ophidiophobes, as people who are irrationally afraid of snakes are called, with training as to how to handle snakes, this time using a live boa constrictor. A resident snake expert showed participants how to perform the tasks. Participants had a chance to train on each task one at a time, achieving a sense of competency before going on to the next. Some of these tasks were broken down into steps to make the training easier. In other cases, the snake expert first helped participants get the feel of the task by performing it with them. After participants had gotten a specific task down pat, they rated how good they felt they were at the task. If they felt competent, they continued on to the next, harder task.

Some participants continued with this training until they felt they could approach the snake and interact with it, but couldn't touch it. Others continued until they had reached a greater sense of mastery, thinking themselves capable of physically handling the snake themselves. A final group of ophidiophobes continued until they reached an even higher level of perceived competency: they believed they were skilled enough to have the snake actually crawl freely on their lap.

When participants finished their training, researchers tested again how afraid they were of snakes and how well they performed snake-related tasks. Researchers turned up a striking pattern: the more capable that participants *believed* they were at interacting with the snake, the better they actually did at a behavior that they had previously perceived to be extremely scary. It might seem that our fears are instinctive or automatic and hence beyond our control—some of us just have irrational phobias about snakes, spiders, or bats that we can't shake. Yet we *can*, in fact, shake them: our sense of our own competency enhances our ability to behave courageously, even if we're quite terrified initially. When we possess confidence or "self-efficacy," as Bandura has termed it, we feel more in control of the situation. We're more empowered to take risks, and we're more likely to keep fear in check.

We start to cultivate self-efficacy when we're infants. We realize that we can effect change in the world, say by knocking a toy over with our hands. Over time we build more self-confidence and agency, a belief that things don't just happen to us—that we also *make* them happen. Sometimes, frankly, we take self-confidence too far. We fall prey to a bias in which we think we're more capable than we really are. If you've ever hurt yourself while taking on a DIY home repair, then you know what I'm talking about. By overvaluing your ability to operate effectively in a particular arena, you might take actions that later seem misguided or foolish.

Much of the time, though, the opposite problem arises: we have too little confidence and so shrink from taking bold action. As research has shown, we tend to underestimate our abilities when we face tasks that we regard as difficult and complex. Underlying this bias, we're prone to think that others are *always* better suited to tasks that we find difficult, even if that's not true. This tendency to doubt our own abilities prompts us to refrain from tackling difficult tasks, leaving them to others whom we perceive to be braver and more capable. We decide not to gun for that big promotion, thinking other candidates are more qualified. We refrain from speaking up in meetings, presuming that others are smarter or more informed.

The courageous individuals I studied weren't simply confident about their ability to succeed—they built a perception of self-efficacy into their very identities. Developing a courageous mindset, they came to think of themselves as strong, effective, well-prepared, and brave people. We can do the same, shifting how we think about ourselves and our abilities and building up our sense that we really can do it. The key is to *build our actual skills*—not just in the abstract, but in ways that support our own, internal narratives about our competency in complex, real-life settings. As Bandura noted, "Perceived self-efficacy is concerned not with the number of skills you have, but with *what you believe you can do with what you have* under a variety of circumstances." You might excel at certain important skills in the classroom, but if in real-life settings you find yourself doubting your abilities given your particular circumstances, you will be less likely to take action. Courageous people I studied tend to train in ways that leave them with a deep, practical perception of competency that both includes and transcends the task at hand.

But these individuals didn't stop there. Advanced training is one thing, but our self-efficacy still can falter when we actually find ourselves grappling with complex, real-life situations. Although we might feel confident that we possess the right skills, we might still doubt our ability to actually apply them well as we're taking action, especially when we're tackling seemingly impossible challenges. The individuals I studied tended to take additional steps while behaving boldly to boost their self-confidence even further. By breaking down big goals into manageable steps, looking to others for a vote of confidence, and securing vital tools as the need arose, they bolstered their sense that they could conquer the obstacles in front of them. Working to shape their situations in the moment gave them an additional feeling of control and agency that reduced their fear, further enabling their courage. We too can build our courage muscles by not merely training in advance but also attending to our self-efficacy in the process of addressing big challenges.

THE POWER OF "I CAN DO IT!"

How precisely does perceiving ourselves as capable support courageous behavior? For starters, it feeds our sense of control and agency, reducing the fear that comes with venturing out of our comfort zones. Most of us would perceive jumping out of an airplane as a risky—and scary—proposition. In one study, researchers asked young recruits in a paratrooper unit to fill out questionnaires on several occasions during their training process—when they reported for training on the first day, just before they first jumped out of an airplane, and at the culmination of training. The questionnaires asked about their levels of fear generally, how skilled they felt at jumping, the emotions they felt about their first jump, and how strongly they experienced physical sensations related to anxiety (sweating, dizziness, feeling faint, and so on).

They found that two-thirds of the soldiers experienced fear at the outset but proceeded regardless. The soldiers felt "more positive" and less fearful about jumping after successfully completing their first jump, suggesting that the experience had left them more assured about their own capabilities—more in control. To the extent that our self-efficacy strengthens, we experience less fear and can operate better in risky situations. Eventually, increasing confidence leads to such a reduction of fear that people no longer feel afraid at all.

It's easy to find examples that illustrate links between self-efficacy, a sense of control, fear reduction, and courage. If we believe we're strong and competent in our area of professional expertise, we'll take the leap to bold action even in life-and-death situations, simply because our self-efficacy reduces our fear response and enables us to act.

On January 15, 2009, when US Airways Flight 1549 set off on its regularly scheduled flight from New York City to Charlotte, North Carolina, the flight at first was, in the words of Captain C. B. "Sully" Sullenberger, "completely routine and unremarkable." But then, about one hundred seconds into it, the plane plowed into a flock of Canada geese, and all hell broke loose. There were so many birds, and the animals were so large, that it seemed to Sullenberger "as if it were a Hitchcock film." When some of the geese were sucked into the plane's massive engines, Sullenberger heard strange sounds, felt vibrations, and smelled a terrible odor of burning bird flesh. Then the unthinkable happened: both engines stopped delivering thrust. "It felt like the bottom had fallen out of our world," Sullenberger recalled.

Panic spread among the passengers, but Sullenberger knew he had to stay calm. It is very rare for commercial jetliners to lose all of their engines and have to glide to a landing, so much so that pilots don't even train for this specific scenario. As a seasoned pro with decades of experience, Sullenberger knew he had just a few minutes to execute a precise series of actions to bring the plane safely down. As he later explained to journalist Katie Couric, "I needed to touch down with the wings exactly level. I needed to touch down with the nose slightly up. I needed to touch down at a descent rate that was survivable. And I needed to touch down just above our minimum flying speed, but not below it. And I needed to make all these things happen simultaneously."

Incredibly, Sullenberger kept his cool, executed these precise tasks, and landed his airliner full of passengers in the middle of New York's Hudson River. Not a single passenger or crew member perished—a feat some have dubbed the "miracle on the Hudson." How did Sullenberger manage to take decisive action in the face of mortal danger, even though he knew full well how much trouble he was in? As he remembered, he fell back on his training and experience, which also connected back to his identity as a competent, seasoned pilot. Despite not having trained to handle a two-engine shutdown scenario mid-flight, his countless hours in the cockpit had produced an unshakable sense of self-confidence in his piloting skills generally. Not only had he trained in in-flight crisis management, but he taught it to others as well. "I was sure that I could do it," he said. "I think in many ways, as it turned out, my entire life up to that moment had been preparation to handle that particular moment." Because of his sense of his own abilities as a pilot, he was able to step up and act when it counted

In contrast, stories abound of people who become paralyzed by fear in the moment and can't act, because they *don't* feel that intense sense of confidence. On February 14, 2018, when a teenager in Parkland, Florida, opened fire on students on the campus of Marjory Stoneman Douglas High School with an automatic weapon, Sheriff's Deputy Scot Peterson was on duty and armed with a Glock pistol. By the time he arrived at the building where the shooting was taking place, the gunman had already mowed down two dozen people. In a Hollywood movie version of events, Peterson would have raced Rambo-style inside the building to bravely and effectively take out the shooter. But alas, that's not what he did. He stayed safely outside, crouched down next to a wall, while the carnage continued. Even after other officers arrived and raced inside the building, Peterson stayed parked where he was, apparently paralyzed by fear. Meanwhile, six more people inside the school were killed—lives he arguably could have saved had he managed to act.

In the tragedy's aftermath, outrage at Peterson's apparent cowardice led authorities to charge him with crimes that collectively could have landed him in prison for almost a century. If we look closer at what led the "Coward of Broward," as some have called him, to fall down on the job, we find that a lack of self-efficacy seems to have played a profound role. It is extraordinarily risky for a single police officer to race into a building and engage an active shooter—usually squads of highly trained officers tackle that job. Peterson didn't have nearly the kind of relevant general experience in his job that Captain Sullenberger had. Although Peterson had worked as an officer in schools for almost three decades, he had seldom arrested anyone before. He had little experience with violent crime, since the area surrounding the school was considered relatively safe.

Moreover, Peterson had received little formal training about how to handle active shooter situations. The quality of this training was, in his words, "shit" (more on this in a moment). Speaking of a witness who in court portrayed his training as extensive, he said, "When you listen to that guy, you'd have thought we were getting SEAL Team Six training. It's a farce." The most recent training he'd received hadn't encouraged him to boldly take on a rifle-toting assailant. On the contrary, instructors reading from the training script would have told him: "There is no reason to give up a good position of cover. . . . Remember, the cavalry is on their way, so it's better to hold, than to expose yourself to unknown threats." Peterson also wasn't equipped with the gear required for taking on a criminal with an automatic weapon, such as a bulletproof vest or a rifle.

The public expects police officers to immediately show bravery in a crisis situation like this, but in fact Peterson had little reason to think he would succeed in the task of bringing down a shooter armed with an automatic weapon. We can't know for sure, but it seems highly unlikely that he thought of himself as a seasoned, SWAT-team professional.

On the contrary, he knew enough about the challenge of taking out an active shooter by himself to realize how *little* he knew about how to actually get the job done. This narrative—"I *don't* have what it takes," and even "I'm not a competent person"—didn't help him to overcome the tremendous fear he likely felt in this situation. So he stayed put. I am not in any way condoning Peterson's inaction that undoubtedly led to numerous tragic deaths, but I do believe that understanding these underlying dynamics can help us grasp his cowardice a bit better. As one officer memorably put it, "You can't send Officer Snuggles out to face the dragon" of a deranged shooter. You need one that is thoroughly trained in relevant skills. Sadly, Peterson appears to have been an Officer Snuggles, lacking the ability, identity, and confident mindset required to step up.

TRAIN LIKE YOU MEAN IT

Given how important self-efficacy is when it comes to taking bold action, how can you nurture it? How can you go further and create an awareness of yourself as a strong, competent, courageous person? The obvious answer is to *build your actual skills.*

Two kinds of skill-building are important here, what we might call specific and general. First, we need training in the *specific skills* necessary to perform a given task. If we want to feel confident and in control in a new sales role, for example, we need training in the specific skills related to pitching clients, nurturing sales relationships, and the like. If we're trying to become a primary care doctor, we need training in medical skills like the diagnosis of disease and the framing of treatment protocols as well as nonmedical skills like how to communicate with patients and interact with insurance companies.

Of course, there's training, and there's *training*. The courageous few train with an unusual intensity and focus, one that allows them to feel confident that no matter what the circumstances, they can handle it. They are intentional about their training, practicing not in a rote, repetitive way but with an eye toward always pushing themselves and taking their performance further—what some have called "deliberate practice." Rather than simply seeking to acquire a skill, they want to master it and even become the very best at it. By progressively improving and experiencing fewer failures, we not only build up our mastery of the skill, but a deeper understanding of how and when to use it in the most effective manner.

Regardless of the kind of specific skills we need, it's important that training gives us a chance to practice under pressure. Recall the observation of psychologist Albert Bandura: what's most important isn't just that we know how to perform tasks, but that we feel competent doing so in specific, real-life settings. Sitting in a training course where an instructor conveys knowledge about a topic in the abstract might leave you more informed, but when you're out in the field contending with a specific situation, will you really feel confident enough to take action?

Scot Peterson technically received active shooter training. But some have argued that he and other officers didn't get enough training, and they also didn't get high-quality, specialized instruction in the specific skills they would need to handle a real-life scenario involving a crazed perpetrator with an automatic weapon holed up in a school full of students. "If the public knew how poorly some police officers are trained and, more importantly, how poorly those undertrained officers perform—thank goodness crooks don't know," one expert said. Again, I am not condoning Peterson's inaction, but we can only imagine how he might have responded had he trained with intensity, determined to truly master ensuring public safety in situations such as this. The chances are better that he instinctively would have stepped up and taken bold action.

Many of us in the workplace struggle to access the specialized skills training we need to feel confident at specific tasks—potentially including simulations, expert instruction, a chance to practice and master skills, and so on. Given how busy we are, we might feel tempted to let this lack of training slide or to engage with it superficially, figuring that we'll pick up what we need to know along the way. That's a mistake: we're passing up a vital opportunity to build more self-efficacy, foster a stronger sense of our own power, and build our courage muscle. And most important, embrace these learning moments with intensity and a desire to internalize those skills.

At the same time, focusing on learning specific skills isn't enough. To maximize the sense of control we feel and in turn activate our courage, we need to pursue a second kind of preparation: training and experience that affirms our *general competency*. This is the sense that we possess a broad capability to obtain results across a variety of situations—that we are resilient, adaptive, and committed to excellence no matter what. As courageous people the world over will tell you, such empowering beliefs are absolutely vital.

I've always wondered how astronauts muster the guts to strap themselves onto a giant rocket and blast themselves into space. When I asked NASA astronaut Terry Virts, he told me that the survival training he received early in his career as a military aviator and later at NASA proved pivotal by nourishing a general confidence grounded in toughness. After spending time in nature suffering from cold, lack of food, and other privations during his NASA survival training, he emerged with a general sense of "I can do it" that he hadn't had before. "Afterwards I had so much confidence," he says, "I'm like, man, I can do that. . . . Maybe I'm better than what I thought." As he wrote about his survival training: "Spending intense time with my comrades, being pushed to our physical and mental limits, did more for my self-confidence than anything I've experienced."

Military training often makes use of similar hardship experiences to build a general sense of confidence. The training that young recruits to the US Marine Corps undergo is designed to be tough. At boot camp, recruits are subject to sleep deprivation; they experience hunger due to limited caloric intake to simulate operational stress; and they are required to hike long distances as part of their endurance and resilience training—perhaps even with an angry, menacing drill instructor watching them. They also undergo extensive training in fighting, including hand-to-hand combat and tactical decision-making. As one famous Marine Corps recruiting poster reads, "We didn't promise you a rose garden." After completing their training, most marines feel a strong, general sense of pride and empowerment. Many of my students who are former marines have expressed this deep sense of "I can do it" to me. In their eyes, they're now part of an elite group of performers who have shown their ability to persevere and prevail in the face of hardship, and who have the general training and toughness required to be world-class warriors. If they could get through these intense training challenges, they think, they can get through anything. A general competency is built into their very identity as soldiers.

Unfortunately, many of us don't undergo general, confidence-building experiences like Virts and Marine Corps recruits endure. Here again, we can find workarounds for ourselves. In your spare time, take on personal challenges that push you into your discomfort zone—just to prove to yourself that you can. If you're a student, try taking a year to live in a foreign country whose language you don't know.

At work, volunteer for an assignment that affords you a chance to get to know a whole different function or area of the business. In your spare time, try running your first marathon or taking up a physically demanding sport like rock climbing. Find ways to really stretch yourself and boost your resilience and determination to excel, no matter the circumstances. You might learn an array of specific skills, but as you persevere through challenges and achieve goals, you'll also walk away with a general sense of power and confidence.

SHAPING THE SITUATION

As helpful as skill-building can be to boost self-efficacy and hence courage, courageous people go further. To truly internalize self-confidence and infuse it into their identity, they also take steps to actually change or influence the situations they're in. They understand that their ability to feel in control of a situation lies at least in part in their capacity to shape it. The very act of working to turn a situation to your advantage can give you a boost of confidence that makes a difference, especially when you're tackling big challenges. Three strategies are most helpful here.

CONFIDENCE BOOSTER #1: GO SMALL TO GO BIG

Mentally breaking down a challenge into smaller parts and focusing on one part at a time can lead to more courageous behavior, allowing us to develop greater perceptions of self-efficacy over time. We get our "foot in the door," feeling more confident than we did at the outset and then moving on to tackle other, bigger parts. All along, the tasks feel more manageable, and we feel a sense of power over the situation. As the courage researcher Pauline Schilpzand argues, a "foot-in-the-door" dynamic seems to hold when it comes to bravery, with smaller, less remarkable feats paving the way for more substantial acts of risk-taking. A person who rushes into a burning building might seem impossibly heroic, but in fact that person might be a professional firefighter who gradually gained a sense of competency thanks to a long period of training and the tackling of progressively riskier experiences. Courage, Schilpzand suggests, is very much like a muscle, in that it strengthens incrementally over time. The way to start is to get your foot in the door and go from there.

I experienced this foot-in-the-door approach to building courage when I learned to pilot a small plane. Initially I was quite nervous to fly, but Jerry, my instructor, a veteran pilot, put me through a series of scenarios that progressively tested my abilities. We'd be flying and he would switch off the engine of the plane, demonstrating that we wouldn't crash. On another occasion, he purposely stalled the plane. With him sitting beside me and telling me what to do, I took emergency action and got us out of the stall. On another occasion, he flew me into clouds and had me navigate through them. Each time I made it through a challenge he set for me, my confidence in my abilities increased. That sense of control I felt eased my fear and set the stage for bold action in the future, including my first solo flight.

If you're feeling daunted by a challenge, think of how you might be able to break it down into more manageable bites. Sometimes it might be immediately clear how to do that, but if not, ask others who are more experienced, or hire a coach to help you. Give yourself time to notch small, confidence-boosting wins. As you succeed, make sure that you continue to take on bigger, riskier tasks that stretch you and build your confidence even more.

Once we're taking a foot-in-the-door approach, we can up the ante by embracing a related strategy: focusing on the process rather than the end result. When we break down big challenges into numerous small pieces and work on each piece, we tend to stay focused on the ongoing work rather than on the end result. That too can build our courage muscle. An ambitious end result can overwhelm us, arousing fear and sapping our motivation. It can distract us from what we must do to hone our skills and apply them effectively in the moment. By fixing our minds on the process and the small subchallenges we might need to surmount, we maintain a sense of control and steel ourselves to take on seemingly daunting challenges, one small step at a time.

In 1998, Michigan State University's football team was struggling toward the middle of its season. Slated to play the nation's top-ranked team, the Ohio State Buckeyes, Michigan State's head football coach, Nick Saban, decided to consult a faculty member at his school's psychiatry department for advice on how to fire up the team and avoid an embarrassing defeat. The guidance he received was this: "Tell the players to play one play at a time, like it has a life of its own. There's no scoreboard, there's no external factors, your whole focus for 60 minutes is just play the next play to the best of your ability."

Saban took this advice, coaching his players to forget about the scoreboard and just *play* each minute to the fullest. Initially they fell behind and were losing by fifteen points after halftime. But then Michigan State got a lucky break on a play and the momentum shifted decisively in the fourth quarter. Commenting on how his team managed to win the game even when the outlook appeared grim, Saban said, "Nothing changed. Everybody kept that same demeanor. And we won the game. That changed my whole approach to coaching, and not being so outcome-oriented." Research has confirmed that focusing too much on an end result can hurt performance, while immersing yourself on the moment-to-moment process can unlock adaptive, on-the-fly thinking, which ultimately can lead to better outcomes.

Saban went on to become a coaching legend at the University of Alabama. Process thinking underpinned this success, comprising the core of Saban's coaching approach. Players learn what Saban called "The Process," described as "a definition of what you have to do to accomplish the goals you have. . . . You are not *outcome* oriented; you are *process* oriented." Rather than concentrating on winning per se or even on achieving specific performance goals like catching a certain number of passes in a season, Saban has his players adopt broad, developmental goals, such as "I want to be a complete player at my position." He and his staff then lay out subprocesses that players can work on to make progress toward their goal. By working on a daily basis toward their developmental goals, players would in the end be more likely to put out exceptional performance, and to help the team to win. As one player said, "Coach Saban is the most consistent, process-driven person I've ever been around in my entire life. I mean, this man loves the process. I don't think he really enjoyed winning. What he enjoyed was the grind."

Focusing on process—and in turn, on taking incremental, ongoing steps—led Saban's players to increased self-efficacy over time, and reduced their fear. In the face of potentially frightening challenges, knowing that they could limit their gaze to the task right in front of them made the game seem much more manageable and in their control. The athletes came to "trust the process," as a team mantra had it, understanding that if they just focused intensely on the minutiae of their training and the here-and-now, breaking big tasks into a series of much smaller ones, they would improve and surmount big challenges.

CONFIDENCE BOOSTER #2: SEE YOUR STRENGTHS THROUGH OTHERS' EYES

As we embark on bold action, we can further boost our self-confidence and our capacity for courage by relying on others around us. When they affirm our capabilities, such "social persuasion," as Albert Bandura called it, motivates us to act, allowing us to build our skills and feel more self-efficacy. We're all human; when others praise our skills, it feels good. Our sense of self-worth, competence, and potential blossoms. As Bandura cautions, social persuasion works best when those giving us feedback are credible, when their messages are rooted in reality, and when they can point to objective evidence of our competency. In contrast, when people pump us up excessively without regard for our actual capabilities, we might go on to fail in our endeavors, eroding our confidence and in turn our capability to behave courageously. "To raise unrealistic beliefs of personal capabilities," Bandura says, "only invites failures that will discredit the persuaders and further undermine the recipients' beliefs in their capabilities."

In February 2023, *The New York Times* ran a story about Yulia Bondarenko, a middle school teacher in Ukraine who volunteered to defend her city of Kyiv against invading Russian forces. The military gave her a gun and bullets, assigning her to a unit of volunteers that would take on the Russians if they entered the city. Bondarenko was a complete newcomer to the world of guns and fighting. Her first two weeks, she said, were "a constant nightmare"—she felt "like [she] was in a fog." And she was a woman in a unit made up primarily of men, including experienced soldiers.

But over a period of weeks, she learned the basics of combat, thanks to her fellow soldiers, who taught her marksmanship and fighting skills. After some weeks, her unit was sent east to train and eventually fight on the front lines. Given the option of avoiding combat service, Bondarenko chose to go, overcoming her trepidations. The formal training she now received gave her self-efficacy. But what also made a difference was the support from her male fellow soldiers. "It was pleasant when the guys said, 'It's working out with you.' And they said, 'I would go into battle with you.'" Bondarenko's confidence in her abilities, coupled with her belief in the Ukrainian cause, enabled her to overcome her fears and perform her military responsibilities, even in the face of withering Russian attacks. As she remarked, "I am an infantry soldier now." Self-efficacy as a warrior, reinforced by moral support from others, had become woven into her very identity.

Do your colleagues at work provide you with the encouragement you need? If not, you might consider giving them a vote of confidence in hopes that they'll return the favor. Or you might try making yourself vulnerable to them, revealing areas in which you're still learning and indicating that you could use their encouragement. Friends, mentors, and coaches also can affirm their faith in you and your talents. As we'll see later in the book, it's important to surround yourself with a close group of people who can lift you up in a whole variety of ways, including emotionally.

CONFIDENCE BOOSTER #3: GET TOOLS YOU CAN USE

A final way that we can shape the situations we're in, further boosting self-confidence, a sense of control, and our capacity for courage, is by securing the tools we need to perform. These tools can include confidence in physical devices, people on whom you can rely, or even pre-rehearsed processes that will help you address a situation if it arises. When an individual feels they're well equipped to perform a task, and when their toolbox is so comprehensive that they know they'll be able to improvise solutions regardless of the situation, they are more likely to stick their necks out and take action in the face of fear.

A corollary of the existing research is that we should seek out environments that equip us with what we need to succeed. Another is that teams and organizations should take steps to ensure that people feel confident in their own abilities and the team or organization's ability to perform. One organization that does this particularly well is the industrial conglomerate Danaher. Emphasizing the development of self-efficacy among its people, the company offered a suite of versatile management tools that leaders throughout the organization can draw upon that could help them tackle any difficult situation. The "Danaher Business System" (DBS), as this suite is called, included dozens of tools covering everything from strategic planning to accounting, new product development, and leadership development. Using DBS, leaders felt secure in knowing that no matter what challenge arose, they would have powerful tools to help them get the job done.

This system had helped Danaher drive extraordinary results across a diverse range of its portfolio of businesses, so leaders across the company trusted it. A strong culture for sharing best practices among teams also figured prominently. Managers felt emboldened at knowing that they could reach out to colleagues and quickly obtain the information or guidance they needed. This set of tools along with access to executives who had used them successfully gave leaders a sense of confidence that they could take courageous action and solve what in others' eyes might have seemed like intractable challenges.

On the strength of DBS and the sense of efficacy it supported, commitment to winning became the norm, as did gutsiness. The result was extraordinary business performance. Between 2007 and 2018, Danaher generated returns of 381 percent, far above the 155 percent produced by the S&P 500. Between 2009 and 2015, Danaher's share price tripled in value, and over the past two decades its earnings have far exceeded those of other technology-intensive conglomerates like 3M, Ingersoll Rand, and Honeywell. In an interview, former Danaher CEO (and current General Electric CEO) Larry Culp noted that DBS helped make Danaher a more innovative company in ways that many outsiders don't fully appreciate. By empowering and enabling people to take creative risks and make small, daily innovations in their work, DBS boosted efficiency and productivity, which allowed the company to invest more heavily in forward-looking initiatives. All these little innovations accumulated to produce extraordinary results.

If you're embarking on a challenge, have you taken the time to assess the tools you'll need and to provide for them? If you lead a team or organization, have you outfitted your team members with tools, systems, and processes so they feel confident enough to take risks? Securing the right tools might require an investment of time or money—it's sometimes tempting to jump right in and figure out the details later. But making sure you or those you lead are equipped for success can pay important dividends, allowing people to feel confident about what they're doing and to proceed boldly.

FREEZING IN MIDFLIGHT

Although taking steps to build our confidence can allow normally fearful people to perform brave feats, we should heed Albert Bandura's concern that our perception of our capabilities not become unduly inflated as a result of others' feedback. As research has found, overconfidence can benefit us in social situations, allowing us to wield more influence over others. People like being around confident individuals and see them as strong leaders. But overconfidence doesn't necessarily help our performance, and it can hinder our ability to behave boldly once we're confronted with our own, actual limitations. Overconfidence also can lead us to reckless behavior, which can damage us and prevent us from pursuing our goals.

I saw how potentially devastating an inflated sense of self-efficacy can be while earning my pilot's license. Should I have given so much weight in my mind to the positive feedback about my abilities that I received from my instructor Jerry? Beyond a point, maybe not. Soon after my first solo flight, I spent an afternoon flying from the Seattle area to an unfamiliar airport in the San Francisco Bay Area. Several other students and our instructor were flying as well, each in their own airplane. Midway through the trip, we ran into some clouds. All of us handled it well, except for one of my fellow students, "Ben," who panicked. He became disoriented while flying in the clouds and the unfamiliar airspace and had a meltdown in midflight. "Help!" Ben shouted. "I don't know where I am. I don't know what I'm doing. I don't know where I'm going. I have no idea what is going on." Our instructor had mistakenly overinflated his confidence. Ben was a quick study, but flying solo without an expert on board was a whole different animal.

It was a terrifying moment for all of us who were listening on the same radio frequency, and nearly catastrophic for Ben. Fortunately, our instructor managed to calm him down over the radio, helping

Ben to orient himself by looking at his compass and altimeter. It was a memorable lesson in the importance of keeping self-confidence—our own and that of others around us—tethered to our actual capability.

I hope that reading about the power of self-efficacy will prompt you to build your confidence using the strategies I've presented. Seize opportunities small and large to build your skills, both the specialized ones you need for specific tasks and those that lead to a generalized sense of confidence. If you lead others, give them as many opportunities as you can to develop their capabilities and take more control. Be sure also to give them a self-efficacy boost as they take action, helping them to break down big tasks, affirming that they're performing well, and giving them access to the tools they need to succeed. Let them know as well that if they don't have the tools they'll need, you'll help to find them.

Research shows that developing more self-efficacy can benefit you in many areas of your life. Depending on the situation, it can help you overcome personal difficulties, regain your health after illnesses, and feel less anxious. But it can also help you take bolder action. You can feel less fear by instilling in yourself a realistic belief that "I can do it!" Of course, there are other emotions besides fear to consider when it comes to forging a courageous mindset. As we'll see in the next chapter, you can help yourself behave boldly not just by trying to shrink your fears but also by arousing other emotions that motivate you to act, including love, joy, excitement, determination, awe, and even anger. You can tap these other emotions by committing to a broader mission that you feel passionately about and that inspires you.

Chapter 3

COMMITMENT

The stories we tell about ourselves galvanize our courage, fueling our commitment and motivating us to sacrifice ourselves for a noble cause. The most inspiring stories of all are anchored in deep purpose and take the form of a hero's journey.

It was 1995, and Patrick Awuah, a young immigrant from Ghana, faced a momentous decision, one that would affect his life's trajectory. He had achieved what most would consider to be the American dream, working at a well-paying job at Microsoft and enjoying a nice, upper-middle-class life in Seattle. His wife had just given birth to their first child, and with the dot-com boom in full swing, his prospects seemed bright. And yet, something didn't sit right with him. The woes of his native Africa were prominent in the news headlines—civil war in Somalia, genocide in Rwanda, economic distress in many countries, including Ghana. How, he thought, could he just live his prosperous life when his continent was on fire?

For months, Patrick had been thinking of quitting his job, moving to Ghana, and starting some kind of entrepreneurial venture that would contribute to the country's advancement. Considering the many conditions that were holding Ghanaians back, such as water scarcity, unemployment, and inadequate health care, he noticed that a deeper dynamic was at play. "Underlying every challenge," he later said, "were people in positions of responsibility who were neither fixing problems nor creating solutions. Very few seemed to care, and even those who did were resigned to the status quo."

Patrick concluded that the most fundamental problem facing Ghana and Africa as a whole wasn't economic or technical in nature. It was a moral malaise that had taken hold, particularly among a corrupt, unenlightened leadership class that lacked the skills and values to build a productive society. This malaise in turn reflected the weakness of higher education in Ghana and elsewhere in Africa, which failed to impart a strong sense of ethics. If Patrick could somehow improve the way the top 5 percent of Ghanaians were educated, he could make a profound and lasting difference in his home country. On an even greater scale, he thought, he could help fuel Africa's transformation, changing the narrative about the continent's endemic corruption, dysfunction, and misery.

Growing up in modest circumstances, Patrick attended Swarthmore College in Pennsylvania on a scholarship, and he came away with a profound appreciation for a liberal arts education and its ability to render people more tolerant, thoughtful, and ethically minded. Education was very different in Ghana, focused on memorization rather than the critical thinking that feeds into ethical judgments. Now Patrick wondered if he might create a new, American-style institution grounded in a humanistic, liberal arts approach, one that would teach young Ghanaians the technical skills they would need to compete in the marketplace, but that would also help them to develop an appreciation for integrity and an ability to think carefully through ethical dilemmas.

This line of thinking confronted Patrick with an ethical dilemma of his own. The idea that a new kind of university would transform Ghanaian society was far-fetched. Even if such an institution could have an impact, Patrick knew nothing about how to build a new university from the ground up. Was it responsible of him to think of uprooting his family and giving up a lucrative career at Microsoft to pursue this seemingly crazy dream? Did he owe it to his family to set the idea aside and continue on with his comfortable life as before?

Patrick decided to risk everything and go for it. He went to his boss at Microsoft and told him that he was leaving. Then, with his wife's support, he got to work on what would become Ashesi University, named after the word for "beginning" in Fante, a Ghanaian dialect. His first move was to enroll in the MBA program at the University of California, Berkeley, to gain more clarity about his goal and how to achieve it. He researched and developed a full business plan, pinning down the financial resources he would need to get the school up and running as well as an operational model that would allow it to eventually become self-sustaining.

Having a plan in place was a step forward, but the challenges before Patrick remained daunting. Somehow Patrick would have to build a physical campus in Ghana. Recruit the right faculty. Obtain funding from donors. Attract capable students. Convince local regulators to allow him to grant degrees. Overcome opposition from an accreditation board that was suspicious of private universities. As he later admitted, these challenges aroused "a measure of fear" in him. "The goal that I had set for myself seemed as difficult as climbing Mount Everest."

But upon graduating from UC Berkeley in 1999, Patrick remained as committed as ever. Remarkably, so was one of his fellow students, a young woman of Japanese descent named Nina Marini. Nina had no personal connection to Africa, and in fact she'd planned to return to her native Japan after receiving her MBA. Nevertheless, Patrick asked her to cofound the school with him. She was reluctant at first, mulling over the decision for weeks. "It felt like a risk. It felt like an unknown, an uncharted territory for me," she told me in an interview. But meeting Patrick and working with him on his feasibility study made an impression. "This classmate with a dream and vision—it was a discovery for me," she said. "He's not afraid to think big." She was in.

In Nina's mind, any fears or hesitations she had paled in comparison to her enthusiasm for Patrick's vision of contributing to a renaissance in Africa. "I often talk about how it's like we were taking on a quest," Nina said. "Ashesi was like a vision that was so compelling and meaningful and clearly impactful, it just sucked a lot of people in." More than merely a vision, Patrick seemed to be telling Nina and himself a kind of story that implicitly cast him, her, and others who joined them as heroes embarked on an epic quest. It was a narrative about a series of actions that could culminate, against all odds, in a glorious accomplishment.

THE POWER OF PERSONAL NARRATIVES

The stories we tell ourselves about our lives and goals, and that we sometimes communicate publicly to others, have an enormous influence on our sense of self, our understanding of the wider world, and our ability to behave courageously. We know from our earliest childhood that stories have motivational power, arousing compelling emotions and in that way inspiring us to rise up and help others. Stories affect us imaginatively, allowing us to enter a different world and put *ourselves* in the action. There is actually a biochemical mechanism for this motivational and imaginative power of storytelling. Narratives can trigger the release of the neurochemical oxytocin, which floods our brains when we feel empathy or connections with others and that scholars have linked to altruistic action. Have you ever felt emotionally transported while reading a story, to the point where you feel what a character is feeling? That's oxytocin at work. As the neuroscientist Paul Zak has shown, the release of oxytocin thanks to a compelling story leads people to take positive actions, such as donating to a worthy cause.

Patrick's goal might have been a long shot, but through the story he crafted, he positioned it as a noble adventure that he and others could join, and one with at least some chance of success. As Nina Marini remembers, Patrick's story didn't simply present a vision: it also laid out concrete, practical steps for overcoming the obvious challenges. "The way Patrick had painted the vision, it was very easy to believe that that could happen," she said. This quest was so compelling that Nina committed to it despite the obvious risks, perceiving that if she didn't, she would regret her choice.

Many others would commit to Patrick's heroic quest, from the American teachers who set aside their careers to spend time at this experimental school, to the local villagers who sold him the land at below-market prices, to the skeptical government ministers who agreed to back his project, to the former Microsoft colleagues who donated money to his venture, to local students who agreed to give a new academic institution a chance. Each was willing to take personal and professional risks to make Patrick's dream a reality. They made his dream theirs, in the process taking on a shared identity and a sense of common fate.

For some of them, the sheer boldness of the quest Patrick outlined, his absolute determination to make it a reality, and his sense that it *was* possible to achieve were reason enough to sign on. "I was talking to him one time," a former Microsoft colleague and early Ashesi backer remembers, "and said, 'What's Plan B?,'" and "[Awuah] said, 'There is no Plan B. We're going to make this work.'" A local village chief likewise recalls being "highly impressed" by the story Patrick told about his mission. "The way he talked, wanting to establish the school to help Ghana and Africa . . . this man is not somebody who is just making up a story."

Today, over two decades since it was launched in 2002, the institution Patrick and Nina founded and that their team built—Ashesi University—has formal accreditation, its own campus, and thousands of alumni making a positive impact across Africa. Establishing the university took over a decade and required significant risk-taking on the part of the founding team as well as donors, local residents, and others. Patrick couldn't guarantee that his unlikely project would succeed, and at times it nearly foundered for lack of funding. What he could do—and what we all can do to build our courage muscles—is to shape how he and others around him thought about the project, conveying it as a morally resonant heroic quest. Attaching himself to the quest fired up deep-seated emotions, inspiring him to overcome his fears and take that first, bold step into the fray. Conveying that quest to others inspired them too to close their eyes, swallow hard, and join him in attempting the seemingly impossible.

COURAGE FOR AN INSPIRING CAUSE

If conceiving of our actions as an epic quest can instill boldness, how can we narrate that quest to ourselves and to others so that it motivates us most powerfully? The content and form of these stories—what they're about and how they're structured—both matter. Let's first consider the content. Patrick's story for himself revolved around an impressive goal, but not just any—it was one with salient moral overtones. Patrick wasn't going to perform some arduous feat for its own sake. Rather, he was determined to do some good in the world, to help people. He sought to improve life in an entire country and maybe even a continent. One key to expanding our capacity for courage is to pursue quests that have moral content, putting ourselves in the role of doers of good, vanquishers of evil, or both.

Adopting a quest that is decidedly moral unlocks tremendous emotional power. The connection between courage and morality runs deep. All of us have moral values that we hold dear, concepts such as truthfulness, justice, or compassion. These values often inform our deepest sense of identity and purpose. When we see these values violated around us, we may feel compelled to spring into action, especially when we feel a sense of ownership or duty and perceive that we're in a position to make a difference. As psychologists teach us, emotion plays an important role in these kinds of situations. We feel *personally* aroused by a sense of what psychologists call "felt responsibility."

Behaving courageously on behalf of moral principles satisfies some of our most basic drives, including our need for a sense of belonging and a positive personal identity. You might take bold action to affirm your connection to a group—a phenomenon we'll explore later in this book. You might feel a strong sense of patriotism, for instance, and a willingness to risk your safety in pursuit of a principled vision of national glory. Some of us also identify with the very *idea* of behaving morally. You might relish what researchers have called "moral potency," a perception that you possess "ownership over the moral aspects of [your] environment." This psychological state in turn allows you to take risky action on behalf of your higher ideals. You might see sticking up for what you believe and advancing a morally significant goal as something that is core or essential to who you are. And you might feel a sense of meaning and self-worth knowing that you're doing good in the world.

By framing a morally resonant quest for himself and later communicating it to others, Patrick Awuah could feel like he was living up to his idea of himself as a moral actor, one whose actions matched his principles. He had the energy and drive that come from understanding clearly his purpose or reason for being. Certainly, he could feel a greater sense of coherence than he could living his old life as a Microsoft employee. To behave more boldly, you can follow his lead and tell yourself a story in which you're the hero who takes on risk not just for its own sake, but to do some good in the world.

Be careful, however—particularly when you're signing on to quests that others have created. People sometimes engineer quests they *think* are good but that most other people perceive as blatantly immoral. Extremists of various stripes have performed heinous acts of terror, thinking that they're fighting forces of evil and bringing about positive change. Members of religious cults have surrendered their agency to morally challenged leaders who, on account of their personal charisma, have deluded them into thinking that they're on a virtuous path. When it comes to inspiring bravery, the pursuit of purpose is a psychologically potent weapon that can be used for both good *and* evil. When assessing a heroic quest, you must scrutinize the ambitions of its authors, making sure that they conform to your own values and moral sense.

STRUCTURING A POWERFUL STORY

To frame compelling quest stories, focus on the structure or organizational schema of the narrative, not just its moral content. The stories that do it best, keeping audiences' attention and allowing them to become transported emotionally into the worlds of characters, are those structured to depict rising tension—what literary types call a "narrative arc." Such stories typically unfold across a series of events, in which the protagonist's desire comes up against obstacles of mounting size and seriousness. We seem to have a cognitive and perhaps biological bent toward the classic "hero's journey" kind of story, where a protagonist survives a number of increasingly harrowing trials, eventually achieving a lofty goal while undergoing some personal transformation in the process.

Scholars have mapped out the tension-filled hero's journey in all kinds of complex ways. But for everyday purposes, compelling, tension-filled quests usually display three core narrative elements: a vision of a desired future, an elaboration of the obstacles or challenges, and the outlining of practical steps we could or will take to make our vision real. Quests with these three elements create tension by putting grand ambitions in contact with challenges, and they point to the resolution of the tension by presenting practical steps on the road to making the dream a reality.

If we look closely at courageous people around us, we often find them weaving together highly motivational, tension-filled stories in their minds and communicating them to others. They don't necessarily do so consciously, and the elements we have outlined might sometimes emerge in uneven and shifting ways. Nevertheless, the three elements of goal, obstacle, and means come together as a powerful "story," a heroic quest that affects them and others both cognitively and emotionally and allows them to override their fears.

The Russian politician Alexei Navalny is a good example. Think about this scenario: You've dedicated years of your life to vigorously opposing an authoritarian government known for its brutal repression. You've finally found personal safety with your young family in a neighboring country, having narrowly survived an ugly assassination attempt. Would you then leave your family and *go back* to your home country, putting yourself at immediate risk of arrest, imprisonment, or death?

Navalny did just that. In August 2020, he fell sick and was placed into a medically induced coma after being poisoned by what German officials later identified as Novichok, a nerve agent associated with the Russian government due to its Soviet-era origins. Brought to Germany for medical care, he might have stayed there and lived out his days in safety and comfort. But he didn't. In January 2021, he and his wife flew back to Russia, leaving their two children behind. "Good man," one prominent Russian wrote on social media, "but he's taking a risk." Indeed he was. Upon touching down, Navalny was immediately detained by Russian authorities. In February 2024, after being transferred to a remote Siberian penal colony, Navalny died in prison.

For years Navalny had depicted for himself and others a heroic quest marked by the three elements of goal, obstacles, and means. As for the first of these elements, Navalny defined interlinked goals of combatting corruption in his home country, fighting back against authoritarianism, and promoting democratic governance. His ambition, as he and his colleagues put it, was to create "the beautiful Russia of the future." Beauty was, he suggested, tantamount to a kind of normalcy. As Navalny remarked in 2018, "I want to live in a normal country, and refuse to accept any talk about Russia being doomed to being a bad, poor or servile country. I want to live here, and I can't tolerate the injustice that for many people has become routine." Elsewhere, Navalny clarified that the goal was to turn Russia into a prosperous, safe country with Western democratic ideals. In 2021 he wrote: "My country could right now become a rich, successful state moving along the European path of development. We are specific, like any nation, but we are Europe. We are the West. The basic political structure should be parliamentary democracy, and fair elections, independent courts and full freedom for the media. . . . [These] should be sacred concepts in the new Russia."

In the course of fighting to bring about "the beautiful Russia of the future," Navalny unmasked the primary obstacle preventing the realization of that vision: resistance from an entrenched and corrupt elite led by Russian president Vladimir Putin. In a 2011 radio interview, he famously labeled Putin's United Russia party as "the party of crooks and thieves." The fundamental obstacle, he suggested, wasn't just these bad actors but a sense among ordinary Russians that they couldn't be opposed. That kind of fatalism was "the basis of Putin's regime," he once said.

Over the years, Navalny articulated a series of steps that he and his supporters could take to root out corruption and transform Russia. First among them was investigating and drawing attention to the elite's corrupt dealings, which he did on his blog and via the Anti-Corruption Foundation he founded. But Navalny also sought to contest Putin's power by working within Russia's electoral system to gain power. As the journalist David M. Herszenhorn observed, Navalny didn't want to be another dissident who might adopt a morally righteous stance but fail to make actual change. He sought to work within the system to one day be elected president of the Russian Federation.

Navalny made a series of moves designed to help him gain political power, including organizing political demonstrations, becoming a candidate for mayor of Moscow, and later announcing his intention to run for president of Russia. As an interim step to reforming the political system, he also created strategies in 2018 that Russian voters could use to express their desire for reform in elections that were otherwise rigged, a "smart voting" scheme that involved marking their ballots for certain candidates more likely to unseat Putin-backed candidates. The goal was to send a political message via elections that might over time lead to more freedom.

For some of us, the idea of highlighting the obstacles that might prevent us from realizing our dreams might seem strange. Pop psychology tends to talk about the power of positive thinking, and it warns us against dwelling on the negative. If we want to psych ourselves up, we're supposed to forget about the challenges we face and imagine ourselves achieving our goals.

Research suggests that our greatest motivational boost comes from acknowledging the challenges we face and then considering them alongside our goals. It's the *tension* between the two that truly energizes us to act. As the management scholar Jim Collins tells us, we must have faith in difficult circumstances but also be willing to confront brutal truths. If we only think positive, we enjoy a virtual experience of achieving our goals, but we wind up making less effort in the real world—our brain tells us that we've already achieved what we're seeking. Studies show that people who contemplate their dreams alongside the real-life challenges they face enjoy more success in achieving their goals, whether it's losing weight, eating more vegetables, getting a job, or doing well in school. When individuals also envisage a rudimentary plan for overcoming the obstacles they identified, identifying the actions they would take if the obstacles materialized, they do better still.

On some occasions, Navalny evoked all three of the heroic quest's narrative elements in a single breath. In his last court appearance in 2023, he took the opportunity to "explain why I continue to fight that unscrupulous evil that calls itself 'the state power of the Russian Federation.'" At one point in the speech he implicitly outlined the contours of a heroic quest for his audience, likening it to the act of raising a child. In just a few lines, Navalny evokes a morally resonant goal: birthing a "new, free, rich country." He alludes to obstacles, acknowledging that the birth will be painful and require effort and "some kind of sacrifice." And although he doesn't specify the actions that it will take, he suggests what they might be: personal acts of resistance to the status quo that carry some danger. "Not everyone has to go to jail," he says, but people of conscience do need to stand up and "make some sacrifice, some effort" in the political struggle.

It's a potent message, one that frames an evocative, tension-filled quest. Expressed in such a way, Navalny's self-narrative inspired him to undertake almost unimaginable acts of courage. And to date it also has inspired thousands of Russians to bravely oppose Putin's government, at the ballot box and beyond.

Consider a big pursuit in your life that requires courage. Maybe you're thinking of starting a community organization or taking on a new initiative at work that you hope will make a big difference for your company and the wider world. How might you tell a story to yourself about that pursuit that contains these three simple elements of a vision, obstacles standing in your way, and practical steps to surmount the obstacles? If you need to mobilize others to join you in your cause, how might you then communicate this narrative to them?

Might you join up with a team or organization that already has such a story in place? Doing so can give your efforts a powerful boost of energy that will fuel your boldness.

MORE THAN A LITTLE PINK MUSTACHE

As the examples of Navalny and Patrick Awuah suggest, individuals not only use storytelling to frame a motivational purpose for themselves. If they happen to occupy leadership roles, they can translate their own self-narrative into a message that inspires others, spurring what I call "collective courage" (more on this in Part II).

Founders of small startup companies, for example, often convey tension-filled heroic quests to boost courage and help their teams persevere through tremendous adversity. We tend to think of successful entrepreneurs as squarely focused on realizing big, pathbreaking business ideas, but in my research I've found that many of them also pursue grand *ideals* quite early on when founding startups. They energize stakeholders with visions of revolutionizing their industries and bringing positive change to the wider world. This big thinking lends itself to compelling heroic quest stories, fueling bold action.

Consider the rideshare company Lyft. I doubt that early inventors of the automobile ever would have imagined that one day perfectly intelligent people would think to affix cute pink mustaches to their front grilles. But that's what drivers for Lyft did during the 2010s. Compared to its archcompetitor Uber, Lyft was seen as the "nicer," more ethical, more socially conscious company because of the welcoming nature of its brand and the friendliness of its drivers.

At first, niceness and pink mustaches didn't cut it for Lyft. Shortly after its founding in June 2012, the company came under immense pressure not just from regulators, who challenged the very concept of ridesharing, but from Uber. As Lyft cofounders John Zimmer and

Logan Green recall, Uber not only copied their rideshare business model but then tried to brutally crush the company. At one point, they called potential investors that Lyft had just pitched and convinced them not to fund the company. With limited access to capital, Lyft was very nearly forced out of business.

But although they were afraid of their larger and seemingly unscrupulous competitor, Zimmer and Green stayed in the game, bravely sticking to their original vision for the company even when their prospects were at their bleakest. Their fortitude was rewarded. In 2016 and 2017, the market changed in their favor as Uber was hit with bad publicity on account of its allegedly toxic culture, its conflicts with drivers, and its harshly competitive business practices. All of a sudden, Lyft's moral values gave it an edge with customers, allowing the company to rapidly increase its market share.

As I discovered when I interviewed Zimmer and Green, Lyft's "niceness" wasn't superficial, but linked to a deeper, morally resonant vision that the two entrepreneurs had long held for the company. In a letter included as part of a 2019 filing to go public with the Securities and Exchange Commission, Green and Zimmer noted that Lyft's goal was to "improve people's lives with the world's best transportation." Ultimately, the company sought to shift the transportation system away from driver-owned cars by providing a ridesharing service that would reduce the need for car ownership. The service would effect change by bringing people together in new ways, by making transportation more affordable, and by helping to reduce humanity's carbon footprint. As Green recalls, reimagining the transportation system was "the core purpose that lit a fire under us and that we built the culture and the team around. We weren't just going to go out there to build a better taxi or try to build a big company."

Green emphasized how important this ambition had been in allowing the founders to cultivate a sense of courage for themselves and rise to the challenge posed by Uber. "At so many points," he said, "failure seemed the most likely outcome. It often seemed like the rational thing would have been to give up. Our strong sense of purpose was the only reason why we stuck with it, were able to raise the capital we needed, and managed to build such a strong team." At times when the company was on the brink, its goal "gave us something to fight for, and a source of resilience when our backs were against the wall. Survival truly became part of our DNA. We also wanted to prove that you could build a winning business by taking care of people. Had Lyft died, Uber would have triumphed, and it would have given the impression that you can behave horribly and still wind up with a monopoly."

Looking more closely at how Green and Zimmer sought to rouse stakeholders to support their efforts, we find a narrative arc defined by the key elements of vision, obstacle, and a plan to surmount the obstacle. Their 2019 filing put the company's vision front and center and in big, bold print: "Improve people's lives with the world's best transportation." The letter contained in this filing went on to paint a vivid picture of a dream of sustainability and personal connection that Lyft sought to realize through ridesharing: "Imagine for a minute, what our world could look like if we found a way to take most of these cars off the road. It would be a world with less traffic and less pollution. A world where we need less parking—where streets can be narrowed and sidewalks widened. It's a world where pedestrians, bikers, and children can navigate a city just as quickly and safely as an automobile. That's a world built around people, not cars." Sharing a ride, the two cofounders suggest, also makes life better by bringing people together with one another so that they can share personal interactions and help one another.

In its filing, Lyft founders also acknowledge one of the biggest challenges Lyft faced in realizing its vision, which was transitioning consumers away from the dominant transportation system in the United States: self-owned cars. "Mass car ownership in the twentieth century brought unprecedented freedom to individuals and spurred significant economic growth," the filing notes, so Lyft, like its competitors, had to wean consumers off car ownership and toward a whole new way of getting around—a process that required creating new rideshare infrastructure as well as changing consumers' minds and behavior. In effect, Lyft was attempting to "deliver one of the most significant shifts to society since the advent of the car"—a monumental task, to say the least.

The founders also sketched out elements of a practical plan for making this change happen. They laid out key principles to which Lyft would adhere: providing service to the drivers and riders in their network, keeping the business financially stable, and investing to grow the business. Elsewhere in the filing, the founders described a number of specific strategies that the company would pursue to further its mission, including investments in marketing, launching new offerings, increasing how often users use the service, continuing to invest in technology, and more. All told, Lyft and its founders articulated a cohesive quest narrative for themselves and others, unleashing dedication and a capacity for bold action among team members, even at moments when the dream seemed most elusive.

COMMITTING TO A QUEST...TOGETHER

The writer George R. R. Martin, whose work inspired the popular *Game of Thrones* television series, has remarked that "we're all the heroes of our own stories." What we might not always realize, however, is how helpful our internal and external storytelling can be in allowing us to become *actual* heroes. Even the most fearful and cautious among us is capable of taking big risks and making personal sacrifices. But we need to feel as if we're part of a grand narrative of struggle and achievement, that we're making history despite the odds and because of our sacrifices. The epic stories we tell ourselves penetrate deep into our psyches, shaping our identities and imbuing our lives with meaning. By weaving them, we gain a sense of power and control over our destinies, feeling like courageous people *in our bones*.

For all he accomplished, Patrick Awuah wasn't a fearless, impulsive risk-taker. After first coming up with the idea of starting a university, it took him a year to muster the courage to leave his job at Microsoft. "The reason [I stayed] was that I was afraid," he said. Commitment to his quest was what ultimately led him to take action. He realized that if he didn't go for it, he would never achieve his dream, and he'd "regret not having even made an attempt." His lofty ambition was "the motivation for everything. It's the motivation for [persevering] through their fear. It's the motivation for [persevering] through difficulty." And the courage to take a stand is what he today seeks to instill in Ashesi's students. "To really make change, we must have courage," he says, "the courage to imagine something new, the courage to act, and the courage to persist through setbacks." Awuah has tried to build that courage by exposing students to the liberal arts, but he has also tried to do so—perhaps unconsciously—by evoking a heroic quest that they too can claim as their own as Ashesi graduates entering leadership positions across Africa.

You can be quite frightened yet still manage to transcend your emotions, simply by adjusting the way you frame your everyday life in your mind. You can inspire yourself to tackle seeming impossible challenges—the kind that make you pinch yourself afterward and think, "Did I really do that?" But storytelling isn't the only way to spur yourself to face your fears. As we'll see in the next chapter, research suggests that you can draw a similar strength from others around you—that, as the Beatles said, we "get by with a little help from [our] friends."

Chapter 4

CONNECTION

> Behind every Great Hero stands a team of helpful supporters. To build your courage muscles, work on fostering your connections with others, building a squad that can provide you with the emotional support, tangible resources, and feedback you need to excel.

Most of us take for granted our ability to zip around the world in the comfort of an airplane cabin, ice-cold beverage in hand. If the free Wi-Fi doesn't work or they're out of Diet Coke, some people become upset. During the early twentieth century, however, before the invention of the airplane, cross-continental voyages were much more time-consuming and dangerous. Out on the high seas, you were vulnerable to the vicissitudes of nature. Heavy storms could be so severe and life-threatening—with strong winds and torturous seas—that even atheists might have started to believe in God.

This was the situation legendary explorer Sir Ernest Shackleton and his band of adventurers faced in April 1916, some eighteen months into their famous expedition intended to cross the continent of Antarctica. Their three small lifeboats—the *James Caird*, the *Dudley Docker*, and the *Stancomb Wills*—were plunging through the rough, icy waters of Weddell Sea, near the South Pole. It's a place that even today is, according to a writer for *National Geographic*, "one of the wildest and most remote corners of the planet," and that Shackleton himself regarded as "the worst sea in the world." Temperatures on the boats were colder than your average deep freezer. The men were soaked to the bone and plagued by frostbite, seasickness, and dysentery. "At least half the party were insane," one of them later wrote. Food was scarce, and what there was of it wasn't exactly cruise ship fare. The nearest human settlement was hundreds of miles away.

To make matters worse, one of the three boats, the *Stancomb Wills,* the least seaworthy, was struggling to keep up in the rough, icy water. Recognizing that the *Wills* wouldn't make it on its own to the boats' common destination, sailors on the *James Caird* had attached a line to it, hoping to drag it along to moor it on dry land. With the seas so rough, it seemed that even this wouldn't be enough to keep occupants of the *Stancomb Wills* from a watery grave. Adding to the danger, Shackleton and his men were nearly depleted, having already encountered a series of devastating setbacks since departing on their expedition in August 1914.

The first of these catastrophes occurred fifteen months earlier, in January 1915, when Shackleton's ship, the *Endurance,* became wedged in a massive ice floe. The group was stranded there to wait out the brutal polar winter until the ice melted enough for the ship to come loose.

Some ten months later, in October 1915, another disaster struck: shifts in the ice floes caused the *Endurance* to be damaged beyond repair. As the men watched the ice slowly destroy their ship (it would sink about a month later), their spirits were crushed: this was the group's only lifeline, their connection to the world they left behind. And now it was gone. To survive, Shackleton and his men were forced to camp on vast sheets of floating ice and had to sacrifice their sled dogs due to declining food rations. As one recent recounting of their story reminds us, "It would be almost impossible today to be as isolated as the *Endurance* party was in 1915. They were marooned at least 1,500 miles from the nearest human and had no radio to communicate with the outside world. Tents were pitched on a constantly moving floe barely 10 feet thick and beneath them the Weddell Sea plunged to a depth of 11,250ft." Enveloped in darkness, they had to process the reality that they wouldn't achieve their goal of crossing Antarctica; the goal now was simply to survive and get back home alive.

In April 1916, after five more torturous months (for a total of fifteen months on the ice), the men lost their campsite when the ice floe they were on splintered. Now, as they huddled in their three small lifeboats, the crew's last hope for survival—and a slim one at that—was to cross the sea and make landfall on Elephant Island. If they succeeded, a few members of the crew might be able to make their way to the nearest human settlement to get help. But in this roiling, raging sea, with storms pummeling them from overhead, success seemed but a distant hope. Shackleton himself was on the verge of despair, although he couldn't betray these feelings to the group. "It seemed from moment to moment that we should have to part the line and leave her [the *Stancomb Wills*] to her fate," one member of his expedition, Frank Hurley, wrote in his diary. "Sir Ernest [Shackleton], in the stern, strained his eyes into [. . .] the dark torment and [shouted] at intervals words of cheer and inquiry."

Fortunately, a member of Shackleton's inner circle, second officer Thomas Crean, was by his side. Shackleton had known Crean for years, having served with him on a 1901 expedition led by the explorer Robert Scott. Since then, Crean had joined a torturous 1910 expedition to the South Pole with Scott, which ended unsuccessfully with Scott's death. At one point during this expedition, he walked thirty-five miles by himself to save the life of a fellow crew member, later receiving a medal for his effort.

Respectful of Crean's extensive experience, Shackleton counted on him to come through in tough situations. He also appreciated that, in the words of one historian, "Crean was trustworthy and no sycophantic yes-man. Crean had a particularly forthright manner and was not afraid to speak his mind." Now these qualities put Crean in a good position to calm Shackleton and buttress his courage. As Shackleton worried over the fate of the *Stancomb Wills*, Crean again and again reassured Shackleton that the ailing boat remained, for the time being, safely afloat.

When we discuss courageous people, we often overlook others in their orbits, portraying the brave individuals as "great heroes" who single-handedly bring glory to themselves and others. Such is Shackleton's case. "Sir Ernest Shackleton's name will always be written in the annals of Antarctic exploration," fellow explorer Roald Amundsen said. Building on our discussion in Chapter 3, humans seem to have a basic psychological need to connect with narratives that feature a single, strong hero on a journey of transcendence and redemption, with the hero returning with gifts for humanity. Lone heroes serve as role models for us, inspiring us to behave ethically and prosocially. They motivate us with their force of personality and ability to lead full, integrated lives.

What we don't often recognize is that heroes seldom act alone. Behind every hero we usually find other, less visible supporters. Shackleton's group would succeed in their quest to survive and make it back to civilization not because of the great explorer alone, but because he had a small, dedicated circle of confidants around him to rely on—what we today might call a support squad. There was Crean, whom Shackleton relied on for his raw physical strength as well as his experience. If Shackleton had something physically demanding and important that needed to be done, he knew he could count on Crean. But there was also Frank Worsley, the captain of the *Endurance*. With two decades of maritime experience, Worsley was known as "a first-class seaman and navigator," according to a letter of recommendation written by the high commissioner for New Zealand. Shackleton had hired him on the spot when first meeting him in 1914. Not only was he impressed with his technical ability, but Shackleton also perceived him as something of a kindred spirit, a person he just instinctively connected with.

Shackleton could also count on Frank Wild, his second in command. Wild had known Shackleton for years, having accompanied him on two previous Antarctic journeys, the *Discovery* expedition in 1901–1904 and the *Nimrod* expedition in 1907–1909. As another member of the *Endurance* expedition remembered, Wild possessed "a rare tact and the happy knack of saying nothing and yet getting people to do things just as he requires them . . ." He was also extremely loyal. In an interview, Shackleton's granddaughter later remembered that Wild "was utterly, utterly reliable. My grandfather described [Wild] once as 'my other self.'" Indeed, Wild's loyalty continued to the very end. Prior to his death in 1939, he requested that he be buried next to Shackleton's grave. When this wish was fulfilled, his gravestone bore the inscription, "Shackleton's right-hand man."

Together, these three confidants stanched Shackleton's own fears in extreme situations, enabling him not only to behave boldly but to rally and inspire the larger crew. Shackleton turned to them for help at a number of critical moments, asking their advice and assigning them vital tasks. In December 1915, after the *Endurance* sank, the group had to find a new campsite on another ice floe, since their current one was melting. Worried about the crew's morale, Shackleton talked it through with Wild, and the two agreed that the vigorous work of marching around the large ice floe and scouting for a new camp would refresh them. A few days later, when the men moved to a new camp, Shackleton wanted to take only two of the smaller boats, which they would need if they were to have any hope of returning home. Frank Worsley prevailed on Shackleton to bring a third boat—a decision that saved lives. After that, in April 1916, when the navigator Hubert Hudson experienced physical difficulties and was no longer able to command the *Stancomb Wills*, Shackleton turned to Crean to step in.

When faced with a daunting task, many of us who lack a courageous mindset might feel reluctant to ask others around us for help. We might not want to impose, or we might view our need for help as a painful hit to our egos. We might also on some level buy into the myth of the lone hero, seeing self-sufficiency as a virtue and equating our need for help with weakness. The brave people I have studied had no such compunctions. Knowing that they had connections with people who could deliver multiple kinds of support in a pinch boosted their confidence. On a deeper level, it changed how they saw themselves, giving them a new sense of agency that allowed them to overcome important challenges.

THE MANY REASONS TO BUILD A SQUAD

Research in the social sciences shows that people tend to "turtle up" in the face of adversity and refrain from seeking outside support. In fact, those who need this support the most tend to seek it out the least. The truth is that help from others really matters when it comes to handling difficult, frightening, or risky situations—despite appearances, we're not adept at handling adversity alone. Having a squad to rely on certainly helps people become more resilient. One study analyzing data from over 300,000 people found that social support is literally a matter of life and death: connections positively influence our physical and mental well-being, lowering the likelihood of developing conditions like heart disease, depression, anxiety, and cognitive decline. Individuals who had "adequate social relationships" were 50 percent more likely to survive over the period of the study than those with weaker social connections.

Our objective in this book isn't simply to become steelier and more adaptive when life gets tough. We want to go further and develop a capacity to take action, including in moments of extreme danger. Can social support help with that too? Our daily experience suggests that it can. Many people commonly known for courage—first responders, military, pilots, sports figures—tend to function as part of close-knit teams, not as lone actors. Think back, too, to grade school: even your typical schoolyard bully probably seemed more emboldened when they had a posse backing them up. And quite possibly there were moments when having friends by your side emboldened you to talk to that potential date or raise your hand to ask a question in class.

When we consider precisely *how* having others by our side might help nurture boldness, the case for building connections with others to pump up our courage muscles becomes more compelling. In investigating stories like Shackleton's, I've drawn on scientific research to identify *four ways* that social support can help most anyone to act with courage. As this research suggests, social support can give us an emotional lift, provide us with information we need to succeed, offer us tangible resources, and present useful feedback on how we're doing. Courageous people tend to draw on these four forms of support not just to cope with adversity but to overcome fear and take more risk. If you want powerful reasons to build or tighten your support squad, here they are. And if you're already relying on a posse in some respects, reviewing these four types of support might lead you to identify some additional ways that you can draw strength from your comrades and confidants.

REASON #1: THEY PUMP US UP

The first and perhaps most important form of support that others around you give to boost your courage is *emotional*. All humans want to feel loved, validated, and accepted. We want to feel like we matter to others, that they respect us, that we're heard by them, and that we belong to a group. But when we face adversity or are contemplating bold action generally, feeling emotionally supported becomes even more important. Receiving validation of our feelings and our own value pumps us up, giving us strength to persevere and allowing us to feel better about our situations, so that we don't fall prey to gloom, anxiety, and despair. Feeling seen and accepted by others also bolsters our capacity for action. We might feel more confident and ready to take action simply because we hear others around us confirming that we're strong, competent, powerful people, reinforcing personal stories we tell ourselves that might support risk-taking. Ultimately, emotional support helps us to believe that we have what it takes to behave boldly when it really matters.

When the pathbreaking Indian journalist Meera Devi first joined the grassroots newspaper *Khabar Lahariya* in 2006, she knew that some in her town would be displeased. Like many young women in the poor, rural, deeply conservative Indian community where she lived, Meera was married off when still in middle school but lived with her parents until her late teens. Her parents and in-laws had kindly allowed her to go to school—a big concession in a culture where women were supposed to stay in the home, raise children, and serve their husbands. Meera ultimately took a job at *Khabar Lahariya* to pay for college, which she attended while also raising her two daughters. Members of her community disparaged her job and accused her of immorality. "I had to bear a lot of such comments," she remembers, "but I chose to ignore them and move forward."

For Meera, *Khabar Lahariya* was a social movement to inform and uplift her fellow lower-caste members, but it was also her personal community of friends to which she felt she belonged. Established in 2002, the newspaper reported from India's most underprivileged areas, challenging the mainstream media's tendency to cover only the largest, most affluent cities. Instead of employing male journalists who were educated and could speak English well, as most news outlets did, *Khabar Lahariya* hired members of India's lowest caste (caste being a social class inherited by reason of birth), who were roundly persecuted and excluded from other social groups in Indian society. As a lower-caste woman, Meera found kindred spirits at the newspaper with whom she could finally muster the courage to push back. As she remarked, "*Khabar Lahariya* is not just a job for me. It is a relationship. It is a family . . . we participate in each other's joys and sorrows, both personal and professional."

Given how entrenched traditional gender roles were in India, Meera's work as a journalist was anything but easy. Male government officials whom she sought to interview for a story "either ridiculed or chose not to speak to us and dismissed our questions." In their minds, the mere idea of being questioned by a woman was offensive. On one occasion, when Meera's fellow journalists uncovered a tuberculosis outbreak in a local village, the officials there not only refused to be interviewed but afterward accused them of defaming the village and seemed poised to confiscate their press credentials. Government press liaisons often denied Meera and her colleagues the same access to political events that male journalists got. In other cases, people in powerful positions threatened Meera and her colleagues in an attempt to intimidate them, suggesting that they would have the paper shuttered or even cause physical harm to them or their families.

Staying strong in the face of constant family pressure, physical threats, and social censure wasn't easy. But Meera and her colleagues who came from similar backgrounds had a secret weapon at their disposal that buttressed their courage: each other. Colleagues at work created a supportive environment by serving as empathetic sounding boards. "I consider my colleagues as family who play an important role in my life," Meera says. In confronting daily challenges, the women turned to one another for emotional support. When a founder of *Khabar Lahariya*, Kavita Bundelkhandi, herself faced ostracism after deciding to leave her husband, her colleagues helped lift her spirits. "Everyone has their struggles, and we share our stories. My colleagues greatly inspire me, and I continue to draw strength and courage from them."

The emotional support Meera and her colleagues provided one another fed their self-confidence, powerfully affirming each other's ability to prevail in the face of hardship. By sharing their own stories of tackling challenges, her peers implicitly confirmed that Meera too was capable of rising to the occasion. And because the journalists knew and respected one another, this message came across as both credible and meaningful. As Meera remarks, colleagues at the newspaper tended to buttress one another's confidence regardless of rank through the stories they shared with her. She inspired members of the team she oversaw, while younger colleagues continued to convince her of her own capability to make a difference in the face of social censure and threats of violence. "My story is not unique, many others at *Khabar Lahariya* face such fears and threats, and we will continue to do so. We all draw courage from each other and from sharing our stories. My juniors inspire me more since they spend more time on the field and face [risk]."

REASON #2: THEY'VE GOT OUR BACKS

You'll recall that our self-efficacy reflects in part our awareness that we have the *tangible* means required to succeed in a risky endeavor. More friends backing us up can often mean more resources, including money, manpower, tools, and so on. This in turn translates into more self-confidence—and more courage. With a safety net beneath us, our fears ebb—we worry less and feel more in control knowing that we have the tools or resources we need. Material support also can serve as a source of emotional support. When people help us in tangible ways, we take that as a sign that they care about us and want us to succeed, further boosting our confidence.

In 2016, Bertrand Piccard flew around the world on an experimental, solar-powered airplane along with copilot André Borschberg, setting a world record. The two became media celebrities, covered in outlets like *National Geographic*, *Time*, and the *Atlantic*. Yet many others worked behind the scenes to help the pair fly a remarkable 40,000 kilometers (25,000 miles) without fossil fuel. Piccard and Borschberg relied on a team of dozens of specialists, all of whom provided instrumental support that was vital to the mission's success. A group of engineers constructed the airplane, an engineering marvel called the *Solar Impulse 2* that included innovative electric engines, batteries, solar cells, composite materials, insulation, and more. Another team tested and helped to maintain the plane prior to its record-setting flight. Yet another team was charged with serving as a ground crew, taking care of the plane in its hangar. Still other teams focused on providing financial, marketing, and communications support for the mission.

Without these specialists providing various kinds of tangible assistance, Piccard and Borschberg would have been grounded, their dream of promoting a sustainable future by piloting "the most energy efficient airplane ever built" would have been elusive. More to the point, they might have lacked the great courage required to fly an experimental plane long distances through unforeseen weather. They could feel confident knowing that thanks to their team they had the tangible resources they needed to safely achieve their mission.

In business settings, we often find that having tangible resources at our disposal boosts our confidence and willingness to act. Entrepreneurs are a good example. Starting a company is fraught with risk, and entrepreneurs often take second mortgages and max out their credit cards to fund their enterprises. Having so much on the line can render them hesitant to take bold risks. But the situation looks a lot different once they obtain funding from a venture capital firm. Knowing that they now have the financial support they need gives them confidence to make risky growth investments. They also feel empowered to take strong action because they know that success on their part will unlock future investment dollars. Access to resources bolsters them emotionally. If a group of serious, seasoned investors is willing to take a bet on them, they can feel all the more confident facing danger head-on.

REASON #3: THEY KEEP US IN THE KNOW

We might have the emotional backing and tangible money, tools, or other resources we need, but do we also have the *intangible* knowledge and expertise we need to get the job done? With a support squad backing us up, we can call upon the brainpower of others to help us surmount obstacles and achieve goals. Supplementing our know-how with that of our comrades, we avoid those potentially frightening moments when we might feel utterly baffled and uncertain about what to do. Equipped with the right knowledge, our sense that we have what it takes to succeed increases, and with it, our capacity for action.

You might shrink from buying your first house, unfamiliar as you are with the legalities and fearful that you'll make a bad choice. By consulting with friends who have bought homes, and some who might even have legal training, you can feel more confident making decisions and moving ahead. Similarly, successful CEOs of companies often rely on the knowledge and expertise of team members when making important decisions, many of whom are selected precisely for their know-how. Sometimes leaders even go beyond their established support crews, turning to rank-and-file employees to get the knowledge they need and in turn boost their courage muscles. A memorable example of a leader who did this is Xerox's legendary CEO Anne Mulcahy.

During the early 2000s, when Mulcahy was trying to save the

company from almost certain bankruptcy, she contended with a frightening array of challenges including problems with operations, sagging revenues, a government investigation into accounting irregularities, and no cash reserves to fall back on. Having worked mostly in sales and human resources, Mulcahy wasn't deeply familiar with the operations of Xerox's core copy machine business. She also didn't know much about the critical area of finance. "I certainly hadn't been groomed to become a CEO," she later remarked. "I didn't have a very sophisticated financial background, and I had to make up for my lack of formal training. I had to make up for it with intense on-the-job learning."

At this critical moment, Mulcahy turned to some of the junior members in her team for support. "Folks in the controller's department would spend hours with me just making sure I was prepared to answer all the ugly, tough questions from the bankers," she recalled. Others with expertise in engineering, new product development, and research did the same. Mulcahy's drive to educate herself and her ability to cull the information she needed from others around helped her to pull off a momentous turnaround of the company. She was able to make bold moves that included selling the company's China business and drastically reducing its cost base. Ultimately, Xerox saw its earnings soar, from losses of $273 million in 2000 to nearly $900 million in profits in 2004. Meanwhile, its stock price rose 75 percent, even as the overall stock market declined 6 percent.

REASON #4: THEY GIVE YOU A REALITY CHECK

When we face adversity, or when we're taking on any kind of risky action, it's hard to know exactly how we're doing. Are we truly executing the plan we set for ourselves? Are we unknowingly making mistakes that might damage us? This blindness can amplify any sense of uncertainty we may feel, arousing our fears and causing us to hesitate. Conversely, having others in our corner giving us information to help us judge our performance—what social scientists call "appraisal support"—can reassure us that we're on track and in control. We can talk through with others the contradictory signals we're getting, noticing patterns, making sense of our situation and our options, and gaining more certainty about a course of action. Performance feedback can also help us feel better about ourselves in general, improving our sense of self-worth and feeling less angst-ridden.

Appraisal support is like the intangible knowledge we've discussed already, with one difference: it's information that pertains to *us* and how we're doing. That can include direct feedback but also simply knowledge about performance benchmarks, which we can then use to evaluate ourselves. Let's say we work at a pharmaceutical company and are training for a sales role. If a mentor of ours tells us that the average new salesperson generates $400,000 in revenues the first year, and we've generated twice that with a full quarter still to go, we'll feel a boost of confidence. Knowledge of benchmarks and how we measure up to them might make us more inclined to take risks in our job role, like trying out a new and untested sales pitch or volunteering for a new, stretch assignment.

When it comes to feedback, appraisal support might include praise about what we're doing right, which can be quite powerful in fostering confidence. One study of youth swimmers found that those whose coaches praised their performance during their season felt more competent in what they were doing and also more connected to their coach. At especially tough moments, having a squad of friends and confidants that provide appraisal support can calm us down, reassuring us that we really are doing just fine. And if we're not doing fine, they can nudge us toward making necessary adjustments, saving us from a downhill slide.

A great example of appraisal support comes from competitive tennis. Since top players spend large parts of each year traveling to tournaments, they bring entourages with them that provide all the types of support described here. Appraisal support plays a prominent role. Craig O'Shannessy serves as a "strategy analyst" for superstar Novak Djokovic. As he has explained, the essence of his role is not just to observe and understand Djokovic's opponents, but to understand the player's own performance, including aspects of it of which Djokovic himself might not be conscious. "I analyse everything Novak does," O'Shannessy said, "and look at it match by match but also at bigger-picture trends in his game where things may be changing, getting better, or something that has gone off that we may not have been aware of." Armed with an informed perspective on his game and able to make changes on that basis, Djokovic can feel even more confident and empowered to take bold risks.

Appraisal support is poised to play an even bigger role in tennis thanks to recent rule changes that allow coaches to convey feedback to players during matches. New technology that tracks data about how many balls players manage to hit, where their serves land, and so on will only enhance players' ability to gain real-time evaluations of their performance. To the extent that having this information helps their game, their self-efficacy will increase and feed their courage.

THE DEEPER POWER OF A POSSE

Having others around to help you doesn't just support boldness by boosting your self-confidence and firing up your passion. On an even deeper level, it alters how you think about yourself and your ability to effect change in the world.

We should recognize, first of all, that our identities are fundamentally social in nature. Sociologists dating back to the great nineteenth-century German thinker Georg Simmel have explored the complex ways our relationships help to create and shape our own sense of who we are. As we've seen, we have the power to give meaning to the social world through shifts in how we view it. But the social world also works on *us*, influencing how we see ourselves, what scholars have called our "social identity." In other words, we understand who we are *in relation* to the roles that others play and how they behave toward us. A prime example of this can be seen in the early development of children, which hinges on their interactions with their parents. Insecure attachments to parents can leave children permanently unsure of themselves and doubtful of their own worth. The opposite holds true as well. As some scholars have pointed out, we might harbor nascent notions of who we are, but these can take root and grow as others validate our identity for us, leading us ultimately to regard it as natural and obvious.

The identities we forge in social contexts contribute mightily to our ability to take bold action. In some cases, our relationships might lead us to see ourselves in particular roles—as an explorer, for instance, or a war hero—that give us confidence to take action. In these roles, we might also feel a strong sense of *responsibility* to act. Because our relationships affirm our identities as, say, parents, citizens, employees, military service members, and so on, and because these identities themselves often entail certain obligations to others, we might feel more duty bound to take risks than we otherwise would. We might risk our lives to save a drowning child if others around us revere us as a "super" parent to our own kids. We might be more inclined to volunteer for hazardous duty at work if we're known as a loyal and dedicated employee and team member.

According to one recent theory, courageous acts can sometimes arise out of our attempts to negotiate *conflicts* between the various personal and social identities that we have. In many situations, our sense of who we are in one context might collide with the demands placed on us by our roles in other contexts. When this happens, we can feel unsettled, anxious, or confused, so much so that we're willing to behave courageously to resolve our internal tension. If you're an advertising executive who is a visual artist at heart, you might feel you are "selling your soul" by working in a well-paid, commercially focused job. To resolve this tension, you might decide to leave your job and take one in the nonprofit sector. Courageous acts are thus a mechanism for revealing to ourselves who we *really* are—what we're truly made of. The need for coherent, stable identities propels us to behave bravely in specific situations, but also to do so consistently across the various contexts that these situations impact.

Our social relationships also enable boldness in another way: by helping us deeply internalize our own view of ourselves as *courageous people*. When we have a strong support crew behind us, our own sense of who we are shifts. Above and beyond our perceived self-efficacy when facing a specific task, with a support crew we begin to think of ourselves *in general* as bigger, stronger, and more capable of taking action. We feel better about ourselves, imagining new possibilities for what we might achieve. Over time, as we continue to take bold risks with others' participation or help, our sense of our own agency can become even more expansive, further increasing our potential for bold action. Instead of regarding ourselves as individuals who on occasion might behave bravely, we can begin to think of ourselves as inherently brave individuals who take risks in support of noble causes.

Research suggests that people use small groups as settings in which to confirm their sense of self-worth or self-esteem. In the workplace, our interactions with colleagues shape our identities, allowing us not only to become more attached to our work but to think of ourselves in positive ways as, for instance, competent, adventurous, or important. One-on-one coaching and mentoring relationships likewise enable us not only to expand our skills, but also to increase our self-esteem and alter our sense of self. Put another way, mentors can help us to see ourselves as leaders capable of effecting change in the world. As we come to identify with mentors who are older than us and more advanced in their careers, we can start to see ourselves in *them*, taking their present as our potential future.

You can draw on your social relationships not just to take action in specific situations, but to heighten your sense of yourself as a courageous individual. You should take care to surround yourself with others who can give you the four key forms of social support discussed in this chapter. This might mean seeking out close friends and confidants with diverse talents, skills, and resources at their disposal. It might mean ensuring that some of your coterie are more experienced than you, capable of providing the informational and appraisal support that only trusted mentors can provide. You also should nurture these relationships, doing your best to ensure that your squad endures long enough to underpin your broader sense of agency. Members of our support squad give us so much. You should also ask yourself: What am I giving *them*? Just as you rely on others to build your courage muscles, so you too can help others build theirs.

DON'T WAIT TO FORGE CONNECTIONS

One question, though, is whether you should be doing any of this right now. You might not be embarking on an epic adventure like Ernest Shackleton was, or taking on an urgent business crisis like Anne Mulcahy, or making a conscious decision to take on oppressive social norms like the *Khabar Lahariya* reporters. You might just be going about your normal life. Is it really worth it to spend precious time and energy building a support squad? I believe it is, if only because you never know when you might need to rely on it. My research turned up a number of everyday heroes who found themselves called to perform seemingly impossible feats they never imagined taking on. In these situations, they managed to succeed because they happened to have people around them whom they could count on to provide all four kinds of social support.

In the summer of 2021, a former student of mine named Frances Haugen sent shock waves around the world by making public thousands of pages of internal Facebook documents. These documents were highly sensitive and damning; they confirmed suspicions among some observers that Facebook knew its products were contributing to ills such as eating disorders among teens, the spread of misinformation, and human trafficking, yet had refrained from taking action.

For anyone interested in courage, the sheer audacity of Haugen's act was astonishing to behold. Like other large and powerful companies, Facebook could easily destroy those who challenged it. It could unleash highly paid attorneys to sue whistleblowers for violating confidentiality provisions. It could spend millions on public relations efforts discrediting whistleblowers. It could blacklist whistleblowers in the industry, preventing them from getting jobs. In short, blowing the whistle on Facebook was an extremely risky move with potentially life-changing consequences. Yet Haugen had done it.

As Haugen suggested in her published memoir and in an interview with me, she hadn't planned to take on this role and in fact never liked receiving attention from others. She first became sensitive to the problem of misinformation on Facebook after a close friend of hers became radicalized online, leading to a rupturing of their relationship. When a recruiter subsequently approached her about a job at the company, she saw an opportunity to help Facebook root out misinformation like that which had victimized her friend.

As Haugen got to see Facebook from the inside, she became increasingly disturbed by what she saw as the company's ongoing refusal to tackle misinformation, extremism, and other serious problems on its platform. "Facebook," she wrote in her memoir, had repeatedly "*failed to warn* the public about issues as diverse and as dire as national and international security threats, the Facebook algorithms that drive political party platforms, and the fact that Facebook had knowingly been harming the health and well-being of children as young as ten years old."

On various occasions, she saw that others around her who tried to help Facebook fight misinformation were being ground down by the company's bureaucracy, fueling her sense of injustice as well as a recognition that someone needed to take on the system. "A large part of what would push me over the edge into whistleblowing," she wrote, "was that I watched that formula play out tragically over and over again. People would drive themselves into the depths of burnout trying to fight the institutional decay because Facebook couldn't heal itself with the system of incentives that existed."

But recognizing injustice and the need for someone to speak up wasn't enough for Haugen to go public. She also had to develop sufficient self-confidence. Here her support squad played an important role by providing the four kinds of assistance described in this chapter. While hunkering down with her parents during COVID, Haugen spent many hours talking with her mother about her distress at what she was discovering about Facebook. Receiving this emotional support helped her clarify her thinking and feel stronger about going public. "If you're having a crisis of conscience," she said, "where you're trying to figure out a path that you can live with, having someone you can agonize to, over and over again, is the ultimate amenity."

Tangible help from others was also important. A *Wall Street Journal* reporter with whom Haugen collaborated, Jeff Horowitz, helped her structure the process of collecting documentation and making it public. As Haugen told me, "the top thing he did for me was provide an external source of accountability because we all have a lot of stuff going on in our lives. Once I decided that he was going to be the one I was going to collaborate with, the fact that he texted me and was like, 'When can we talk again?'—that gave me a cadence."

At one point, Haugen received intangible knowledge and expertise from Larry Lessig, a Harvard Law School professor who counseled her and connected her with a communications firm that could help her with the process of going public. Finally, she received appraisal support from her parents. As she explained, a devastating challenge afflicting many whistleblowers is the cognitive dissonance they experience by knowing an unpleasant truth about their company. "You're like, 'The sky is blue,' and everyone else is saying 'the sky is purple.' The sky is actually blue and you feel like you can't tell anyone. And that destroys people." While living with her parents, who served as her trusted confidants, Haugen could reality-check her own impressions of what she was experiencing at Facebook with them. Her parents could confirm that yes, her observations of the company were correct—the sky really was blue, despite what others might have been saying. As Haugen relates, that simple feedback made all the difference, allowing her to achieve a degree of mental stability while going public that eludes many whistleblowers.

Confronted unexpectedly with the challenge of operating as a whistleblower, Haugen could overcome her fears and jump into the unknown at least in part because of the group of supporters around her. Social support in its various guises boosted her self-efficacy; she could remain confident that she had the many resources she needed to complete her mission. Critically, this support was open-ended: Haugen knew that whatever happened, others around her would provide her with the necessary help. The world recognizes Haugen as the heroic whistleblower, as it should, but she arguably never could have mustered the strength to take on Facebook if she hadn't had a strong support team around her, including some newer faces and others who had been by her side all along.

Even if you're not currently facing an urgent challenge, the time to start building close connections with others is *now*. Make sure you have people on your team who can give you the broad mix of help that you need. I also urge you to adopt the other three C's we've discussed so far in this book: Coping, Confidence, and Commitment. But don't stop there. It's one thing to build up your courage muscles in advance, but it's quite another to actually use them in the moment as you stare danger in the face. To increase the odds that you'll step up when it truly counts, you can keep some additional strategies in your back pocket, calling upon them to act even when every fiber in your body is screaming *no*.

Chapter 5

COMPREHENSION

Radical uncertainty destabilizes us, to which our natural response is to freeze up. By learning to act our way toward more comprehension and clarity, we can prevent ourselves from becoming stuck and behave more courageously in the moment despite our fears.

It's August 12, 2022. The novelist Salman Rushdie is onstage at a large, open-air amphitheater at the Chautauqua Institution in western New York State, about to give a lecture as part of a summer arts festival. The scene is calm, peaceful, and decidedly literary—a "faculty-lounge atmosphere," as one report described it. Suddenly, a young man dashes toward him, knife in hand. As Rushdie later recalls in a memoir, this man is dressed head to toe in black and comes at him "hard and low" like "a squat missile." Rushdie feels surprised, but also not. The Iranian ruler Ayatollah Khomeini had issued a decree, or fatwa, condemning him to die, but that was in 1989, decades earlier. Rushdie had long ago assumed that he was no longer under threat. Why, he wonders, is an attacker materializing before him now? At the same time, Rushdie has long expected an attack to take place and imagined what it might be like. His first thought, therefore, is: *"So, it's you. Here you are."*

With an audience in the thousands looking on, the man stabs Rushdie numerous times—in the neck, eye, chest, hand, thigh. "He was just stabbing wildly, stabbing and slashing, the knife flailing at me as if it had a life of its own." Onlookers are shocked—they're not certain that what's happening is real. Some think it's a preplanned spectacle designed to accompany Rushdie's talk, which ironically enough is slated to deal with "the importance of keeping writers safe from harm." Henry Reese, a colleague seated nearby onstage who like Rushdie is a septuagenarian, realizes what's happening and darts over to wrestle with the attacker. Others in the audience follow to help take him down. The entire encounter, which leaves Rushdie on the verge of death and costs him an eye, lasts precisely twenty-seven seconds—about as long, Rushdie notes, as it takes to recite a Shakespearean sonnet.

The spontaneous courage shown by Reese and the audience members that day was exemplary. Once he processed that Rushdie was under attack, Reese didn't hesitate to come to his defense, even though he was decades older than the assailant. In Rushdie's view, it was an act of "pure heroism." The audience members joining Reese all put their lives at risk as well, doing so instantly, without hesitation. As Rushdie later reflected, the response was "remarkable" and "the opposite of the so-called 'bystander effect.'" It was, he said, "the intuitive response of an empathetic community." In Rushdie's judgment, the collective effort was pivotal. Without it, he asserts, he would have been killed.

Thankfully, most of us don't have a bounty on our heads, but we might imagine how we would react if an attacker rushed at us from out of nowhere, shattering a previously normal moment and confronting us with a mortal threat. Decades of research suggests that acute danger arouses intense emotions as well as physiological responses like an elevated heart rate or quickened breathing. Scholars long presumed that such responses led us to do one of two things: either fight back or take flight. More recently, scientists have observed a third response. Gripped by fear, some people freeze up and become utterly incapable of taking action. Their heart rate slows and they go quiet, much like many animals do when they spot a predator.

That's what Rushdie did when he faced down his attacker on that amphitheater stage. He remembers himself "just standing there, staring toward him, rooted to the spot like a rabbit-in-the-headlights fool." Rushdie artfully reconstructs the experience as only a world-renowned novelist could: "My eyes follow the running man as he leaps out of the audience and approaches me, I see each step of his headlong run. I watch myself coming to my feet and turning toward him. (I continue to face him. I never turn my back on him. There are no injuries on my back.) I raise my left hand in self-defense. He plunges the knife into it. After that there are many blows, to my neck, to my chest, to my eye, everywhere. I feel my legs give way, and I fall."

How could Rushdie just stand there? It's true that he was much older and less physically capable than his attacker, but reason would compel him to do *something*—hit his attacker, push him away, move his own body aside. Rushdie professes to be puzzled and ashamed by his almost total inaction. But he does hazard an explanation, one that has to do with the working of his mind in that extreme situation. As he suggests, the brutal violence against him caused a kind of cognitive short-circuiting, rupturing his sense of everyday life as he was used to experiencing it. Here's how he memorably describes it:

> *The targets of violence experience a crisis in their understanding of the real.... Suddenly they don't know the rules—what to say, how to behave, what choices to make. They no longer know the shape of things. Reality dissolves and is replaced by the incomprehensible. Fear, panic, paralysis take over from rational thought. "Thinking straight" becomes impossible, because in the presence of violence people no longer know what "thinking straight" might be. They—we—become destabilized, even deranged. Our minds no longer know how to work.*

> *On that beautiful morning in that attractive setting, violence came running at me and my reality fell apart. It is perhaps not very surprising that in the few seconds available to me, I didn't know what to do.*

We've seen that uncertainty about our situation can arouse intense fear, and that's precisely what Rushdie experienced. As his attacker charged, reality "fell apart" for Rushdie, and he simply didn't "know what to do."

We've talked about how you can mentally shape your understanding of your own reality, thinking about both your external world and your sense of self in ways that help you build your courage muscle. But our ways of seeing—whether we've created them consciously ourselves or developed them unconsciously over time—are inherently fragile. Sudden threats might destabilize, confuse, or overload us. We can experience these situations as moments of extreme uncertainty, ones where we question our present or future reality. Our minds might freeze, and thereby our physical bodies. Most of us have experienced traumas that, for a moment at least, leave us unable to think. These traumas might involve physical violence, but other sudden, shocking changes in our circumstances can thrust us into a radical, terror-inducing uncertainty. We might have become disoriented and experienced a strange, out-of-body sensation after being diagnosed unexpectedly with a major illness. Or when a bully terrorized us during high school. Or when we received unexpected news that someone close to us had passed away.

Some crises in everyday life aren't as short and compressed as these situations. Instead of seconds, they might last a few days, as in the case of a storm or other natural disasters. They might even last weeks or months. These more prolonged crises might not cause a lasting bodily freeze such as Rushdie experienced. But they might still cause our minds to become frazzled and disoriented as we experience overwhelming uncertainty and loss of control. We might perceive a kind of rupture in time: the sudden dissolution of our familiar reality and its replacement with a new, less comprehensible one. We might feel a sense that we're floating through our daily experience, fumbling about for a sense of direction, unsure what to do. And while we might be physically able to move, we might still find ourselves singularly incapable of taking *bold* action. We might fall back instinctively on our ingrained habits, entering into a kind of autopilot mode.

The anthropologist Anthony F. C. Wallace spoke of a "disaster syndrome" that occurs in times of crisis, one marked by a "temporary paralysis." Dazed and confused by what they've experienced, survivors of natural disasters "simply sit or stand motionless, or wander aimlessly, or 'putter about' at inconsequential tasks." One factor contributing to such a response might be what psychologists call "status quo bias," our preference to behave in familiar ways that uphold what already exists. Another might be our inability to face up to extreme uncertainty; the shock we experience triggers our fear response, which in turn limits our ability to take decisive action. We experience a form of cognitive overload that numbs our faculties and prevents us from acting decisively.

When hurricanes strike, for instance, some people opt to ignore government evacuation notices, wrongly assuming that the storm won't drastically impact their lives—an assumption that can lead to preventable tragedies. We do this for any number of reasons: it might seem too difficult to behave differently, we might fear losing what we already have if we depart from the status quo, we might feel attached to our past decisions or ideas and the tangible or emotional investments we've made in them. In times of uncertainty, we might easily fall back on what feels familiar and safe rather than taking a risk. We might instinctively "putter about" and bide our time in a state of confusion. Further, we might conceal our less-than-valiant responses, rationalizing our inactivity in our minds after the fact to make ourselves feel better.

Business leaders freeze all the time when confronting fear-inducing threats. A famous example comes from the tire maker Firestone. The company was renowned during the mid-twentieth century as one of the best tire manufacturers in America. At the time, every American car came with bias tires, which Firestone could produce at scale. Then, during the late 1960s, a new technology emerged: radial tires, which lasted longer, were safer on the road, and were more economical than bias tires. Radials were what business analysts today call a disruptive innovation—very scary for a leader of an established company like Firestone, which had built its entire business manufacturing bias tires. Switching over to radials would mean converting existing factories' production capabilities and, ultimately, building new factories dedicated to producing this new product. In turn, it might also mean closing down its old factories and laying off workers.

Faced with this reality, Firestone's management didn't freeze in the sense of doing absolutely nothing. They probably didn't experience the visceral fight-flight-freeze response in their brain, as they might have if confronting an immediate physical threat. But they did become paralyzed in some sense, relying on established habits and ways of thinking and preserving their stake in the bias tire as much as possible. One researcher who studied this in detail has described their response as one of "active inertia," defining it as a company's "tendency to persist in the activities that contributed to its past success despite even the most dramatic changes in its competitive environment."

At first, Firestone's leaders tried to manufacture the new radial tires using existing equipment rather than building entirely new plants. This decision led to poor product quality, eventually compelling Firestone to recall 8.7 million tires, at the time the most extensive recall ever seen in the United States. Meanwhile, as Firestone began manufacturing radial tires, the plants that it hadn't converted over to this new product became increasingly obsolete. Leaders persisted in keeping them open, a decision that by the late 1970s left Firestone taking steep losses and bleeding cash until it was ultimately sold off to the Japanese competitor Bridgestone.

How can you stop yourself from freezing in the face of extreme uncertainty, whether by doing nothing when facing a sudden, visceral shock or hewing like automatons to established patterns? How can you rouse yourself to step up and truly address the situation? When the threats you face last just a few seconds, you might not be able to escape your physiological freeze response. Like Salman Rushdie, you might be stuck in cognitive overload until the crisis passes and you can recover. But in crises that last minutes, hours, or longer, there is a simple strategy that works.

Conventional wisdom holds that you should think first and then act, but the secret to preventing yourself from freezing is actually to do something a bit more nuanced: build your comprehension of the situation by thinking and acting at the same time. You can notice your situation and take an initial stab at interpreting it. On that basis, taking stock of what you *believe* you know, you can take a small step forward as a way of learning *even more* about your radically changed circumstances. This allows you to then take another small step forward that is even more informed and more likely to get you to your goal. Taking a series of these small steps and refining your sense of reality in the process can allow you to progressively get your bearings, so that you can move ever more boldly to address what threatens you.

ACT AND THINK AS YOU GO

On March 11, 2011, a massive earthquake struck off the coast of Japan, triggering a forty-five-foot-high tsunami that hit the prefecture of Fukushima in Japan, killing almost 20,000 people and knocking out the energy supply at the Fukushima Daiichi nuclear power plant. Within seventy-two hours, with cooling functions at the plant inoperative due to lack of electricity, three nuclear reactor cores had partially melted down. Explosions and releases of radiation forced authorities to evacuate hundreds of thousands of people and declare a no-fly zone around the plant. It was the worst nuclear disaster since Chernobyl in 1986.

Another nuclear power plant, located just over six miles away, also was hit that day. At that plant, Fukushima Daini, the tsunami also took most of the power supply offline, threatening a meltdown and explosions as had taken place at the Daiichi plant. Fortunately, workers at the Daini plant were able to take bold action, bringing new sources of power online to run the plant's cooling system before the core melted down. After two days of grueling, round-the-clock effort in extremely dangerous conditions and with just hours to spare, the facility's four hundred employees, led by site superintendent Naohiro Masuda, managed to bring the plant's cooling functions back online, avoiding a catastrophe.

In my research into the response to this extraordinary crisis I uncovered astounding tales of courage. At one point, dozens of team members had to leave a "safe" facility and head into the flooded reactors to assess the damage, braving electrocution hazards, debris, potential explosions from gas canisters stored on-site, and of course the risk of radiation exposure. Midway through the frenzied efforts to restore power, workers saw smoke rising from the nearby Daiichi plant and knew that it was likely radioactive—yet still they soldiered on. Not long after, workers had to enter a section of the plant where large containers of liquid hydrogen had toppled over in order to turn them back upright. Despite the extreme risk of explosion, they got the job done.

The workers' bravery seems especially impressive when we examine their situation more closely. Workers at Fukushima Daini weren't simply in a high-risk situation. They were in a situation that was profoundly fluid, uncertain, and disorienting, and therefore fear-inducing. Although nuclear plants are built and workers trained with natural disasters in mind, this particular set of circumstances was both unexpected and unprecedented for the workers at the Daini plant. A typical control room of a nuclear power plant is a dizzying array of dials that are connected to sensors outside that monitor every aspect of its operations. In this instance, most of the dials in the room had ceased to function. Minute to minute, workers had little sense of the extent of the damage to the plant, how much real danger they were in, when help would arrive, or even whether family members who lived nearby were safe. They were flying blind and yet called upon to save the plant.

Why didn't workers at Fukushima Daini become paralyzed with fear? Let's take a closer look at what transpired. Masuda, the plant manager, had decades of experience and knew the plant intimately. It might have been natural for him as the boss in such a tense environment to aggressively map out the best plan he could muster and bark out orders. Instead, at the outset of the crisis, he stepped back and stood almost professorially before a whiteboard facing his hundreds of crew members in the emergency control room, sharing what he did and did not know about the earthquake and its impact. He wanted the group to work together to take stock of the situation, considering how they might be able to fill in vital gaps in their knowledge. He sought to motivate them to take action to learn more about conditions at the plant and how they could remedy them.

Masuda knew that if his people had waited to act until they understood the situation well enough to come up with a detailed plan, they might never have taken action, certainly not in time to make a difference. They would have huddled in a protective crouch, allowing chaotic and seemingly incomprehensible events to wash over them without mounting an effective response. On the other hand, a reckless, *move fast and break things* approach wouldn't work either. If he had simply given orders, failing to acknowledge the complex and uncertain situation they were in, trust and morale would have plummeted, making swift, decisive action difficult if not impossible.

So, Masuda did something ingenious, toeing the line between excessive caution and recklessness. He motivated his team to act with an eye toward mapping out their terrain and discovering together what they were dealing with. And act his team did. Late in the evening after the earthquake hit, forty workers volunteered to go out to investigate conditions at the plant's reactor cores. They spent hours in the field, all of them returning safely by 2 a.m. Thanks to their reconnaissance, Masuda and the team had a better sense of which equipment was still working and which wasn't. Based on that information, he could start to make some provisional plans for repairing damaged machinery and hopefully avert a meltdown.

In this instance, Masuda treated action not simply as a means to a desired end result, but as *a pathway to comprehension*. As he understood, if the team started to take small steps with an eye toward making sense of the situation, circumstances at the plant would become increasingly more intelligible and hence less threatening. Meanwhile, the team would be increasingly equipped to take next steps. In this way, by leading his team through a process of progressively making sense of the situation as they worked, Masuda would help them work through the crisis and get to the other side rather than remaining stuck and stymied.

COPING WITH THE BIG ONE

When I first heard about Masuda's response, I was a bit puzzled. What kind of leader responds to a life-or-death situation by turning it into a kind of educational seminar, one in which participants learn as they go? Then I thought about the work of the sociologist Karl Weick. In research dating to the 1970s and captured in his 1995 book *Sensemaking in Organizations*, Weick describes a process called "sensemaking" in which individuals and groups adapt to uncertain situations by observing cues from their environment, interpreting them in light of past experiences or understanding, and progressively creating meaning. Critically, they frame this meaning not by philosophizing off to the side, away from the flow of events, but in the very course of moving in the world.

You can think of sensemaking as an ongoing process comprised of three basic steps. *First*, something surprising or unexpected happens to (or around) you. If you're alert to such surprises and mindful of the emotions they arouse in you, they can trigger you to begin making sense of a disorienting situation. *Second*, you notice cues in this unfamiliar environment and craft an interpretation or story in your mind about them—an initial hypothesis you have about the event and its meaning. This is a preliminary assessment of vital aspects of the event, such as what has happened, why it happened, and what the consequences may be. And *third*, you take steps based on this imperfect meaning you've been able to glean, which in turn allows you to learn in-action and to notice new cues.

Let's go back to those harrowing days at the Daini plant as the Fukushima disaster was unfolding. Relying on eyewitness testimony, we can trace how the ongoing sensemaking process got off the ground step by step. Masuda and his team members didn't engage in this process self-consciously—it's not like they had all read their Karl Weick. Rather, they intuitively understood that the best way not to become frozen or mount an inadequate, status quo response is to *lean into* uncertainty, taking some small, initial actions as a way to better map out their situation.

STEP #1: STAY MINDFUL AND ALERT FOR A SENSEMAKING TRIGGER

The initial trigger for sensemaking—Step #1, the surprising event that throws established meaning into question and creates confusion—was twofold. First, it was the earthquake, which at 9.0 on the Richter scale was the most powerful ever recorded in modern Japan. The quake was so powerful, so jarring, that it left Masuda utterly shocked as he sat in the main office of the Daini plant. "It was the biggest earthquake I had ever experienced," he said. "When we are small, Japanese people are all taught to duck under a table when an earthquake happens. . . . I had never done that before, but I did this time."

A second trigger was the resulting tsunami. After the earthquake struck, Masuda made his way to the plant's emergency response center (ERC), where he and his four hundred colleagues had assembled. They went through protocols to shut down the plant's reactors, cool down their cores, and contain any radiation. From what he could tell, the plant had not sustained significant damage, so cooldown seemed like it would be no problem. But then the tsunami alerts started coming in.

At first, authorities advised them that a wave up to ten feet high would soon hit, then they revised that upward to twenty feet. The plant was built to withstand a wave of about seventeen feet, so a twenty-foot wave could perhaps inundate the plant and compromise its cooling system. When it finally hit, the wave was *fifty-five feet high*—enough to flood the plant's reactors and knock out its power supply.

For a couple of hours after the tsunami hit, other, smaller waves continued to batter the plant. With many of their control and monitoring systems knocked out, it was impossible to know the full scope of damage. Masuda did, however, learn the bad news that three out of the four reactors no longer had operational cooling systems. If they did nothing, a catastrophic meltdown might occur. Normally the team had an array of dashboards and meters feeding them information, but none of them were working. Masuda didn't know exactly what at the plant had been damaged and how badly—again, he and his team were flying blind in an incredibly complex technical environment. Causing even more distress, since phone lines were down, nobody at the plant could check on their families. If the plant experienced a meltdown, members of the surrounding community might die too.

Sensemaking is an unnatural way of responding to disruptive events. Yet some people like Masuda and his team manage to do it. One way that you might prevent yourself from instinctively freezing up is by practicing a kind of mindfulness in the moment, staying attuned not just to the external situation but to your own emotional response to it. You try to step outside of what's happening and how you're reacting and look at events more dispassionately. As scholars have pointed out, the fact that earthquakes occur is not necessarily what triggers us to either freeze up or engage in sensemaking. It's the *emotions* that such unexpected events produce and our response to those emotions.

We can prime ourselves to respond with sensemaking in times of uncertainty by understanding the value of this approach and sensitizing ourselves to recognize events as triggers. If we make a habit of looking for relatively minor disruptions of our normal reality and regarding them as triggers for a sensemaking process, we can increase the odds that any unusual events we encounter—including big, dramatic ones like an earthquake—will prompt us to try to act our way toward knowledge.

Now that you know about sensemaking, incorporate the practice into your everyday life. Pay attention to moments in which you feel suddenly disoriented or confused. Notice the thoughts running through your mind as well as physiological signs like a racing heartbeat or quickened breathing. If you find yourself becoming distressed or freezing up, notice this response. Gently remind yourself that you need not become stuck—your disorientation could simply mark the beginning of a new learning process. If you're leading a team or company, you also can create cultures that nudge people to look for potential problems, treat them as opportunities to learn progressively by taking action, and take time to understand circumstances rather than mindlessly rushing in.

STEP #2: NOTICE AND INTERPRET CUES

Rather than cower passively in the ERC, Masuda and his team members began crafting potential interpretations in their minds of the earthquake: the destruction it might wreak, the steps Masuda and his team might have to take to save the plant, and the safe ending that they would all be working toward. In this second step of sensemaking, their task was to scour their environment for *any* information they could get their hands on—even small, seemingly insignificant cues—and assemble them into a broader interpretation or story.

Weick likened cues in our environment to "seeds from which people develop a larger sense of what may be occurring." How might these seeds fit together? What patterns do you notice? How does what you're seeing relate to other situations you've encountered in the past? Can you begin to categorize or classify what you're seeing in some way? With just a few tantalizing scraps of knowledge, you can try to create some initial meaning around them, stringing together some possible accounts that make sense of the reality you're in. You can create a set of hypotheses about your reality, choosing the one that seems most plausible.

In crafting an interpretation, we're in effect like a person who is trying to assemble a jigsaw puzzle without the cover box. We don't know what the full, assembled puzzle actually looks like, but we can work with individual pieces, interpreting them and gaining some rough sense of the picture. As Weick emphasizes, we don't need perfection here, just an interpretation or story that is *plausible enough* to energize us to move forward. Operating on the basis of our chosen interpretation, we will go on to identify more cues that can allow us to further validate, refine, adjust, or build upon our hypotheses. "Sensemaking is not about truth and getting it right," Weick and some coauthors have observed. "Instead, it is about continued redrafting of an emerging story so that it becomes more comprehensive, incorporates more of the observed data, and is more resilient in the face of criticism."

That evening, as aftershocks continued to strike, Masuda focused his team on gathering these little seeds of information and forging hypotheses. As he stood at the whiteboard writing down what little information they currently had at their disposal, the team was already beginning to craft interpretations of what had happened that enabled them to map out next steps. When the workers returned from the field, they shared new information that allowed Masuda and the team to further refine these initial interpretations. Processing this data, Masuda continued to note it on his whiteboard—sensemaking in this instance was a collective process of story creation, with Masuda organizing the raw material for their interpretation and keeping the process going.

Based on what the team learned, they crafted a provisional interpretation: the pumps were down, leaving the reactor buildings flooded. Meanwhile, the plant's cooling system was out of order because of a lack of power. This interpretation led immediately to potential actions their team could take. The first priority was to bring in necessary supplies to fix the pumps and at the same time to connect the cooling system to a power source at the plant that was still functional. The team would only have a day to make that happen, and that included installing about five and a half miles of massive power cable lines.

As Weick noted, a number of factors can contribute to how precisely you notice small cues and construct stories. First, your own sense of self comes into play here, influencing what you see. When you face crisis situations, you can shape your sensemaking by asking yourself what specific roles you play in life that might be useful in the situation. Mobilizing your relevant knowledge or training, what might you notice? When others are involved, you should consider their perspectives too. What skills or knowledge might they contribute? How might those shape their interpretation of the situation in helpful ways? How do their interpretations differ from yours, and how can you blend insights from both to gain a better picture of what is truly happening?

In identifying cues and building possible interpretations, you also can look to your personal experience, matching what you're seeing to reference points and patterns you've encountered previously. As we saw in Chapter 1, experienced firefighters who enter burning buildings spot particular signs—for instance, black smoke billowing from the kitchen—and flash back to a similar scenario they've seen, drawing on that connection to make quick decisions about what to do. You can do the same when taking initial plunges into the unknown during crisis situations.

Looking about you, do you notice any elements that might be familiar? If so, can you better understand or classify the challenges before you? By remembering experiences from your past, even ones that seem somewhat tangential, and incorporating them into your meaning-making, you can break unhelpful emotional and mental responses and help yourself to take action.

Masuda and his team members were drawing on their past experience and collective knowledge in exploring the plant and mapping out the damage. Although the team hadn't prepared for an unprecedented situation like this, Masuda's intimate knowledge of the plant allowed him to alert team members to investigate specific areas, looking for data that might help them piece together what had happened and what they should do. As he recalled, "I knew almost everything about the inside of the plant. When I had a report about a fire, or machines under water, I could easily picture where those were happening. I could give concrete instructions when it came to which power and cables to use for which equipment because I had in mind almost everything that had been done at which location." Again, the point wasn't to produce a definitive, expert interpretation of their situation. Rather, he and his team were just trying to amass enough insight or information to serve as a reasonable basis for taking the next step.

STEP #3: TAKE ACTION

After we've created meaning, we take action based on the most plausible interpretation or story, in the process exposing ourselves to new cues that enable us to adapt or revise our understanding of the situation and of the environment. A balanced approach works best here: you force yourself to act decisively while also understanding that your action might turn out to be incorrect and that you'll need to pivot and adapt as new information emerges. When you're overconfident or adopt a "tunnel vision" associated with a seemingly powerful interpretation, your curiosity can wane. You might not update your knowledge and adapt accordingly. If you're too cautious, you might likewise become locked into an existing course of action, this time out of fear.

In group settings, a second kind of balance becomes important. An individual leader must drive the process and solicit the right amount of information and advice from others. If the leader allows for too little input, the group might become vulnerable to blind spots and lack motivation to execute. Too much input from others, though, and the group gets bogged down and can't act decisively. As a leader

I know puts it, "People in crisis situations want to be heard, but they also want to be led."

At Fukushima Daini, Masuda could craft a strong, helpful interpretation because he got these two forms of balance right. He didn't hesitate to modify his plan as new information became available. For example, at one point it became apparent that it would be too ambitious to draw power from one of the buildings on-site that Masuda had originally chosen, as that building was located too far away and it would require more time to lay the massive cables. So they switched to another potential power source: the plant's last functioning generator. In another instance, the team had planned to repair the cooling system at one of the reactors to prevent it from melting down. However, when they found that pressure was building up more quickly at a different reactor (suggesting a greater risk of a meltdown), they shifted midstream to prioritize the one where pressure was rising the quickest. Throughout the crisis, Masuda allowed for an appropriate but not excessive amount of group input. As he tracked information on whiteboards, team members could stay current with what was happening and offer insights. Masuda used the whiteboards when giving orders, enabling team members to understand their rationale. But at all times, he was clearly in charge and didn't hesitate to forge and implement his plan in a determined way.

—

Although arrived at intuitively, Masuda's actions and those of his team map nicely onto Weick's notion of sensemaking. Thanks to these three sensemaking steps, undertaken iteratively with very little time to spare before a potential meltdown, Masuda and his team managed to step up and generate an initial plan for stabilizing the plant. They then repeated these steps multiple times during the few days after the earthquake to deal with new, unexpected challenges that developed. If any of the reactors at the Daini plant had suffered a catastrophic meltdown, the radiation release might have rivaled or exceeded that from the 1986 accident at the Soviet Union's nuclear plant in Chernobyl, Ukraine, and would have utterly devastated Japan. In fact, then–prime minister Naoto Kan was even contemplating the evacuation of Tokyo in a worst-case scenario.

Fortunately, such extreme measures weren't necessary. By March 14, about three days after the crisis began, all of Daini's cooling systems were online, and a day after that all the reactors were fully and safely shut down. The cooling system for one of the reactors had come on just hours before pressure at one of the reactors would have reached a dangerous level. All told, the team at the Daini plant narrowly managed to avert a catastrophe. As for Naohiro Masuda, he received the Chevalier of the National Order of Merit from the French government and has been lauded among his peers as an "engineering hero" for his bold action.

SENSEMAKING IN EVERYDAY LIFE

Although the trigger for sensemaking in this example was quite extreme, the same approach of using action as a pathway to comprehension can help you in everyday situations. Destabilizing surprises can take many forms. It might be noticing some frightening medical symptoms that leaves you spinning, or learning of unpleasant developments in your business, or being given a new assignment at work that utterly baffles you, or even just graduating from college and suddenly facing the prospect of "the rest of your life." In these situations, people commonly become paralyzed. Rather than staying stuck and waiting for some magical development or intervention to jar them loose, they can *act* their way into more clarity, certainty, and calm, like the team at Fukushima Daini did.

Consider the situation of having to embark on a career. As exciting as launching into the world can be, it's also anxiety-producing. Graduating college seniors might craft rough, hypothetical interpretations of their desired careers based on their interests, capabilities, and their own sense of self. They might want a career in business, or to have a creative job that offers work-life balance, or to settle down in a foreign country. New developments might disrupt those interpretations and force them to adapt: the economy might make it hard to get a job, or new laws might make emigrating much more difficult. Falling prey to the status quo, other students might throw up their hands and opt for careers laid out for them by their parents. They might work a series of temporary jobs to avoid having to make a decision. Or they might waste months or years trying to find the "perfect job," which never quite seems to materialize. Much of their lives will involve crafting an interpretation of their professional life and adjusting, however anxiously, as the job market evolves.

Practicing sensemaking in this situation can help you bypass status quo responses and open up possibilities for bold action. Instead of trying to figure out in excruciating detail how to achieve a general career goal you might have, just take an initial step. Try an internship, for instance, or take a part-time job in the field. See how you feel and what you learn about yourself and the opportunities out there, and use that to determine your next step. Keep going like this, learning as you go. Be prepared to go down a false path every now and then. Over the long term, you'll make steady progress toward your goal and avoid becoming frozen by anxiety and disorientation.

THE POWER OF BEGINNER'S MIND

More than just a strategy, sensemaking is actually a comprehensive way of approaching the world, one that fuses action with a posture of humility, openness, and curiosity. Rather than wait to figure out a comprehensive plan, we proceed with an awareness of just how much we *don't* know. In effect, we practice what Buddhists call "beginner's mind." Someone adopting the mindset of an expert allows assumptions and established beliefs to color their view of reality. All of us do this to some extent—we go through life with fixed ideas about what we're encountering. With beginner's mind, we let go of this mental baggage and adopt a posture of curiosity. As one commentator describes it, beginner's mind entails "dropping our expectations and preconceived ideas about something, and seeing things with an open mind, fresh eyes, just like a beginner. If you've ever learned something new, you can remember what that's like: you're probably confused, because you don't know how to do whatever you're learning, but you're also looking at everything as if it's brand-new, perhaps with curiosity and wonder. That's beginner's mind."

Uncertain situations are perfect opportunities for us to exercise beginner's mind. If we behave as "experts" sticking stubbornly to our preexisting assumptions and ideas, we'll gravitate toward status quo actions that are inadequate to the realities at hand, as Firestone's leadership did. With sensemaking, we allow curiosity and wonder—the essence of beginner's mind—to guide us and inspire action. As chaos roils around us, we step forward with the aim not of resolving our situation once and for all, but of simply comprehending our situation a little better so that we can take another step, and then another, and then another. As with beginner's mind, we don't presume that we have everything figured out; we give up the notion that we must have the perfect plan. We open ourselves up to possibilities, trusting that the landscape will progressively become clearer and we'll get where we need to go.

It's not easy walking through the world as a beginner, especially when we face situations of extreme uncertainty. Mobilizing a sensemaking strategy takes grit, a determination to hang tough and figure things out even when our prospects seem bleak. It takes faith in ourselves, a belief that we *can* figure things out little by little if we try. It takes persistence, a refusal to accept defeat. It takes patience, a willingness to stick with a process of learning rather than just rushing to a potentially half-baked and reckless decision. And it takes flexibility, a capacity to adjust our thinking and quickly throw out preconceived notions that turn out to be incorrect. All of us have these capabilities latent in us—we just need to nurture and develop them, and we need to surround ourselves with others who can give us encouragement and support.

Sensemaking might not have helped Salman Rushdie—the danger before him materialized too quickly. In many other circumstances, however, it can help us stay active and engaged in the early stages of an uncertain situation, and it can keep us pointed in the right direction as we move toward clarity. But it often isn't enough to see us through. It's important in these situations to attend to our emotions, taking extra steps to limit our fears and prevent them from spiraling out of control. As we'll see in the next chapter, everyday heroes intuitively adopt simple tactics that let them stay calm at times when the world seems to be falling apart around them.

Chapter 6

CALM

Dangerous situations can cause our fears to run wild. Some simple mental strategies can preempt this natural response, calming us and allowing us to behave more boldly.

The winter of 2022–23 was an excruciating one for the people of Ukraine. Russia had sent ground troops into the country's eastern regions earlier in the year, and starting in October it began a massive bombing campaign against Ukraine's vital infrastructure. Week after week, ballistic and cruise missiles, along with Russian drones, attacked Ukrainian population centers, raining down destruction in barrages that lasted hours and left hundreds of civilians dead or injured. Ukraine's power systems suffered catastrophic damage and, just as Ukraine's notoriously brutal winter was fast approaching, millions of Ukrainians were left without power—a situation that a World Health Organization official described as "life-threatening" amid snow and freezing temperatures. In Kyiv and other cities, residents had to do without streetlights and were tormented by the wail of air raid sirens. It was a "cynical strategy" on the Russians' part, French president Emmanuel Macron observed, one that sought "to put Ukraine on its knees."

As the country's armed forces fought on, Ukraine president Volodymyr Zelenskyy made numerous public statements aiming to bolster the courage of troops on the front line, civilians on the home front, and supporters worldwide. "We are now showing that Ukrainian life cannot be broken," he said in an October 22, 2022, video address to his fellow Ukrainians. "Even if the enemy can leave us temporarily without power, it will still never succeed in leaving us without the desire to make things right, to mend and return them to normal." Addressing a joint session of the US Congress on December 21, Zelenskyy vowed that Ukrainians would "celebrate Christmas—and even if there is no electricity, the light of our faith in ourselves will not be put out. If Russian missiles attack us—we'll do our best to protect ourselves. If they attack us with Iranian drones and our people will have to go to bomb shelters on Christmas eve—Ukrainians will still sit down at a holiday table and cheer up each other." Four days after that, in a Christmas address to Ukrainians, he again reassured them that "the darkness will not prevent us from leading the occupiers to their new defeats."

Amid so much serious rhetoric, one appearance of Zelenskyy's stood out. On December 27, his office released a video of a conversation he'd held weeks earlier with the American comedian and longtime television host David Letterman. As the two sat together in an underground subway station to stay safe from Russian bombs, Zelenskyy told a joke that echoed his ongoing themes of Ukrainian strength and Russian weakness: Two men from Odessa, Ukraine, are meeting one another, and one asks the other what's new. The second man says that a war has apparently broken out between Russia and NATO. Asked by the first man how the war is going, the second man describes horrific Russian losses: 70,000 soldiers dead, huge losses of equipment. But what has NATO lost so far? "NATO?" the second man says, delivering the joke's punch line. "NATO hasn't arrived yet."

This joke, which quickly spread around the world on social media, alludes to Russia's subpar military performance up to that point. President Vladimir Putin had justified its invasion in part by referencing its tensions with the NATO alliance, arguing that a Ukraine aligned with Western powers posed a threat by potentially giving NATO a position right on Russia's border. In invading Ukraine, Russia was ostensibly pushing back against NATO. But as the joke suggests, Russia's military was so incompetent that despite having a population dwarfing Ukraine's by roughly a factor of three, it sustained heavy losses. The joke also took a jab at NATO, which was perfectly content having Ukraine—a nonmember—do its fighting on its behalf.

It might not be surprising that Zelenskyy would weave humor into his public statements. He was a well-known comedian in Ukraine prior to being elected president in 2019, the star of a humorous television show called *Servant of the People* in which he played an ordinary person who became president of Ukraine. What's striking, though, was the extent to which everyday Ukrainians relied on humor while facing aggression from a much stronger foe. Not only did the stand-up comedy scene in Ukraine flourish during the war; comedy actually became a feature of everyday life. As one Ukrainian wrote from Kyiv, telling jokes while eating breakfast had become a reassuring ritual, a way to start the day off right. Humor was so pervasive that local newspapers were publishing the city's funniest jokes.

Ukrainian social media accounts circulated funny memes referring to acts of resistance as well as the ineptness of Russia's military. Even Ukraine's Defense Ministry got in on the action, posting humorous messages of its own. In one instance, after explosions hit a Russian military base in occupied Crimea, the ministry lampooned Russia's own disinformation tactics with posts suggesting that errant cigarettes smoked by Russian soldiers had caused the blasts. Humor was also widely present among frontline soldiers. Ukrainian comedians visited the front lines and soldiers developed a black humor all their own. "Oh, man, the guys are *so* funny," remarked one Ukrainian stand-up comedian who had served for eighteen months on the front line. "I went through a lot with them, and people tend to open up to you after these tough shared experiences. That's when the comedy really thrives."

The Ukrainian reliance on humor suggests an important strategy we can use to help us muster courage as we face adversity: shaping our emotional response so that we can calm ourselves and find new meaning in otherwise negatively charged situations. Strategies described in previous chapters will help us minimize fears far in advance of adverse situations, but we can reinforce those preventative efforts by taking additional steps in the moment to limit fear right when it seems poised to arise. Comedy is a great way to do so. More than just a diversion for Ukrainians, it functioned as a way for them to stabilize themselves emotionally in the face of the Russian onslaught. As the founder of a comedy club in Kyiv remarked, "Comedy works as an anesthetic for the soul. People laugh about things that scare them. And then they stop being afraid of it, because they remember the joke about their fear."

While the Ukrainian reliance on humor might seem like a fairly obvious coping mechanism, it's not clear that laughter always holds the solution to dealing with adversity. Rather than acknowledging our negative feelings, including our fears, we often feel tempted to suppress them, pretending they're not there. Yet, as research suggests, suppressing emotions such as fear once they've materialized generally isn't a long-term solution. It taxes our cognitive resources, stresses us out, and causes us to alienate others around us. We walk around with a nagging sense that we're not being true to how we really feel. Our well-being is compromised rather than enhanced. When it comes to behaving courageously, it's better to address our emotions directly, so that they don't hijack us. Humor is one powerful way of doing this, but there are others. By acknowledging how debilitating fear can be and taking steps to prevent it from overwhelming us, we can rise to the occasion and take bold action in dangerous situations.

OUTWITTING OUR FEARS

Many of us work through emotions by talking them through with others around us. We do this with close friends, relatives, professional therapists, sometimes even complete strangers. At so-called climate cafes, a new kind of physical or online gathering that is becoming more popular around the world, people come together to work through a range of painful emotions about climate change, including fear and anxiety, sometimes with the help of trained therapists. The very process of analyzing, understanding, and accepting our emotions can help galvanize people to take action, with some groups evolving into forums for grassroots climate activism.

At one such meeting in New York City, participants brought up different ways that they could take action and thereby reestablish a sense of control, from composting their food waste to becoming more politically involved. As one therapist participating in a climate cafe in Illinois remarked, "The dread, the hopelessness is getting exiled in all of us, and that's why we're not talking about it, because it's too painful. If we can't heal what we're all feeling, we can't heal our planet either."

Yet working through fears isn't easy. As anyone who has tried it knows, it takes time, effort, and commitment, and often we really do need the help of a trained professional. It's not so practicable to process feelings when you're in a situation of extreme adversity—when you're facing a potential nuclear meltdown, like the workers at the Fukushima Daini plant were, or when you're a Ukrainian soldier in a trench dodging Russian shells. Are there quicker, less arduous ways of addressing our emotions so that we can act boldly?

It turns out that there are. Instead of suppressing fear outright or taking time to process it, you can seek to limit fear in the first place, nipping it in the bud. In effect, you can *outwit* your fear in the moment, thereby positioning yourself better to take bold action.

Psychologists have closely analyzed the workings of what they call "emotional regulation," including as it pertains to fear. James J. Gross, a Stanford professor and renowned expert in human emotions, has created a general model of how emotions are formed, suggesting how you might track, assess, and alter them while they're emerging but before they take hold of you. If you make the right mental moves, either consciously or not, you can mute your fear, diminish how long it lasts, or change how you express it. Gross's work points us to three mental moves you can make to stay calm and enhance your courage.

MENTAL MOVE #1: RETURN TO A RITUAL

One way to prevent our fear response from fully taking hold is to alter the situations we're in so that we can interpret them differently. Even small actions on our part can subtly adjust or shape an otherwise frightening situation, turning it into one that feels more comfortable and unthreatening. We've already encountered a powerful way to help tailor situations and their emotional tenor: rituals.

As we saw in Chapter 1, people perform ritualistic acts of various kinds to help them feel more comfortable in risky situations. To the extent that rituals relate to religion or folklore, they can ease our fears and help us cope with uncertainty and the lack of control that comes with it by strengthening our belief in something bigger. But what rituals of many kinds *really* do is subtly alter the situations we're in, normalizing what's going on in our minds. Through rituals, we inject an element of familiarity and predictability into our lives that allows us to perceive these circumstances as less threatening. The routine nature of rituals can help us to compensate for the disorientation and lack of control we might otherwise feel when adversity rears its head.

From an emotional standpoint, rituals help us favorably alter situations and their meanings in two ways. First, the *physical movements* you might perform may calm you and reestablish a sense of order. By focusing on performing those movements, you can keep your mind off the uncertainty of the situation. The pop star Adele has been open about the extreme fear she feels before performances. During her residency in Las Vegas, she is said to have made a habit while heading onstage of kissing a photograph of the singer Celine Dion, who served as an inspiration for her, believing that doing so brought her good luck. Adele might have centered herself in the moment by repeating the physical act of walking past the picture of Celine Dion and kissing it. The predictability of the gesture would have helped her to reestablish a sense of order.

Rituals also ease our fears because the *specific meanings* they hold for us give us a sense of control over the situation and allow us to get out of our own heads. The repetitive gesture of kissing Celine Dion's picture had emotional implications for Adele. Since Adele saw Dion as an artist whom she admired, kissing her picture would have been a way to feel a connection to Dion. This in turn would have allowed Adele to make the moment more personally meaningful to her and also to get out of her own head. It would have made an otherwise frightening moment feel less daunting.

Although minor and seemingly insignificant, the repetitive actions that comprise rituals can change situations and their meanings in critical ways, allowing us to behave boldly even in situations of extreme uncertainty. On July 19, 1989, at about 3:16 p.m., a blast on United Airlines Flight 232 flying from Denver to Chicago knocked out an engine. The airplane's hydraulic system went down as well, disabling the flight controls that the plane's captain and copilot were using to fly the plane. It was a full-blown emergency; the cockpit crew had no easy way of controlling the plane, and it seemed like they wouldn't make it to the runway for a safe landing. The crew didn't know what to do. Nobody had ever heard of a situation in which a DC-10's entire hydraulic system had failed all at once.

Thinking quickly, the plane's pilot, Al Haynes, and the copilot, William Roy Records, managed to steer the plane manually as best they could by manipulating the throttles, giving more or less power to the two remaining engines, one on either side of the plane. But this was a difficult and subtle task that required making adjustments second by second based on factors like airspeed, wind conditions, and air density. One mistake, and the plane could go down.

Dennis Fitch, a United Airlines flight instructor who taught pilots how to fly the DC-10, happened to be a passenger. Rapping on the cockpit door, he offered his help. Although Fitch was a complete stranger, Haynes asked him to take over the plane's throttles. Meanwhile, Haynes could coordinate with air traffic control and prepare the cabin for a crash landing. Copilot William Records needed to pay attention to other tasks, and the flight engineer, Dudley Dvorak, lacked experience to handle the throttles.

No pilot wants to ever fly with a disabled hydraulics system, or with a complete stranger manning the throttles. Still, as Haynes realized, it was vital to stay calm. As he later said, "You must maintain your composure in the airplane or you will die." In these intense, chaotic moments, he and Fitch interacted in a ritualized way, falling back on what sociologist Erving Goffman described as an "interaction ritual." These are small, patterned behaviors that we often don't think much about but that structure our everyday encounters. As Fitch took the controls, their conversation in the cockpit went like this:

> Haynes: My name's Al Haynes.
>
> Fitch: Hi, Al. Denny Fitch.
>
> Haynes: How do you do, Denny?
>
> Fitch: I'll tell you what, we'll have a beer when this is all done.
>
> Haynes (laughs): Well, I don't drink, but I'll sure as hell have one.

To limit their fears in a potentially fatal situation, these two men resorted to the kind of formulaic, casual conversation they might have engaged in on a standard flight. The familiar, ritualized nature of the conversation normalized the situation just a bit, infusing it with a sense of comfort and predictability so that it felt less uncertain and chaotic. It wasn't much, but it *was* enough, apparently, for them to save some lives. Forty-four minutes after the initial explosion, the plane crash-landed at an Iowa airport, killing 111 people on board. Remarkably, 185 people survived, including the cockpit crew and Fitch.

MENTAL MOVE #2: PAY SELECTIVE ATTENTION

A second way to regulate our emotions in the moment, preventing the fear response from taking hold so fully, is to perform what James J. Gross calls "attentional deployment." Faced with a perilous situation, you can selectively direct your attention in ways that alter your experience of the situation, so that it feels less frightening.

On the one hand, we can decide to distract ourselves, so that we don't ruminate on dangers that might otherwise wear on our psyches. As we saw in connection with the war in Ukraine, humor can serve this capacity. If we find ourselves in a hazardous environment, cracking a joke can allow us to take our minds off its negatively charged aspects. In fact, we often see soldiers, first responders, and others in dangerous situations using humor in this way when under duress— "To get rid of the tension, let off steam," as a firefighter in one study put it. Even criminals deploy humor as a way to deal with the fears they feel. According to one of the authors of a study of thirty-three drug dealers, "Crime is inherently dangerous, and 'talk'—particularly humorous talk—is a way for people to cope with the dangers of the world." As the comedian Stephen Colbert remarks, "You can't laugh and be afraid at the same time. If you're laughing, I defy you to be afraid."

On the other hand, you can selectively focus on specific parts of a situation that tend to reassure you by affirming your own agency. In Chapter 2, we saw how football coach Nick Saban has his players focus on the step-by-step process of winning a game—executing each play properly—rather than on the win itself. We may feel more confident and in control—and position ourselves to behave boldly—when we focus on the small task right in front of us. But doing so can also build our courage muscle by limiting our fear response. If we care about achieving a particular outcome, we can become locked into anxieties about the future and see every small setback along the way as a potential threat. Focusing on what is right in front of us prevents us from becoming drawn in by our worries, taking the edge off seemingly unmanageable situations.

The sports psychologist Michael Gervais observes that in public speaking or in other situations where we might be concerned about what others think, we can bring fear under control by focusing not on the audience members but our own internal strengths. If we find ourselves starting to grow fearful in the moment, we can remind ourselves that we're great at speaking, that we've put in the work or preparation, that we have great ideas to communicate, and so on. In doing so, we're concentrating on an aspect of the situation that we find empowering. This allows us to think more optimistically about what we're doing and our role in the world, fostering other, more positive emotions like hope, joy, or excitement. At the very least, we might feel security and comfort, a sense that "we've got this" and everything will be okay.

Gervais's advice resonates with me as I've had my own struggles with public speaking. My internal motivation when I address audiences is simply to be of service to others. As a scholar, I want to create and share knowledge that hopefully will help people in their work and lives. When I'm talking to groups of perhaps a hundred students or executives at a time—no problem. But in years past if you put me on a bigger stage in front of many hundreds of people, I would sometimes become gripped by fear. Standing all alone on a stage, the lights blazing in my face, the audience out there darkened and invisible—I found that pretty daunting. Not being able to see their facial expressions during my talk made me wonder how they were receiving what I was saying. That focus in turn led me to microanalyze and second-guess every remark I made and whether or not it "landed." I obsessed on how I looked to the audience and what they thought of me.

After one such intimidating moment when I almost froze before my talk, I realized that I was losing sight of what *I* was hoping to achieve in being there—my long-standing service mission—and instead focusing all of my attention on my audience and *their* minute-to-minute perceptions. A turning point for me came soon after when I started to selectively focus my attention away from the likely audience response. Instead, I directed my mind to look inward and think about my own priorities and purpose in speaking. That small bit of redirection in the moment energized me and calmed my fear. I began taking more chances with my material, diverging from my prepared thoughts and speaking extemporaneously. I felt liberated and inspired by this newfound freedom.

MENTAL MOVE #3: REINTERPRET A SITUATION IN YOUR MIND

You can also preempt or limit your fear response not by tailoring the situation itself or shifting your attention per se, but by directly reframing what a situation in its totality *means* to you. With this technique, you can acknowledge fully the dangers that you face but reassess the situation in ways that shift how it affects you emotionally, in particular making it seem less frightening and more familiar.

Reframing how we see situations is extraordinarily powerful, and there are several framing strategies we can deploy to behave more courageously. Nobel Prize–winning research has shown, for example, that when we must choose between two options, how we frame these options impacts our propensity for risk. When we frame them as two possible sets of gains, we become risk-averse and make the more conservative choice. When we frame them as losses, we select the riskier option. That's because humans experience the pain from a potential loss as greater than the pleasure that comes from a potential gain. We're loss-averse. If we want to take more risk, framing our options as possible losses can draw us toward the riskier choice. Conversely, if we seek to behave more conservatively, we can frame our options as possible gains.

Another helpful way to reframe a situation is to focus on the upside of situations and choices. While acknowledging the downside risk, don't let it terrify and disable you. Examine carefully if your sense of the downside risk is exaggerated, and if you might temper it with a slightly different understanding of the situation. If you're about to go bungee jumping and you get cold feet, you can look at the situation more objectively, telling yourself that many people go bungee jumping every year and live to tell about it.

You might already use the technique of reframing situations to behave more boldly, without realizing it. If you're terrified of flying, you might have read a book or taken a course to help yourself overcome the fear. "Flight anxiety" courses by airlines such as British Airways are designed to facilitate this kind of reframing, and in particular, the variant of it that allows us to become more emotionally detached. They do so by describing in detail how commercial aviation and airplanes work and by breaking down sounds and sensations that might unnerve skittish passengers. At the course offered by British Airways, for instance, the instructor advises participants that commercial jets have large fuel tanks that won't suddenly run out, like they sometimes do in the movies. Participants also learn that turbulence isn't a big deal for pilots and that they need not worry about the plane's wings breaking off in midair.

Reframing is a powerful tool, one that we sometimes turn to intuitively or unthinkingly to fuel our boldness. Aisha Chaudhary was one of the most courageous people I've come across. If you saw the 2019 film *The Sky Is Pink* you know her story. In 2010, at age thirteen, she was diagnosed with a devastating illness: pulmonary fibrosis. The illness had arisen as a side effect of chemotherapy Aisha had received as a baby while receiving a bone marrow transplant to treat a genetic condition. At best, doctors told her she had five more years to live.

Aisha's parents decided to tell her the truth about what awaited her. At first, she didn't quite understand the death sentence she faced. But as weeks and then months passed, Aisha surprised her parents. As her father remembers, "She found this inner strength. I think she just dug deep inside her to the innate wisdom that I think all of us have and she just transformed spiritually into a person who continues to inspire me."

Rather than give herself over to fear, depression, or anger, Aisha decided to take control of her life and find happiness where she could. She set goals for herself, resolving to learn to paint and to continue with her studies even if her illness made it hard. Most of all, she would challenge herself to become a motivational speaker, recounting what had happened to her so that others might learn to be happier and more fulfilled. Many of these moments were frightening for her, but she chose to reframe them for herself in a positive light, which in turn allowed her to proceed. As her father said, "I think she elevated who she was and what she had control of and what she knew deep inside, was able to draw on it and make the most of the limited time she had."

As Aisha's illness worsened, just getting up in the morning and going about her day was a brave act. She never knew if she would experience crippling pain, receive more bad news about her health, or discover that there was some activity she could no longer partake in. So how did she manage to stay active day after day amid the uncertainty?

Again Aisha made a point of framing life and her situation in a positive light, and she shared this message with others in her public speaking. "Happiness," she told an audience in 2013, "is clearly a choice one can make, no matter what, no matter where, you can find it if you look for it."

Aisha passed away in 2015, but up to the very end, she handled her fear by deliberately reframing her situation to focus on the joy, not the fear or sadness. "What I'm going through is actually better than what someone else is going through out there," she wrote in a book penned during the last year of her life—yet another challenge she eagerly took on. She also reminded herself to appreciate experiences that she could still enjoy, such as her times with family. She didn't deny the harsh realities she faced. To an important extent, they became familiar, not scary.

Deliberately shifting the meaning of situations didn't save Aisha Chaudhary's life, but it did allow her to squeeze the most out of it that she could. By regulating her emotions during a prolonged and terrible crisis and establishing a sense of familiarity, she was able to rise up despite her suffering, inspiring countless others around her to do the same.

THE DIFFERENCE A MEAL MAKES

As pervasive as fear is, our discussion in this chapter has shown that we can rally ourselves to behave courageously with some simple mental strategies. We also, of course, can still opt to do the harder work of processing our fears once they've already taken hold of us, understanding and analyzing them so that we can better live with them and act courageously anyway. If we choose this direction, making some belated effort to limit our fear response can help prepare us to perform this processing by opening up some much-needed mental space.

One of my favorite examples of this comes from the epic poem *The Aeneid,* penned by the ancient Roman poet Virgil. At one point, the poem depicts remnants of the once-mighty Trojan fleet, led by the mythical warrior Aeneas, washed up onto a beach following a devastating storm. The fleet had fled Troy following its loss of the Trojan War to the Greeks. The soldiers had suffered seven years of misfortune, including the death of Aeneas's wife, and had been making their way across the Mediterranean, hoping to create new lives for themselves. Now that catastrophe had found them yet again, destroying thirteen other ships in the fleet, it was hard not to feel dispirited. Even Aeneas, for a few brief moments, seemed unsure if he could go on. Somehow he had to find the courage to do so, while inspiring his men to do the same.

The men begin to make camp, and as they partake in the familiar rituals of clearing out a place to sleep, preparing food, and so on, their emotions, including fear and grief, begin to ebb. Taking advantage of this emotional lull, Aeneas decides to try to rally the group by giving an inspirational speech, but it falls flat. The men are so dispirited and lackluster that they can't seem to break out of their funk. Fortunately, a path forward presents itself, one that Aeneas hadn't considered: a good meal. Dinner is prepared, and the men eat and drink together, as they have so often before. Sitting around the fire, they relax into this familiar ritual, which makes the situation feel more orderly, controllable, and familiar.

The soothing quality of this moment—the sense of its basic continuity with the past—gives the men space they need to reflect on what they experienced. A kind of group therapy session ensues; they begin to open up about the mix of emotions they're experiencing: grief at friends who had died, fear about whether they themselves will survive, hope for the future. Aeneas himself talks about friends of his who had perished, mentioning their names: Amycus, Gyus, Cloanthus. The expression of emotions feels good.

As the conversation continues, Aeneas realizes that he was mistaken earlier. After a terrifying, near-death experience on the open seas, a few nice words won't suffice to inspire still more brave action. Attempting to shape the fear response through rituals like meals can help, but even this doesn't suffice given the fears that the men are already feeling about the challenges they will face. Ultimately, in an extreme and prolonged situation such as this, he and his men have to *process* difficult emotions, not suppress them. The group might be able to muster courage anew, but only if they continue to acknowledge the traumas they experienced.

Modern science has a lot to offer when it comes to regulating our emotions and bolstering our capacity for bravery in the moment. But, not unlike Aeneas, many of us also find ourselves in situations when we don't just want to nourish our own bravery but that of others around us. Perhaps you lead a team or organization as a formal part of your job, or you might simply feel called on an informal basis to lead. How can you boost an entire group's capacity for courage? In the next section of the book, I present approaches you can use to build what I call *collective courage,* starting with one of the most powerful of them all: nurturing an especially intense kind of loyalty and affection among teammates.

PART II

Leading for Courage

Chapter 7

CLAN

To unleash collective courage, leaders can take team-building to a new level, creating far deeper connection and commitment. They can help people see the group as a close-knit clan or tribe that is a powerful extension of themselves.

Huu Can Tran liked to dance. A naturalized US citizen of Vietnamese descent, he is said to have spent a good deal of time during the 2000s and early 2010s at the Star Ballroom Dance Studio and Lai Lai Ballroom & Studio, two dance halls outside downtown Los Angeles, California. Patrons, most of them Asian Americans, gathered at these spots to twirl under flashing disco lights and the watchful eyes of professional dance instructors. These establishments were mainstays of the local community, places where you could learn the tango, lose yourself in the music, and make lifelong friends in the process. Patrons at these establishments weren't simply paying customers. They were members of a tight-knit family.

Sadly, Tran's own connection with this family was marked by conflict. He argued with customers and dance instructors and refused to let go of perceived slights. "He was very distrustful of people and he was angry towards lots of people," a former friend was quoted as saying. "He spent years accumulating unhappiness and disgruntlement." After attending events or classes, he would complain about the instructors, claiming that he could dance better than they or that they had uttered "evil things about him." An ex-wife of Tran recalled that merely missing a dance step was all it took to make him angry—he felt that his image in others' eyes was being diminished.

At some point, Tran stopped patronizing the dance halls. But then, on the evening of January 21, 2023, for reasons that remain obscure, the seventy-two-year-old man went back into the Star ballroom, this time not to dance but to commit mass murder. Pointing a gun, he opened fire on a floor of patrons who had come to celebrate the Lunar New Year. Eleven people died, including longtime customers and the Star's seventy-two-year-old manager, Ming Wei Ma.

Tran wasn't done. He appeared about twenty minutes later at the Lai Lai. It was around 10:40 p.m., shortly before closing time, and only a few patrons were still lingering on the studio's spacious wooden floor. Surveillance footage shows Tran entering the studio's lobby and walking into an office doorway, clad in black and wearing a ski hat. A few moments later, we see him backing out of the doorway, a long-barreled submachine gun still in his hand. We also see something that Tran hadn't anticipated, and that would become an inspiration to millions of people: a young Lai Lai staff member bravely fighting back.

Brandon Tsay, the twenty-six-year-old grandson of Lai Lai's founder, was working that evening. A small, soft-spoken man who was fond of computer games and coding, he had grown up helping out at the dance studio and knew many of its patrons well. Since his mother's death a few years earlier, Tsay had taken it upon himself to keep the studio running. As he told me, the sight of Tran standing in the office doorway was the single most frightening experience of his life. Tran seemed to be scouring for targets, gazing past him at a window that overlooked the ballroom floor. From the hardened look in Tran's eyes, Tsay knew then that the gunman had come not to rob the studio but to kill innocent people. "This was it, I thought, this was the end," he said. "My body just surrendered to the fact that my existence was about to end here. It's done. It's over."

But after this initial reaction, which lasted for a split second, something shifted in Tsay. He had never handled a gun, but somehow he decided right then and there to take a stand. "I thought to myself, 'Well, what can I do here? How can I resist this fate?'"

As Tran paused to ready the weapon for firing, Tsay saw his opportunity. He grabbed the weapon and struggled for control, pushing Tran back into the lobby. He managed to rip the weapon from Tran's hands, but Tran tried to grab the gun back, hitting Tsay viciously on the head and face. Tsay fended him off, doing his best to keep the gun's muzzle pointed toward the ground to prevent someone from being hurt in the event it discharged. He was scared—terrified—as the struggle progressed, but he knew that if he let go of the weapon, people would die. That thought, as well as the adrenaline coursing through his body, led him to fight even harder. After a struggle, Tsay managed to separate himself from Tran and point the weapon at him, screaming for Tran to get out.

Tran turned around and fled the scene. Police located him the next morning, sitting in a parked van. Before they could arrest him, however, he shot and killed himself. Police touted Tsay's courage, noting that his actions had likely saved lives. But that was only the beginning of his notoriety. Security camera footage of his incredible bravery went viral, enthralling a nation plagued by a seemingly unstoppable flood of mass-shooter incidents. Tsay was invited to Washington, DC, to attend the State of the Union address, where members of Congress gave him a standing ovation. "In an instant," President Joe Biden reflected, Tsay "found the courage to act and wrestle a semiautomatic firearm out of the way."

The question, of course, is how Tsay spontaneously found this courage. When I interviewed him some weeks after the attack, he didn't quite know. He was still trying to process what had happened to him—not just the trauma of that fateful evening, but also his newfound fame. He had never had any inkling that he was capable of such bravery. In the past, when he and his friends learned of other active-shooter tragedies and speculated aloud how they would handle themselves, he had always imagined that he would flee, not fight. But according to Tsay, in the moment, "this thought of taking action came about, and I don't know where it came from . . . It's just so out of character."

As Tsay explored what he was feeling and thinking in the moment, an important force behind his courage came to light: his *sense of being*—or how he saw himself. We have seen so far that our own, individual background, experiences, and sheer willpower can shape our sense of identity, all within a broader social environment. But our relationships as well as our affiliations with larger collectives like teams and organizations can also profoundly influence how we see ourselves.

One formulation sees our identity as comprising three levels: how we think about our own self (level #1—personal), the roles we take on in relation to others (level #2—relational), and the groups to which we belong (level #3—collective). For example, I might think of myself as a well-meaning person who cares about ideas, but I also identify myself relationally as a father and a professor. Finally, I identify myself as an American and as a faculty member at Harvard, both collective facets of my identity. These three levels of identity might in turn motivate me to take action for, respectively, my own self-interest, the benefit of other individuals with whom I am connected, and my group's common welfare. Depending on the situation, these factors can work together to motivate courage, or one dimension might wind up taking on more salience than others.

As Tsay came face-to-face with a gunman, he was obviously protecting himself. But his collective identity also came into play. As a family business founded by his grandmother, the Lai Lai dance hall was central to his sense of self, associated in his mind with cherished values of family and community as well as the Asian immigrant experience. Tsay recalled that during those fateful moments when he was struggling to disarm Tran, he wasn't thinking of the extreme danger to himself. Rather, he was focused on safeguarding the community with which he identified. He also knew that individual members of this community—including customers and dance instructors—were inside the studio at the time, and that their lives were on the line. It occurred to him that he was the only thing standing between them and death. "I'm thinking to myself, if I let go of this weapon, if I fail to do what I set out to do, how would the people in my life, the people around me, the people I love, how would they be affected?" Tsay wasn't acting as a boss, colleague, or friend. He was doing so as a member of the group, which itself was deeply intertwined with who he saw himself to be. His collective identity had given Tsay a powerful reason to fight back.

In Chapter 4, we explored how having a squad of supportive people—what we might think of as part of our *relational identity* (level 2) in the framework I've just introduced—can help us take bold action by buttressing our confidence. But as Tsay's story suggests, our *collective identities* (level 3)—those we have by virtue of belonging to organizations, social movements, teams, religions, and other kinds of groups—also enable courage by motivating us to take risks on others' behalf. When we link our sense of self to a larger collective, we feel a duty to promote the common good. Athletes sometimes sacrifice for their teams at key moments, for instance by playing injured in big games so that their teams can win. As we saw in the case of Ashesi University, founders and employees of startup companies risk their careers so that their small, fledgling organizations can succeed.

There's a lesson here for leaders: if you hope to build a team capable of what I call *collective* courage, a powerful strategy is to nurture the kind of loyalty to the group that Tsay felt. But how can you do that? What's the secret to helping team members feel so connected that they're willing to take risks and make sacrifices? How do we encourage more people to act like Tsay, whose instinct in a crisis is to ensure the group's welfare, not their own?

THE POWER OF CLAN

One idea is simply to help team members forge strong, personal relationships with one another. Companies do this all the time, spending billions on team-building exercises. They're not wrong to make these investments. Individuals and teams tend to perform better when people feel like they belong and are connected to others around them. Research also suggests that cultivating relationships with others involved in the same movement encourages people to participate in that movement and thus inspires them to take part in collective courage.

Before we start booking expensive team-building retreats for our squads, however, it behooves us to consider more closely *how* the presence of relationships leads to courage. As it turns out, it's not just feeling close to another person that compels us to take action. Rather, it's also our commitment to a collective identity that does so, *reinforced* by our personal ties. Our sense of belonging is foundational when it comes to our willingness to take risks on a group's behalf. If we merely focus on building relationships, we miss out on a powerful leadership strategy for fostering courage.

During the 1960s, Black people across the American South continued to face severe persecution and political disenfranchisement, part of an enduring legacy of oppression that dates back to the days of slavery. Jim Crow laws in many southern states kept Black residents in poverty, segregated from white people, and unable to vote or exercise other civil rights. In Mississippi, for instance, where white people were bitterly and violently enforcing Jim Crow segregation, fewer than 10 percent of the state's eligible Black people were registered voters. Seeking to spark much-needed change, activists in 1964 brought hundreds of white college students from the northern United States to help with voter registration and educational campaigns in Mississippi, part of a movement called Freedom Summer.

Tensions in the South were running high, and the volunteers knew that their presence would expose them to significant risk of harm, possibly including arrest and physical violence. Those risks were confirmed shortly after volunteers began arriving, when news emerged that three civil rights workers, including two white students from the program, had been kidnapped. They would later be found dead. In addition to physical threats, volunteers would experience poverty conditions—a far cry from what most of them were used to. In short, the summer would be an extreme test of their moral courage, and in the end not everyone was up for it. Out of 1,068 applicants, almost a third never participated.

What about those who did show up? What emboldened those volunteers to put their lives on the line for a cause like voter registration? In a pathbreaking study, Doug McAdam and his colleague Ronnelle Paulsen discovered that it wasn't *only* the presence of strong, personal relationships with other participants that inclined students to participate as opposed to withdrawing. Rather, the collective dimension of identity also mattered a great deal. Students were more likely to participate when they identified with groups relevant to civil rights activism *and* when relationships in their lives reinforced that sense of identity. Belonging to a group and subscribing to their beliefs and values deeply influences our own sense of who we are, contributing in turn to our willingness to behave boldly. The specific relationships in our lives might induce or enable us to behave courageously, but they won't do that unless we're also fired up to take action on behalf of a collective identity we care about.

Young people who courageously decided to participate in Freedom Summer did so because they were identifying with a larger community or an ideal—such as a religion, social activist movement, or profession—that encouraged this kind of bold action. A student might have thought of themselves as a Christian, or as a civil rights activist, or as an educator, and these strong collective identities might have imbued a sense of duty to participate. As one student explained, "If I'm to continue *calling myself a Christian*, I must act NOW to put my abstract conception of brotherhood into practice." Other students, in describing their commitment to Freedom Summer, specifically referenced group identity in ways that evoked a strong sense of duty. "*All of us in the movement* must join forces if the Summer Project is to succeed," one said. "*In my group of future teachers* I make it a point to ask each of them, 'Why do you want to go into education?'" When students also had friends participating in Freedom Summer who shared and affirmed their collective identity and who themselves connected it to Freedom Summer, their willingness to take a risk and participate became more pronounced.

As powerful as the one-two punch of relationships and collective identity are, it still doesn't explain what could compel someone like Brandon Tsay to set aside his fear response in the moment and make a gut decision to risk imminent death. Lots of us identify with groups in our lives, whether it be a work group, a church congregation, or a sports team. Lots of us count close friends as members of those groups. We might be willing to face some dangers to help the group and its members. But we won't instinctively lay down our lives or make other extreme sacrifices for the group's benefit. At a certain point, we'll realize that we must prioritize our own welfare, and we'll shrink back from selflessly taking bold action.

Delving deeper into identity's workings, scholars have developed a more precise understanding of what might compel individuals to sacrifice themselves for a group and a cause that we find worthy. In his book *Talking to the Enemy*, cultural anthropologist Scott Atran describes an unprecedented study in which he interviewed members of extremist groups. His question: Why would people seek to identify with such causes? After "talking to the enemy," so to speak, he concluded: "People almost never . . . die for the Cause, but for each other: for their group, whose cause makes their imagined family of genetic strangers—their brotherhood, fatherland, motherland, homeland, totem, or tribe."

Building off Atran's research, the social psychologist William B. Swann Jr. and colleagues have posited that some people become willing to sacrifice everything for a cause—even their lives—because of a kind of "identity fusion" that takes place in their mind. They feel a particularly intense connection that encompasses both a strong sense of belonging to a group *and* a feeling that they are a unique and valued member of that group. When group membership becomes profoundly personal for them, hitting at what they perceive to be their own, unique core, they become much more willing to make sacrifices for the group, even taking on mortal risk. That is why, as McAdam and Paulsen found, the college students might have risked their life for a greater cause: they identified strongly with other groups who similarly supported civil rights in the 1960s.

Normally when we identify with a group, the strictly individual dimension of who we are—our personal identity—might temporarily diminish. We give ourselves over to the group and act in our capacity as a group member, and we tend to forget about our own individuality and autonomy. We will still feel some sense of our unique individuality, but we'll save its fuller expression for other occasions in our lives, such as when we're at home with our families.

When we experience identity fusion, however, the boundaries between our individual and collective identities become more fluid. We feel a closer, more expansive, more *visceral* sense of connection to the group while still retaining a full sense of ourselves as individuals. In fact the more individual and autonomous we feel, the *more* connected we also feel to the group. When the two levels of identities merge, we feel as if we are utterly one with the group. You know how you sometimes hear people say that they "bleed" the color of the team they're on, so intensely and fully connected do they perceive themselves to be? That's the depth of feeling that the concept of identity fusion captures.

This fusion of individual and group identity is a two-way street: we feel part of the group, but the group also seems to be an extension of us. If we belong to a small startup, for instance, we might come to see that identity as absolutely core to who we are. Conversely, we'll see the startup as projecting our unique selves into the wider world. Perceiving its values and beliefs as deeply consistent with our own personalities, we'll sustain a sense of our own individual agency even as the group operates collectively. We'll also feel extraordinarily close to our colleagues, seeing them not just as faceless fellow team members but as individuals who themselves have become deeply attached or fused to the group and in that sense are extensions of us. We'll regard them as intimates, members of an extended family who share core values. The group will feel like a close-knit clan or tribe.

Think about the idea of a family for a minute. You might belong to the Smith family as a group. But the Smiths wouldn't be who they are without each unique family member in it, including you. Each of you feels a sense of individuality, and you also feel connected personally to the other family members. You have relationships with your mother, father, siblings, and so on. Furthermore, you feel connected to the *group*—you know that for better or for worse, you are a Smith. This connection to the group is that much stronger precisely because it has that personal component layered onto it. This is the dynamic that comes to play in identity fusion with groups that come to feel very much like intimate families.

Identity fusion has practical consequences. When a threat to the group arises, we'll feel more motivated to respond—even if it means taking extreme risks—because we'll perceive that our personal identity is besieged as much as our collective identity. We're nothing without our tribe, and so we'll defend it—indeed, we'll feel *obliged* to take action. In an article titled "What Makes a Group Worth Dying For?," Swann and his colleagues conducted six separate studies in which they asked participants about their willingness to die for a group. They found that people come to feel a "visceral sense of oneness" with a group, perceiving their fellow members as a tight-knit family, even if they are not biologically related. In particular, such "fused" people focus on "core characteristics" they share with group members, whether these are values or biological traits; these values or traits become conduits to the sense of family togetherness. "[W]hen fused persons endorse sacrifice for other group members," these scholars write, "they do so out of a sense of personal obligation to individuals whom they construe to be living extensions of themselves, their family."

Identity fusion helps us to understand how Brandon Tsay could step up in the moment and risk his life for his fellow community members. He certainly had direct relationships with them individually—as friends, colleagues, fellow dance enthusiasts. But he also saw them as belonging to the collective to which he felt fused—as Lai Lai community members. Again, Tsay, didn't see the Lai Lai dance hall as just a place to relax and practice a hobby. He felt deeply attached to it; it was *his* place, a vital part of who he was. As he put it, "The ballroom has been part of my identity for my whole life."

Tsay's sense of himself as a unique individual fused with the collective identity of the dance hall, to the point where patrons and instructors at the establishment felt like extended members of his family. Of course, the dance hall was literally connected to Tsay's family, given their history of owning the establishment and all the years of labor his mother had put in running it. But it also was a surrogate family of sorts, "a very kind and nurturing household," as he describes it. "When I wasn't in school, and if I wasn't at home, I would probably be at the dance studio studying, playing, sleeping. [The lives of the people there], their stories really interested me."

By the time that gunman barreled through the door with the intention of doing harm, Tsay had already made significant personal sacrifices for both his mother and the dance hall. When his mother had fallen sick, he felt obliged to put college on hold to take care of her. As he had seen it, he could always go back to college, but at this moment in time it was more important to help out his mom. After she passed, he again stepped in, this time to help save the family business, seeing this as something he owed to his mother and her memory. Realizing that the dance studio wouldn't make it unless someone stepped in to perform the organizational tasks his mother had long handled, he decided that he could be most true to himself and his values by forgoing college and working at the studio. His sense of self as an individual had become closely bound up—fused—with the studio.

It is in this context that we can best understand Tsay's response to the appearance of a deranged gunman. This gunman was threatening Tsay individually *and* his clan. A community he loved since boyhood and that had felt like an extended family to him was at risk. Tsay felt a visceral urge to fight back and protect his own.

UNLOCKING THE POWER OF IDENTITY FUSION

Tsay's sense of belonging to a close-knit clan grew out of a lifetime of experiences. Leaders in everyday settings usually don't have much time to build group identity, and they often are dealing with team members who lack biological ties, come from different cultural backgrounds, and might even reside in different physical locations. Is it really practical to try to foster identity fusion when it comes to the teams we lead at work or in our personal lives? What might we do to create the deep meaning, attachment, and belonging that propels others around us to behave courageously?

As I've found, some of the world's most successful military organizations, professional sports teams, and startups fast-track the creation of identity fusion—and in turn, more collective courage—by enhancing traditional team-building efforts. They help individuals to form close, family-like bonds with one another, connections that link collective and individual identity in their minds and nurture a capacity for bravery. They do this in three significant ways.

IDENTITY FUSION ENHANCER #1: MOBILIZE THE POWER OF SHARED ADVERSITY

Team-building retreats can be fun and productive, letting you get to know your colleagues and find common ground. But when is the last time you attended one that was truly memorable, even transformative? When was the last time you attended one that had you and fellow team members surmount a difficult challenge *together*?

As research suggests, experiencing and overcoming a shared adversity is much more powerful than traditional team-building when it comes to building relationships. Team members become more deeply attached, seeing one another not merely as trusted colleagues and friends, but as brothers and sisters in arms. They come away from these experiences feeling an intense loyalty and dedication to one another, a willingness to sacrifice courageously for their team members, as well as a knowledge that others around them also have their backs.

Members of the US Marine Corps are known for their exceptional devotion to their fellow soldiers, as evidenced by countless instances of battlefield valor that have occurred throughout the Corps's history. Ask individual marines, as I have, and they'll tell you they feel compelled to fight and perhaps give their lives on the battlefield out of a profound sense of brotherhood and sisterhood with their fellow soldiers. "Leave no man behind," the Marines like to say. "*Semper Fi*—always faithful."

Such attitudes don't crop up by accident. The Marine Corps' training program is designed precisely to forge close, almost familial bonds between individual soldiers. Recruits participate in weekslong training sessions away from civilian society—boot camp for enlisted personnel, officer candidate school for officers. These sessions incorporate intense, shared challenges, culminating in a fifty-four-hour final ordeal called the Crucible, in which teams must go with limited food and sleep while persevering through a series of tests, including obstacle courses, simulated casualty evacuations, and nearly fifty miles of hiking. Teams must work together to figure out technical solutions and make it through. When some soldiers struggle during a given task, other team members help them along. Intense camaraderie takes hold during these experiences, nourishing the team and building a reservoir of goodwill and social "glue."

As a former marine and student of mine, Akhil Iyer, related, recruits are assigned a buddy early in their training with whom to perform specific tasks. These buddy teams become the basis for other teams that are composed for specific challenges: two buddy teams become a fire team, three fire teams become a squad of twelve, and three squads of twelve become a platoon of thirty-six marines. In this way, recruits develop close bonds with their groupmates, an extreme loyalty and a determination to perform on behalf of their team members that deepens their dedication to the collectivity. In effect, team members connect with one another on an individual basis *and* because they see one another as fellow members of the group, making for an especially powerful connection and sense of obligation. Describing one challenge that involved carrying a 78-pound machine gun over a miles-long course, Akhil remembered that "everything was chafing and hurting" and his body was pushed to its limits. "But you do it with your friends, and so the last thing you want to do in formation is fall behind the person in front of you and not carry the machine gun for your allotted time, if not longer."

As Major General William (Bill) Bowers, Commanding General of the Marine Corps Recruiting Command and a former student of mine, points out, individual marines are afraid in the face of danger just like the rest of us, but thanks to the crucible experiences they endured together, loyalty to their brothers and sisters in arms now leads to another, even more palpable emotion: fear of letting down their fellow tribespeople. "You've been trained to count on each other to get the mission accomplished," Bowers says. "The harder the mission is, the closer the bonds become. And then your fear becomes, you don't want to let the team down. You don't want to let the larger team down, you're a part of something bigger than yourself. And you realize in order to sustain this, everyone has to do their part. And so we'll have to do a little more. So that's what you do. You're standing in the group, the tribe, and that's more important than your own well-being."

While the training experiences marines undergo are extreme, you can bring elements of them into your own civilian team-building efforts to spur at least some degree of identity fusion. You can create challenges that team members surmount collaboratively, perhaps in competition with other teams. The hackathons that some companies sponsor are one option, but adding a physical element can increase the intensity.

In providing these kinds of experiences, you should frame shared values in ways that support identity fusion, explicitly reinforcing an ethic of devotion to the team. Like the marines do in boot camp, you should convey to team members that it isn't loyalty to the broader organization and its mission that matters most, but loyalty to the team and to individual team members. You also should make sure to introduce smaller, breakout experiences that allow team members to form close bonds with one another as a way to support and enhance fusion. You want them to feel a sense of intimacy with one another individually *and* as members of a common group, a synergy that will make them feel that the team working together can do anything. If they dedicate themselves to their fellow colleagues, they can best serve the larger, organizational goals.

IDENTITY FUSION ENHANCER #2: MAKE COLLECTIVE IDENTITY MORE SPACIOUS

In addition to fostering identity fusion by strengthening team members' connections to one another, we must ensure that team members' unique sense of individuality doesn't conflict with their collective identity. As my colleague Lakshmi Ramarajan has observed, we don't experience the various layers of our identities one at a time but rather in more complex, overlapping ways. These identities can sometimes seem distant from one another or even come into conflict: a person, for instance, might feel a tug between their roles as a parent and a professional—a serious dilemma that can leave them feeling overwhelmed and anguished. It is extraordinarily difficult to become strongly attached to a group that somehow seems to clash with or even violate a core part of who we are. In corporate contexts, we often see this cropping up in employees' perceptions that they don't feel entirely welcome at work and must leave vital parts of themselves at the door if they are to thrive professionally. The collective identity at work isn't spacious enough to allow for these employees to feel a sense of being utterly and wholly one with the group.

Even as we bolster the integrity of the collective identity, we must maintain a sense of the team as an intimate place where *individuals* are understood and valued for their uniqueness. Fusion requires both: intense group identification *and* an intense feeling of individual selfhood and agency, the sense that the group is a "crucial part of who I am" and that "I am an important part of the group." We can allow for more spaciousness in the collective identity by attending to specific parts of team members' individual identities and harmonizing them with that of the group.

One leader who has done this is Pete Carroll, the former head coach of the NFL's Seattle Seahawks who is now with the Las Vegas Raiders. Early in his career, he became influenced by a concept from the Iroquois Indians called the "long body," special moments in which everyone in the tribe came together and seemed to function as one unified being. To help achieve that, he inculcated three fundamental rules: players had to "always protect the team"; take responsibility for their own conduct; and "be early," a shorthand for "being organized and showing regard for each other." At the same time, Carroll had a strong intuition that the collective couldn't come at the expense of players' individual identity but rather had to grow out of it. As with the Marines, team cohesion among the Seahawks doesn't imply the squelching of players' individual identities, but rather a powerful *fusion* between the individual and the group.

Carroll focuses on helping each player develop as fully as possible both on the field and as a person, understanding that doing so puts them in the best position to contribute to team goals. Whereas many NFL coaches tend to nurture a more impersonal, businesslike environment, Carroll is known for getting to know his players as people on and off the field and for emphasizing their own, individual growth. He also puts resources in place to help them according to their individual needs in areas like nutrition and sports psychology. As he has explained, "It's the whole package of the player that's crucial in helping him be his best, because we see things carry over so much. We recognize that their off-the-field life has something to do with their on-field life. So we're trying to support them and help them find their best in all areas. We take a lot pride in doing that."

Carroll emphasizes the importance of commitment to the team and its rules, but he also strongly affirms players as they express their unique personalities, welcoming in their quirks, outspokenness, and intensity. Research suggests that doing so is a good idea, as humans have a need for *balance* between individual and group identities—we seek to maintain what scientists call an "optimal distinctiveness" in connection with the groups to which we belong. In Carroll's hands, celebrating individuality means making room for and explicitly welcoming other important dimensions of players' identities as opposed to ignoring or merely tolerating them. Acknowledging that many of his players are Black, for instance, he reconciles that aspect of their identity with the larger team identity by creating relevant experiences. He has brought in Black celebrities like the rapper Snoop Dogg and the actor Denzel Washington to speak to the team. Recognizing the importance of neighborhood barbershops in Black culture, he has had a barber set up in the team's training center. During the late 2010s, when some NFL players began the controversial practice of kneeling during the playing of the national anthem to protest racial injustice, some coaches tried to push back. Not Carroll: he encouraged discussion, urged players to follow their conscience, and empathized with their viewpoints, while at the same time encouraging mutual respect among players for their individual decisions.

Do you suppose Carroll's Black players felt more liberated to express their individuality while being part of a team? Absolutely. The result of this delicate balance of individual and collective identity was identity fusion and a powerful sense of team loyalty, summarized well in the team slogan, "I'm In." This team spirit likely has led team members to behave more courageously—to try harder on the field and take more personal risks for the team's benefit. As Doug Baldwin, a former wide receiver for the Seahawks, commented, "When you have an emotional connection to the guy next to you, you're going to fight even harder for him. So when [star running back Marshawn Lynch] is running down the sideline, you see guys sprinting their hearts out to go block for him because they love him, they care for him. That's the kind of culture we built there and it was pretty powerful to be a part of." Just as marines valiantly sacrifice themselves for their teammates, so are Carroll's players more inclined to physically protect their teammate, even if it puts them at personal risk.

Many companies today have tried to make their collective identity more spacious. To open the way for more identity fusion, managers at the team level should take a much more active role. Really get to know your team members as people and invest yourself in their growth both inside and outside of work. Don't just give them resources to do their actual work. Think about what they need to thrive more fully as individuals and do your best to provide it. Make more room for individual expressiveness, whether this means offering more latitude on the dress code, or incorporating various ethnic traditions into the life of the team. It's a paradox, but a delightful one: the more you can create an environment with room enough for diverse individuals to thrive, the more firmly fused those team members can become.

IDENTITY FUSION ENHANCER #3: KEEP THE GROUP FUSED OVER TIME

Identity fusion isn't only all-encompassing for those who experience it: it's enduring. Still, ruptures do occur—what scholars call "de-fusion." Some causes of de-fusion are beyond individuals' control. If a group we're a part of is dissolved because its purpose has been fulfilled, or because the organization no longer needs it (think of the corporate reorganizations that occur as companies adapt to changing markets), members can become distressed and disoriented, unable to exercise the parts of their identity that were directly connected to group membership. Identities are sticky, and as individuals and former members of fused groups, we try to retain aspects of these identities in other settings. In this regard, we might leap at the chance to fuse with a different team, either within our organization or at another, that allows a similar space for self-expression.

Other causes of de-fusion can be participant-led. For example, de-fusion can happen when team members detect that the group has changed and no longer upholds what they consider to be "its core values and beliefs." William B. Swann Jr. and his colleagues cite the example of priests who broke with the Anglican Church because of its decision to allow women to become ordained. We might agree with the church's decision, or not. But to these priests, who harbored more traditional beliefs, it meant that the church's "identity had changed in a manner that was so fundamental that it ceased to be the church that they had joined."

To sustain fusion, we must take steps to renew the collective identity *before* a perceptible erosion can take hold. Here purpose and values become critical. As existing team members leave and new ones come on, we can keep the collective identity vibrant by ensuring that people continue to understand the team's core reason for being as well as the values associated with it. Why *does* the group exist? What noble ambition does it pursue? And what values inform *how* the group pursues that ambition? Such questions help us to uncover what I've described as an organization's "deep purpose." Research has shown that organizations that identify and live their purpose in a comprehensive way perform better, create more alignment among employees, build greater customer loyalty, and more. Asking the "why" question makes it easier in turn for you to clarify your identity, answering the question "Who are we?" By working through these topics as a team, we keep everyone clear about the ideology that ultimately underlies attachment to the group.

For the purpose to feel authentic and true to team members, you should allow room for its modification to fit changing circumstances. Also be sure that the behavior of group members continues to conform to the purpose. The minute even a small amount of dissonance becomes apparent, the collective identity can feel feeble or false, and attachment to it can wane.

Maintaining space for individuality can be a challenge among groups that grow in size over time. Successful startups are a good example. These groups often forge strong ties among team members that feel almost tribal and that fuel courage. These relationships form thanks to what entrepreneurs and early employees will tell you is a crucible experience: the shared challenge of getting a new business off the ground against overwhelming odds. Faced with uncertainty, group members lean heavily on one another, improvising to get the job done just as a team of marines might do in the heat of battle. As one entrepreneurial expert has put it, "Start-ups represent giant experiments. Every initiative is new. One hypothesis after another is being tested. Titles, functional boundaries, roles, and responsibilities are often fluid. The team works as one, inventing, creating, moving toward shifting goals—all while working without a playbook."

For many members of startup teams, dedication and close collaboration with individual team members on an egalitarian basis give rise to an ineffable, almost magical quality, what I've called the "soul" of the startup. But this soul can dry up when startups grow and become established, in part because space for individuality withers and dies. As internal teams become disbanded and newer employees enter the organization, employees might not know their colleagues as well as they once did or feel as connected to them. As leaders introduce formal processes and layers of bureaucracy, informal coordination among teammates erodes. Teammates lose the powerful sense of fighting together in the trenches, protecting one another and convening instinctively as a single, unified whole to tackle external threats. With identity fusion diminished, their capacity for bold action on the company's behalf declines.

As businesses grow, leaders can take steps to keep the soul alive even as they add more size, structure, and discipline. Founded in

2010, the eyeglasses retailer Warby Parker grew rapidly and by 2018 was operating eighty stores and employing a workforce of 1,700. As the company became larger and more established, cofounders Dave Gilboa and Neil Blumenthal worked to define and instill values that had prevailed among the company's early, tight-knit teams and used them to articulate the firm's sense of collective identity. These values included having fun, treating others well, being creative, taking an experimental approach, and adopting an action orientation. But it wasn't enough merely to delineate these values. The company also implemented structures to help bring them alive.

To affirm the importance of creativity and also instill a sense of personal autonomy among the workforce, Warby Parker created a monthly, grassroots competition—memorably named the Blue-Footed Booby award—in which employees could recognize others individually for their innovative work. It also devised a system called Warbles that allowed engineering teams to choose which projects they worked on and how they executed them, providing opportunities for them to exercise their own judgment without needing managers to sign off. Anyone in the company could suggest projects to work on, and senior managers vetted them and voted on which ones had priority, in line with corporate strategies set by senior leaders. Engineers then could pick projects to work on, including ones that weren't top priority. The decision-making process engendered ongoing, transparent conversations about the company's strategies and how specific projects fit in, much as you'd have in a much smaller company.

As former chief technology officer Lon Binder noted, the personal autonomy that Warbles enabled served to inject the feel of working on a small, tightly knit startup where individuals knew one another and expressed themselves. Decision-making didn't happen in some inaccessible executive suite; it played out transparently and involved grassroots engineering teams themselves. "I've spent most of my career as an entrepreneur doing my own startups and in other people's startups," he said. "When you're 20 people in a room, if something is up, you all know it—you're all hearing each other. But when you're 1,500 people, that is gone. How do you ensure that the key people can feel like they're in the loop? Warbles kind of becomes that—a little bit. It doesn't solve the entire business, but on tech-project work, it helps give the sense that you're all in a virtual room together."

Warbles and the company's broader efforts to retain room for individuals to exercise agency didn't necessarily engender the kind of identity fusion prevalent in the Marine Corps or on the Seattle Seahawks, but they did foster more commitment and risk-taking among employees, empowering the company to boldly launch new products and incorporate new technologies. Recent innovations have included glasses that block blue light from digital devices; an app with augmented reality capabilities that allows customers to try on products virtually; and the use of artificial intelligence to suggest eyewear to customers that will be more likely to appeal to them. As leaders, we can learn from Warby Parker and take steps to retain significant space for individual agency and close, family-like bonds in our teams and organizations, in business and beyond. When team members not only are clear about the collective values but continue to feel as if they can exercise their agency as individuals, their commitment to the group soars. They continue to feel an intense, visceral duty to protect it, their capacity for collective courage remains intact, pushing the group to new levels of growth and performance.

FIND YOUR TRIBE

If you think about it, there's something reassuring, even inspiring about collective identity's power to unlock courage. It's easy to think that people are basically self-interested, stepping up in dangerous situations primarily to save their own skin. In truth, we humans have the capacity to feel connected to something bigger than ourselves. Although our survival instinct certainly runs strong, a sense of belonging and the loyalty it engenders can push us *even harder* to take risks and make personal sacrifices. We see this all the time in sports: Olympic athletes who have trained their whole lives to perform at a high level will often perform more boldly when competing on behalf of their home countries. In business too, working in a tight-knit, mission-driven startup can inspire talented employees to work harder and take more risks than they ever imagined. Leaders can call upon the better angels of our nature, harnessing our basic need and capacity for connectedness to inspire more collective courage.

In your capacity as a team member, you also can draw on the magic of identity fusion to become more courageous, and in many cases happier too. Most people want to live to their greatest potential, behaving boldly, feeling a strong sense of purpose, and forming strong, meaningful relationships with others. Most people also have at least some latitude to decide which teams to join at work and in their personal lives. You can seek out teams whose goals and values align firmly with your own, inspiring your intense loyalty and commitment. You can also seek out teams that welcome you in fully as individuals and enable you to forge meaningful, intimate bonds with your peers, who are as committed and integrated as you are. The relationships you'll build and the fusion between your identity and the group's will inspire you to acts of bravery you might never have thought possible. You'll gain the satisfaction of knowing that when it counted, you didn't let your teammates down.

You might find that the act of sacrificing can serve to render you even more committed to your community and more likely to give of yourself in the future. That's what happened to Brandon Tsay. Since his valiant actions at the Lai Lai ballroom, he has experienced a profound awakening. He now realizes, much more than he did before, that "the community is really an integral part of my life and I'm really part of this community and I need to have a bigger play in this." He has played a more public role, leveraging high-profile contacts he has made and starting a fund to help raise awareness around mental health issues. "I think that now that I have a voice, I should really do something important with it for the community, share some positive vibes and positive light . . . a sense of togetherness."

Teams that resemble close-knit tribes or clans aren't for everyone. They require a level of commitment and sacrifice that some of us might not be ready for, either as participants or as leaders. We also must be sure not to spread ourselves too thin: involvement in too many teams will exhaust us and confront us with the pain and stress of overlapping commitments.

In fact, many people today have the opposite problem. Atomization and alienation have taken hold in many societies across the world, leading to what the former US surgeon general called an "epidemic of loneliness." With remote work, many of us feel profoundly disconnected and even alienated—a glaring absence of collective identification. Belonging to a team that gives us a visceral feeling of membership in a deeply enmeshed tribe might be exactly what we need and nothing short of transformational, while also fueling our courage. Assuming that the values and goals that animate the team are morally upright, we might also be able to do some real good in the world. As we'll see in Chapter 8, we can reap similar benefits by finding a charismatic leader to follow, and by striving to become one ourselves.

Chapter 8

CHARISMA

We often think that heroic leaders have some mysterious, inborn charisma that the rest of us don't. In fact, any of us can learn to project charisma through our actions, harnessing it to inspire more collective courage.

The spring of 1940 was a dispiriting time for the British people. For the previous decade, the country's leaders had tried to avoid a bloody, all-out war in Europe by acceding to Germany's aggressive efforts to expand its territory. That policy of appeasement, as it was called, had broken down in September 1939, when Germany invaded Poland. Having committed themselves to assist Poland, Britain and France went to war with Germany. On May 10, 1940, the same day that Winston Churchill became Britain's prime minister, Germany began an offensive against France by invading neighboring Belgium, Luxembourg, and the Netherlands.

Using powerful blitzkrieg tactics, in which they delivered a quick, concentrated attack of tanks, infantry, and air support, the Germans overwhelmed Allied forces, trapping large numbers of troops in western France and Belgium. Miraculously, the Allies managed to evacuate hundreds of thousands of troops across the English Channel in late May and early June. This was the famous Dunkirk evacuation, a military feat that bolstered British morale and allowed the country to fight another day.

In this context, Churchill went to the House of Commons on

June 4 and delivered one of the twentieth century's most memorable speeches. With Allied forces routed, he needed to rally his dispirited countrymen and steel them for a potential German invasion of the British Isles. Churchill did so with rousing rhetoric, proclaiming that "we shall defend our Island, whatever the cost may be, we shall fight on the beaches, we shall fight on the landing grounds, we shall fight in the fields and in the streets, we shall fight in the hills; we shall never surrender." The speech, with its recognition of German victories, left some listeners depressed, but it inspired many others and even moved some to tears. Churchill's secretary recorded in his journal that it had been "a magnificent oration that obviously moved the House." One member of Parliament called it "the finest speech that I have ever heard."

We often presume that the best leaders inspire courage by verbally evoking it at critical moments. John F. Kennedy remarked of Churchill, "In the dark days and darker nights when England stood alone—and most men save Englishmen despaired of England's life—he mobilized the English language and sent it into battle." Great leaders in realms like sports or business make similarly potent attempts to speak courage into existence. In his book *Why Courage Matters,* the late senator and war hero John McCain relates that the legendary college football coach Bear Bryant apparently prepared his quarterbacks to face their fears by following an important ritual. Before a big game, he would stride silently alongside the quarterback and then give them a single piece of counsel: to be brave. "During the course of a game," McCain said, "Bear Bryant would have issued a hundred instructions to his quarterback. None of them could have been as important as his first. Be brave."

As important as direct exhortations to bravery can be, the very presence of great leaders also can rouse followers to behave courageously. The most inspiring leaders seem to possess a force of personality that others find motivational—what we typically call "charisma." Scholars have described the power of charismatic or transformational leaders to inspire followers to perform at their best. Dating back thousands of years, the concept of charisma originally captured the idea of a "spiritual gift" or unique personal abilities that a divine creator bestowed on leaders to serve the public good. Drawing on these earlier notions, the twentieth-century sociologist Max Weber conceived of a form of charismatic political authority grounded in a sense of a leader's heroic personality. Charismatic leaders possessed traits that made them seem "supernatural, superhuman, or at least specifically exceptional." According to Weber, followers were so awed by these traits that they naturally paid deference to their leaders.

Scholars since Weber have observed how charismatic leaders inspire trust, confidence, and respect, all of which make people feel passionate about following them to take bold actions. These scholars also have set forth numerous theories of charismatic or transformational leadership, offering explanations for *how* charismatic leaders inspire performance. They have isolated traits that most people associate with charisma, including how "bold, colorful, mischievous, and imaginative" a leader seems to be. But personal magnetism isn't always such a great asset for a leader to have. Charismatic leaders can dazzle followers with their personal presence and inspire them to act, but they can also lead organizations astray because they fail at the more mundane, operational side of leadership. Further, they can become so central to organizations that they come to be irreplaceable. When they leave, rank-and-file members struggle to replicate what they believe made these leaders so great.

A deeper problem with the notion of charisma is its tendency to affirm popular myths about courage and the "great hero." Whether regarded as a spiritual quality bestowed by the creator or simply a particular combination of personality traits, charisma seems to be the province of a few, select individuals who were mysteriously chosen for greatness. Force of personality is a quality you're born with—you either have it or you don't. Famous speeches by the likes of Churchill, Abraham Lincoln, or Martin Luther King Jr. play into this mystique of the heroic leader as a kind of prophet, one who wields a unique power to attract and galvanize. Still, there's something about the right leader's presence that *does* trigger in others a desire to take risks on behalf of a noble cause. When we experience someone as charismatic and wish to follow them, it's ultimately because we perceive them as intensely competent and trustworthy. Many of us have experienced this ourselves: maybe it was that inspiring high school coach who pushed us to do more than we thought we could; or that manager at work who inspired us to raise our hand with an unusual suggestion.

Research supports a different, more inclusive way of thinking about charisma. It suggests that, like bravery itself, charisma isn't a matter of personality but rather a result of underlying *behaviors* that any of us might cultivate. Great, charismatic leaders, in other words, aren't just born; they're also made through the right training. Instead of simply standing in awe of luminaries like Churchill or charismatic figures we might have met, we should ask ourselves: What do leaders like these *do* that allow them to have such a profound impact?

Scholars of leadership have singled out specific behaviors that motivate others to take action. Building on and refining these more specific dimensions of leadership presence, I've found that under many circumstances leaders help followers take bold action by behaving in ways that create and sustain an aura of heroism around themselves individually and the group. Leaders I studied deploy three specific strategies for projecting their charisma. First, they craft and communicate a heroic quest in ways that followers will find clear and compelling. We've encountered heroic quests in Chapter 3, but here I discuss them from the leader's point of view. Second, they encourage a personal devotion to the quest, modeling it and making their example accessible and relevant to followers. And third, once the quest is underway, they convey strength in the face of hardship, inspiring followers with their extraordinary sense of calm and encouraging them to stay committed.

Although these strategies have a step-by-step logic to them, leaders I studied sometimes engage with them out of order or in parallel. Regardless, adhering to these practices prompts these leaders not merely to preach the heroic quest but to *live* it to the fullest. Through their behavior, leaders connect themselves so powerfully with the quest that followers perceive them as *embodying* it in their very person; in their eyes, the leader becomes the living, breathing form of what otherwise would be merely an abstract ideal.

Perceiving charismatic leaders as authentic exemplars of courage, and feeling more attached to the quest itself, followers aspire to become heroes themselves, a stance that leads them to surmount their fears and take more risk on behalf of the shared mission.

CHARISMA INTENSIFIER #1: CRAFT AND COMMUNICATE THE HEROIC QUEST

To see these strategies at play, let's focus on a leader who was an especially powerful motivator of courage, the legendary civil rights leader Robert (Bob) Moses. Although perhaps lesser known than Martin Luther King Jr., Moses left a legacy that, by many accounts, held similar significance. During the 1960s, he worked to organize and politically empower Black residents in Mississippi and draw national attention to the civil rights cause, helping to bring about passage of the Civil Rights Act. Later in his career, he increased math literacy among Black students through a program called the Algebra Project. Memorializing Moses upon his death in 2021, Derrick Johnson, president and CEO of the National Association for the Advancement of Colored People (NAACP), remarked that he was a "giant, a strategist at the core of the civil rights movement." Activists who worked alongside Moses perceived him as a figure of epic importance, calling him "Jesus Christ in the flesh."

In Chapter 7, we described a famous episode in the civil rights struggle called Freedom Summer, in which students traveled to Mississippi to help organize and politically empower the Black population. Moses was a driving force behind the program, and he personally helped to launch it in June 1964 by leading a comprehensive training in Oxford, Ohio, for students prior to their departure. Moses knew this would be a dangerous undertaking, and he and his staff sought to prepare volunteers for the possibility that local police would arrest them and throw them in jail or that they would be beaten and harassed. As the civil rights leader John Lewis remembered, "[T]hat summer in Mississippi was like guerrilla warfare. You knew that you had to prepare yourself, condition yourself, if you were going to be there."

At one point during the training, it became clear that the dangers the students were facing would be far greater than a beating or a little jail time. Moses learned that three young volunteers—James Chaney, Andrew Goodman, and Michael Schwerner—who were already working in Mississippi were unaccounted for after having been arrested. Given conditions on the ground, Moses understood that the unthinkable had likely happened: they had been murdered.

Moses knew that he couldn't do anything to help the missing volunteers. But he had an immediate challenge before him: What should he tell the college students who were about to be sent into harm's way? He didn't know for sure that they'd been killed, so to keep spirits high he might have decided to downplay the news he'd received. But Moses decided that he couldn't do that. Much as he wanted these students to go through with their volunteer mission, he needed to be honest with them about the risks they would face, even if it meant scaring them off. As he later remembered, "We had to tell the students what we thought was going on. Because if, in fact, anyone is arrested and then taken out of the jail, then the chances that they are alive was just almost zero. And we had to confront the students with that, before they went down [to Mississippi], because they now had—the ball game was changed. I mean, whatever they thought they were coming down to get into—they now knew what they were getting into."

What followed was an encounter for the ages, what one volunteer called a "near sacred moment." Moses told the students exactly what he thought had happened—the three missing volunteers had almost certainly been killed. He didn't adopt a Churchillian approach and urge the students before him to courageously go to Mississippi anyway. He didn't evoke the glory of their potential heroism. Rather, he alerted them to the harsh reality that still more volunteers might meet a similar end, and that some degree of sacrifice would likely be necessary to bring about change. "If for any reason you're hesitant about what you're getting into, it's better for you to leave. Because what has to be done has to be done in a certain way, or otherwise it won't get done."

The room fell silent. Moses, a man who had great gravitas and moral authority in the eyes of volunteers, was calling upon them to make a profound moral choice. Would they join him in possibly sacrificing their own welfare? Just how serious was their commitment? As volunteers would attest, they were scared. But only a few of them gave in to their fears at that moment and left the room—the rest remained steadfast. Suddenly a girl broke the collective reverie by singing a hymn: "Freedom Is a Constant Struggle." As a volunteer later said, this was "one of my most profound experiences of leadership . . . I would have done anything he asked me to do—I trusted him so much."

Several factors contributed to Moses's ability to induce others around him to behave boldly. One was his ability to galvanize others around a shared aspiration for the future. Commenting on charisma, the late sociologist Robert House theorized that leaders who seem to possess magnetism do so in part because they craft a vision for others. They "articulate a 'transcendent' goal which becomes the basis of a movement or a cause," an objective that is "ideological rather than pragmatic and is laden with moral overtones." This goal or vision can affect followers emotionally, attracting them both to the collective identity of the group as well as to the leader personally. As we saw in Chapter 3, individuals also can craft higher goals of their own to fuel their own capacity for courage. Everyday heroes like Patrick Awuah, the founder of Ashesi University, frame a heroic quest for themselves, a narrative of struggle that shapes their own identity as a hero who takes on personal risk in order to do good in the world.

At the June orientation sessions, Moses explicitly conveyed a quest for his followers, tying it to the broader liberation of humanity itself. He told the volunteers not to participate in the program to "save" Black people. Rather, they should "[o]nly come if you understand, really understand that his freedom and yours are one." He explicitly framed the volunteers as heroes, not because they would bring about a breakthrough in the civil rights struggle, but because their very presence in rural Mississippi that summer would mark an important—albeit quite risky—push against white supremacy. "You are not going to Mississippi to try to be heroes," he said. "You are heroes enough just going into the state. This is not a Freedom Ride. . . . You have a job to do. If each of you can leave behind you three people who are stronger than before, this will be almost 3000 more people we will have to work with next year."

Notice the specificity with which Moses evokes the goal for his followers. Leaders tend to communicate visions of the future more persuasively when they use specific details and imagery to evoke it—the vision becomes "sharper" and more meaningful for followers. Leaders further boost the communicative power of the vision when they explicitly alert people to direct connections between their everyday work and the broader vision. Moses's evocation of his heroic quest did both. By not speaking in abstractions and instead asking each student to try to register just three Mississippians to vote that summer, Moses made their goal much more concrete. He also implicitly linked their own, individual work on the ground to the progress of the broader civil rights movement.

In evoking the quest, Moses was not merely welcoming the students to adopt his noble mission as their own. As a respected civil rights leader and the director of Freedom Summer, he was inviting them to identify with the group and to form a direct, personal relationship with him as its leader. Volunteers found his presentations utterly compelling. Despite their intense fears, most were instantly won over and determined not just to sacrifice for the movement, but for Moses personally. At the end of the second weeklong session, one of the civil rights workers noted how emotionally intense the entire experience had been. "Above it all there has been the presence but mostly the spirit of Bob Moses, who is as great a man as any generation could produce: there is not a single person here who wouldn't give his life for him, as he would for any of us."

In communicating your own heroic quest, you might try a range of verbal and nonverbal tactics that charismatic leaders often find effective. Rely on metaphors, stories, and illustrations to make your vision memorable and convincing. Aim big, setting stretch goals for your group while also affirming your belief that these goals are realistic and attainable. Use devices like posing rhetorical questions, presenting lists of possible actions, and sharply contrasting behaviors linked to the quest with those that aren't. Finally, focus on your nonverbals. Charismatic leaders are adept at demonstrating their own, deepest passions through tone of voice, hand movements, and the like.

CHARISMA INTENSIFIER #2: ENCOURAGE DEEP PERSONAL DEVOTION TO THE QUEST

To identify a second dimension of Moses's inspiring force of personality, let's flash back to 1962, a couple of years before Freedom Summer. Moses at the time was a young activist with the Student Nonviolent Coordinating Committee (SNCC) working to register Black residents to vote. At around midnight on August 16, in the small community of Cleveland, Mississippi, Moses fielded a desperate call from three fellow activists stationed in an office in a nearby town. A white mob had surrounded their building, and policemen who had been on the scene had left. Members of the mob were armed with guns and chains. If help didn't arrive soon, the activists might soon be attacked, the latest victims in a campaign of intimidation and violence waged by white locals against efforts to undo the entrenched system of racial segregation.

After calling authorities in Washington, DC, for help, Moses and his colleague went to Greenwood themselves to aid their colleagues, despite the mortal risk. Arriving at 4 a.m., they found the office vandalized and deserted. The activists had managed to escape out a window, and the mob had left. Understanding that the mob could return at any moment, Moses's colleague was petrified. Moses, on the other hand, proceeded to plop onto a couch and fall asleep—a display of nonchalance that stunned his colleague. "I just didn't understand what kind of guy this Bob Moses is," he later said, "that could walk into a place where a lynch mob had just left [and] go to sleep, as if the situation was normal."

On this night, no one was harmed, but on other occasions prior to Freedom Summer, Moses wasn't so lucky. In August 1961 he was arrested, an experience that taught him about "the use of law as an instrument of outright oppression." Later that month, he was beaten bloody by a relative of a local sheriff. Day after day, he exposed himself to the risk of physical violence without flinching. Another activist, Ernest Nobles, remarked that Moses "had more guts than any one man I've ever known."

Moses fostered courage by inspiring devotion to his quest and to himself personally. He did this in two distinct but related ways. First, he *role-modeled devotion to the quest* through his own behavior. He did this not as a conscious strategy, but organically, naturally, reflecting his deepest convictions. As the scholar Robert House has observed, charismatic leaders tend to practice what they preach, behaving in self-sacrificial ways that they hope followers will emulate. House references Gandhi, who "engaged in self-sacrificing behaviors such as giving up his lucrative law practice to live the life of a peasant, engaging in civil disobedience, fasting, and refusing to accept the ordinary conveniences offered to him by others." Other research has found that a self-sacrificial style of leadership serves to rally followers, assuming that the leader doesn't behave in an overly autocratic manner (more on this in a moment). Followers see such leaders as more charismatic, and they're more willing to cooperate with them.

Identity can play an important role here. As you'll recall from Chapter 7, when followers fuse their identities with a group, they "experience a visceral feeling of oneness" with the collective, a sense of belonging wholeheartedly to a tribe. But leaders too can fuse their identities with the group. When they express this fusion via their actions, they shape meaning for their followers. In their own willingness to take risks and potentially suffer the consequences for the group's benefit, leaders demonstrate to group members that they too are fused to the group. Their eagerness to sacrifice their interests and even their life for the cause evokes the intensity of that identification for all to see. In followers' minds, self-sacrificial leaders aren't only acting like "one of us." They are setting a standard for personal devotion to the quest, creating a permission structure for potential risk-taking on the followers' part. "If my leader is willing to go this far on behalf of the group," followers might think, "then why can't I?"

So often in business, we encounter leaders who refrain from sacrificing on behalf of the common cause. They articulate grand ideals for the group and exhort others to behave courageously, but they fail to walk the walk themselves. Pursuing risky strategies for the organization, they stay safely above the fray, falling back on their golden parachutes if need be. Such conduct inhibits identity fusion, displaying a concern with the "I," not the "we." Their leadership comes off as inauthentic, disconnected from what they truly feel and believe. By contrast, self-sacrificial leaders are right there alongside us in the trenches. They're not just delegating, sitting back as others take risks. They're facing danger head-on, demonstrably fusing the "I" with the "we" in followers' minds. Fostering a deep, trusting relationship with followers, their behavior creates the impression that all of us, even those in charge, are facing danger together, as a group.

During the orientation sessions for Freedom Summer, Moses didn't call attention to the many risks he had endured, but he didn't need to: volunteers understood that he and other organizers had sacrificed profoundly. Furthermore, he made clear that while he was asking them to take risks, he would continue to take them on himself. After announcing that the three missing activists were likely dead, Moses remarked that more deaths would likely follow. "I justify myself because I'm taking risks myself," he told the students, "and I'm not asking people to do things I'm not willing to do."

In addition to his practice of role-modeling devotion, Moses adopted a second behavior: he established a strong sense of accessibility and approachability. He engaged with his followers on a personal level, demonstrating a heartfelt respect and concern for them and valuing each of them individually. His followers might not have felt terribly inspired to adopt his example of self-sacrifice for themselves if they perceived that he existed on some fundamentally higher plane than they did. Self-sacrifice might then have seemed like an unattainable ideal, something to admire but not to emulate.

By creating an aura of approachability, the charismatic leaders I studied made devotion to the quest seem more immediate and tangible. Followers were better able to perceive their leaders' devotion as genuine—and well worth replicating. They felt closer to their leaders and aspired to display the same virtue that their leaders did. This is not to say that leaders eroded their own authority entirely. Rather, they sustained a *tension* between empowering their followers on the one hand and wielding authority on the other. They solicited their followers' opinions and allowed them considerable autonomy in their work, *while also* setting forth guidelines for decision-making— what has been called "freedom within a framework." They welcomed team members into the deliberative process even as they retained the power to make final decisions. They supported team members by empathizing with their concerns and coaching them, but they also challenged them by setting high expectations.

Moses was very clear in setting direction for the students and being uncompromising when necessary. During the orientation for Freedom Summer, the issue arose of whether volunteers should use violence to protect themselves in Mississippi. Moses was committed to nonviolence but had recognized the reality that the local Black citizens with whom they were working sometimes carried guns for protection. He allowed a debate to take place in which volunteers argued passionately for nonviolence on the one hand and the permissibility of self-defense on the other. Eventually Moses put an end to the discussion, proclaiming two clear rules for the students that summer: they couldn't keep weapons for self-defense, and if they felt the need to lash out violently, they had to leave the program. As a participant recalled, Moses laid out these rules "slowly" and "gently," but nonetheless decisively. "Questions were [now] resolved. The session ended."

As definitive as Moses could be, he also cultivated a style and presence that was distinctly egalitarian. Although he possessed a master's degree from Harvard, he was known for his profound humility. As one commentator explained, "he believed that an organizer should aspire to a state of near invisibility, by encouraging the skills and decision-making of others. . . . He was uncomfortable talking about himself, and so would tirelessly steer the conversation away from the personal. It was no act: he genuinely felt that an emphasis on personality hindered the course of social justice movements."

Moses was also known for his philosophy of organizing that involved helping his followers to discover their own power rather than directing them from on high. Scholars have argued that the best followers don't just blindly do what the leader directs. Rather, they think critically and take the initiative. They willingly take risks for the group's benefit. Leaders who encourage this kind of followership wind up being "more an overseer of change and progress than a hero." That's precisely what Moses strove to be. As he realized, his very presence as an organizer was enough to galvanize people. He didn't need to direct them or preach down to them. All he needed to do to promote change was to work alongside them, patiently waiting for them to activate their potential. In turn, their own, intrinsic motivation to work hard, grow, and perform at their best would kick in. Ultimately, it was *their* movement, and as an organizer, he needed to cede control. As Moses later reflected, "[A] lot of what turned out to be organizing, turned out to be patience," waiting for people to be ready to act rather than forcing them. The organizer's mere presence and commitment to a shared goal such as voter registration inspired action. Once people were ready, "the organizer has to be prepared to move with them, to accept whatever consequences they might face."

In accordance with these views, Moses spoke softly and deferentially, without a hint of arrogance or condescension. He was content to give *others* the limelight and take his own ego out of the picture.

Consider this account of how he first greeted volunteers at the orientation for Freedom Summer: one who was there observed that after the group sang together, a "slender" Black man "with glasses rose from the front row and waited for the group to grow quiet. He was dressed in a white tee shirt and blue denim overalls. When he spoke, his voice was very gentle. The room became still in the effort to hear him. He introduced himself as Bob Moses."

Moses's modesty and serenity, along with his unassuming strength, fueled a mythology about him as a leader who was both extraordinary and an everyman. "The more he withdraws to the last row at meetings," one observer said, "the more he broods and introspects, the more he lives with the people who are his sustenance, the less he says to anyone, the more his legend grows." Ultimately, Moses's more egalitarian approach to leading greatly enhanced his ability to foster collective courage. His followers perceived that he was accessible to them and that they too could enact his example of heroism and identity fusion. "[O]nly rarely are people willing to risk life and limb for someone's charisma alone," his biographer reflects. "Still, his example in risking life and limb *with them* helped others in reaching the courage to risk theirs."

CHARISMA INTENSIFIER #3: EVOKING STRENGTH AMID HARDSHIP

Once the pursuit of a quest is underway, leaders adopt a third behavioral strategy that allows them to embody the quest and inspire courage: they role-model emotional fortitude. Here we return to a topic we've considered previously: emotional regulation. Throughout history, societies have expressed ideals regarding how leaders should manage their emotions, mindful that followers are watching. Ancient philosophers like Sun Tzu and Plato emphasized the importance of remaining stoic during challenging times, a "tough" approach that many military leaders and sports coaches continue to favor. In recent years, however, some have viewed emotional expression and transparency as hallmarks of strong leadership. As noted earlier, a foremost advocate for this style of leadership is the research professor Brené Brown, who has argued that leaders can best inspire others by showing vulnerability and authenticity in their dealings with people.

Although it may generally hold true that "today's leaders need vulnerability, not bravado," as some have contended, the reality is that leaders need both in some measure; either approach may not be advisable in all situations when it comes to inspiring collective courage. Some situations might call for more vulnerability on the part of leaders. You'll recall how, in the wake of losing the Trojan War, along with countless friends and family, the fictional leader Aeneas transparently processed his emotions with his men while eating a meal together.

In dangerous situations, by contrast, it might be best to temper our vulnerability with some calmness and confidence. Raw emotions like anger and love can certainly prompt people to behave courageously. But as the courage scholar Monica C. Worline notes, the "deliberate cultivation of calm may be important in the expression of courage, and . . . processes of collective courageous action may require ways that members maintain calm in the midst of duress." After all, in situations that require courage, team members are typically under duress. Their fears and anxieties are aroused, and the most pressing risk is that they will freeze up. As leaders, we do best in these situations to help team members remain calm, confident, and focused on the heroic quest.

A powerful way of instilling a sense of calm is by manifesting your own detachment from events. You don't need to do this perfectly—you still can and perhaps should express some measure of vulnerability. But if you deliberately set aside your own anxieties in the moment at least in part, focusing instead on your followers' emotional needs, you can project a poise and confidence that strengthens your followers' own resolve. Scientists know that emotions are contagious in social situations; individuals tend to adopt emotional responses that they observe without even realizing it. As you regulate your emotions and evoke a sense of calm, others around you feel calmer in turn. But controlling your fears also helps on a conscious level to shape meaning, underpinning the notion that you are a hero worth emulating. By projecting calm, you demonstrate just how selflessly committed you are to the heroic quest. As others perceive, you care so much about the cause you're serving that you're capable of overlooking all distractions, including your own fears. Even if you feel frightened, you demonstrate an admirable resolve to sacrifice your own self-interests on the altar of your heroic quest.

As Harvard business historian Nancy Koehn has suggested, the greatest leaders have an ability to regulate their emotions at times when expressing them might do damage to their ability to lead. Keenly aware of their followers' emotional needs, they rise to the moment by preventing their own feelings from taking hold and determining their behavior. She cites Abraham Lincoln, who was deeply tormented by the Civil War yet "rarely revealed his doubts and fears to anyone other than his closest confidants." His reserve, apparently, was motivated by an understanding of emotional contagion. "He knew that if the president displayed such anxiety, it would quickly spread to his generals, his advisors, and the American people, and this contagion would damage his mission to save the Union."

A number of the courageous leaders I studied inspired courage by projecting a sense of calm. Xerox CEO Anne Mulcahy, whom we met in Chapter 4, recognized the importance of conveying outward confidence during the turbulent months when she led her company through near-bankruptcy. This didn't come naturally to her, as she wasn't emotionally reserved by nature. In her words, "The hardest thing for me, as a touchy-feely person, was that my new role required some distance that I wasn't prepared for. When you're worried and when you're really wondering whether you're going to make it, at times like that people need a sense of direction. They want leadership and clarity, and the confidence that we can succeed." What helped her maintain this emotional reserve in public settings was the presence of a support squad, a small group of confidants with whom she could be more vulnerable. She recounts a particularly "dismal" day when her fears got so bad she had to pull her car over on the side of a parkway and take time to collect herself. At this moment, she happened to check her voice message where she heard from a confidant reminding her that others believed in her and the future would be brighter. "That was all I needed to just drive home and get up again the next morning."

Bob Moses too felt afraid while performing civil rights work, despite the great courage he showed. But he became practiced at working through his emotions so that they wouldn't overwhelm him. "The question of personal fear just has to be constantly fought," he once remarked. "I don't know if there is any answer at all." Never did Moses keep his cool and project confidence more than during the orientation when sharing the news about the three missing students. The apparent deaths were an immense blow for him. Months later, he still was "absolutely haunted" by them, according to a fellow activist who had interacted with him. But as we've seen, during the orientation he didn't cry, shout, or shake his fists in anger. He certainly didn't exploit strong emotion to convince the volunteers to go forward with their mission. He spoke quietly and matter-of-factly, acknowledging the pain of the situation and evoking the danger that volunteers would find themselves in if they proceeded with their mission. He seemingly *wanted* volunteers to back out if their hearts weren't in it. With just a few exceptions, the volunteers responded to his quiet, stoic resolve by showing courage themselves, deciding to make Moses's heroic quest their own.

THE POWER OF AN INSPIRING LEADER

You might not possess the eloquence of Winston Churchill nor the bold, impetuous personality traditionally associated with charisma. But as the case of Bob Moses suggests, you don't have to in order to foster collective courage. You can inspire others to sacrifice for a higher mission by adopting a set of courage-boosting leadership behaviors. You can articulate a compelling heroic quest for your followers. You can inspire personal devotion to the quest by role-modeling it through your own self-sacrifice, and by nurturing an egalitarianism that invites and enables followers to adopt your example as their own. You can further accentuate the intensity of your devotion by projecting calm to meet the particular demands of difficult situations, even if you would naturally express yourself differently. Combined, these behaviors help you to frame meaning for followers by positioning yourself as a model of courage for them to emulate. You come to embody the quest in their minds, becoming a vessel through which they can connect with the heroic quest, feel emboldened by its motivational power, and identify as heroes themselves.

You might already perform some of these behaviors, but are you adopting all of them, and are you leaning in on each as much as you might? Embodying a cause as charismatic leaders do isn't about superficially adopting a behavior or two when you happen to think of it. It's about committing to these behaviors and giving yourself over to them, consistently and intensely, so that they define your leadership. It's about deeply understanding and internalizing the quest. It's about fusing your identity with the group, showing a willingness to give everything you have to ensure its success. It's about identifying with your followers and elevating them, so that everyone partakes in the "we." It's about remaining conscious of how others are perceiving you, and the emotions that they need to see you express, especially in times of adversity. Ultimately, it's about living out the quest and its ideals to such an extent that it goes to the core of your being and defines your very essence. This level of commitment seems authentic to others—because it truly *is*.

As a beacon of courage, Bob Moses inspired student-volunteers to emulate his extraordinary heroism and devotion to the cause. It was a dark episode in American history, but the volunteers who followed him could soon take comfort in knowing that their sacrifices were not in vain. Freedom Summer didn't single-handedly give political power to Mississippi's Black population—in fact, only 1,600 new Black voters were added to the voting rolls as a result of the volunteers' efforts, out of approximately 17,000 who applied. But the initiative had an important impact by bringing national attention to the civil rights struggle. By some accounts, the political pressure it created helped lead to the signing of the Civil Rights Act of 1964 and Voting Rights Act of 1965, which enforced voting rights and pushed back against various forms of discrimination. Many volunteers went on to continue their advocacy on behalf of Black political empowerment, making a difference in other local communities and creating the conditions that would eventually enable a Black person to become president of the United States.

Like these volunteers, you can boost your own, individual capacity for courage by seeking out inspiring leaders to follow. You might harbor stereotypes about inspiring leaders: that they are loud, egotistical, extroverted, brash, aggressive, and exuberant in front of a crowd. Some great leaders certainly are like this, but a quieter, humbler, more egalitarian kind of leader can do just as much if not more to inspire courage. When selecting someone to follow, look beyond the stereotypes to see if leaders exhibit the three behavioral strategies outlined in this chapter. Once you've found such a person, try to become what scholars call a "courageous follower." Instead of blindly agreeing with everything a leader says, think critically and speak up when you believe leaders are making mistakes. If you truly have found a humble, egalitarian leader, you'll find that they'll welcome this behavior. They too want to learn and grow.

Of course, some leaders are adept at pulling the behavioral levers of charisma, even if in reality they don't serve an elevated cause. Looking around the world, any number of leaders today use personal charisma primarily to benefit themselves and their supporters. You also find historical leaders like Adolf Hitler, whose charismatic behavior served a manifestly immoral quest, leading to the suffering of millions. When seeking out leaders to follow, always maintain a critical posture, making sure that the charismatic leaders you encounter possess a strong moral sense and values that conform with your own.

Leaders can foster collective courage by thoughtfully framing their own behavior and, as we saw in Chapter 7, by building close, almost familial relationships among team members. To maximize the potential for bold behavior, they also must attend to the wider context. Some companies and other organizations mobilize a trifecta of collective courage: cohesive, tribe-like teams, inspiring leaders, *and* collective norms of behavior that supports boldness. We're used to crediting individuals for stepping up in moments of adversity, but as we shall now see in Chapter 9, the organizational systems we build as well as their distinct cultures can play a pivotal role, inspiring fearful employees to step up and perform seemingly impossible acts of bravery when it matters most.

Chapter 9

CULTURE

Most large organizations are designed for cowardice. You can remake your organization's culture to instill a courageous mindset and enable your people to behave boldly.

Picture an exquisite banquet hall in a grand old hotel. The tables are a symphony of light and color, with gold table runners, candles, and centerpieces with yellow roses. As dusk falls, glassware and settings for an extravagant seven-course meal glitter under the light cast by crystal chandeliers. Waiters and waitresses work the room, serving several dozens of senior business leaders and their guests, while Mallika Jagad, the young assistant banquet manager assigned to the event, looks on. Laughter and friendly conversation fill the air.

At about half past nine, waiters wheel out the main course on food trolleys. They're placing plates before the guests when a series of popping sounds come from outside. Firecrackers, Mallika thinks. The hotel, the Taj Mahal Palace in Mumbai, India, often hosts weddings during the month of November, and Hindu festivities traditionally end with a celebratory bang. But then, a few minutes later, her phone lights up with text messages and calls. It isn't a wedding. Gunman are apparently roaming the hotel shooting people at random.

Although just twenty-four years old and younger than many of the waitstaff, Mallika doesn't panic. As the ranking employee in the room, she takes charge. Following protocol for a situation like this, she and her colleague order that the lights be turned off, and that the dining room door be closed and blocked by the food trolleys. "Please," she urges the guests, "if you could move away from the doors and windows, and get down on the floor, up against the wall. We need to stay quiet. It's for your own safety."

Taking their cue from her, the waitstaff help the guests to the floor and join them there, remaining every bit as calm and collected as Mallika. "Don't worry," they tell the guests. "We'll be safe here." But will they? Mallika calls a friend on the hotel's security team to ask what is happening. He doesn't know. Nobody does. The situation is fluid.

Mallika's gut tells her that for the time being, they are safer staying inside the barricaded room than they would be trying to escape. As more information comes in, maybe they'll find the right time to make a move. So for the next hour, the group of about sixty-five people hunkers down, frightened and bewildered. More gunshots ring out. Is it gang violence? A domestic dispute? Are the police coming? The SWAT team? And how long will they stay stuck in this room? Anxious guests want to know. But Mallika has no answers.

Mallika and the waitstaff do their best to comfort the guests, chatting with them and passing out drinks. Her friend from security calls with an update: it's a terrorist attack, and similar attacks are taking place at other hotels and restaurants around the city. There are four terrorists, and numerous staff and guests are already dead. Local police are on the scene, but they are only lightly armed, while the terrorists have automatic weapons. It will be some time before the government's specially trained antiterrorist commandos arrive. Mallika and her group must stay calm and quiet. It is essential that the terrorists not discover their presence.

For a moment, Mallika becomes emotional. How can this be happening? India is not a war zone. It is a safe country. It's unfathomable. Yet she steels herself and carries on. Although she knows every corner of this hotel, including out-of-the-way corridors and back exits, she doesn't consider deserting her post to save herself. The waitstaff doesn't either, despite being equally familiar with the hotel. Their job is to care for their guests. And that's what they'll continue to do.

Over the next several hours, the situation outside worsens. On the floors above, the terrorists set off grenades. Each time one goes off, the room shakes and debris falls from the ceiling, including shards of glass from the chandeliers. The gunfire continues as well. Hotel guests' pleas for information grow more insistent.

In addition to continuing to calm the guests, Mallika passes the time calling for more information and coordinating with the director of security. Sometime after midnight, he informs her that there might be a way to evacuate the group. The hotel is vast: 285 rooms, nine restaurants and bars, and several banquet halls. The terrorists can't be everywhere at once. Together they map out a plan for her group to sneak out through back corridors. When the director of security gives the okay, Mallika will take the group out. To minimize the risk to guests, she will go first, with guests following behind her in groups separated by staff members.

Another hour passes, and then one more. Mallika checks her phone constantly, looking for the go-ahead from security. By three in the morning, she still hasn't received a call or text, and the guests are losing patience. Some express their determination to leave on their own and find their way out. These are senior business leaders, after all, used to taking charge. "Absolutely not," Mallika says, a new firmness in her voice. Not only would these individuals likely perish if they encountered the terrorists; they would alert the gunmen to the group's existence, compromising everyone's safety. All of them had to stick together. If they did that, she promises, they would make it.

Despite her strong front, Mallika experiences her own moment of despair. She can't believe she has found herself in such a dire situation. As she would later tell me, "For a few minutes, I was thinking, 'Is this how it's going to happen? Is this how it's going to end?'" She quickly puts such thinking to rest, telling herself, "Snap out of it, no time for melodrama." She's in charge of this group's safety. And damn it, she's going to do her duty.

Mallika's phone chimes with news: elite antiterrorist forces have arrived and are preparing to engage the terrorists. Her group continues to wait, alert to every sound, hanging on every text Mallika and other staff members receive. Another hour passes. And then another. As day breaks, guests and staff are stunned by smoke billowing in through the door frames. Mallika rushes to call security: the corridor outside is on fire.

Staff and guests race to place wet towels around the door, but the smoke continues to engulf the room. The automatic sprinkler system activates, sending the guests into a full-blown panic. Screams and sobs fill the air. There is no escape—the heavy glass windows require a special key to open, and nobody in the room has it. Staff and guests throw chairs and other objects at the windows, trying to break them, but they can't: the windows are made of reinforced glass. Mallika tries to calm everyone, but nobody listens to her or the other staff any longer. It's absolute chaos.

A half hour later, someone manages to crack one of the panes of glass. A fire truck is outside, attending to a fire raging on the fifth and sixth floors. Guests and staff attract the attention of the hotel's general manager, Karambir Kang, who is standing in the street. He directs the fire truck to lower its long ladder to the ledge outside the window.

As Mallika coordinates with Kang, guests step out onto the ledge one by one. They maneuver onto the ladder, moving slowly so as not to fall, and continue down to safety. Only after all the guests evacuate do staff members take their turns on the ladder. Twenty-four-year-old Mallika is the last one down.

Upon hearing of Mallika's brave response, I was deeply moved. If

I were a twenty-four-year-old employee, with my whole life ahead of me, like Mallika, would I have stuck around to help guests? None of her bosses had ordered her to do so. Yet she did, as did the rest of her team.

As it turned out, it wasn't just Mallika and her team who behaved gallantly—it was the entire contingent of several hundred employees and managers on duty. "The easiest thing for our staff to do . . . was to drop whatever they were doing and run out of the hotel," said Abhijit Mukherji, executive director of hotel operations. "Not one did that. Not one." On the contrary, many staff put their lives in jeopardy to save guests, with some making the ultimate sacrifice. In one heartbreaking episode, terrorists mowed down chefs who had formed a human shield around guests as they escaped through a back entrance. At another point, a troupe of telephone operators who had been rescued surreptitiously returned to work on the premises, phoning guests in their rooms and advising them on how to stay safe.

Other employees who had managed to escape likewise went back in—not because managers ordered it, but because they felt personally responsible. General manager Kang, who had been off-site when the terrorist attack started, rushed back to the hotel and ran inside looking to help guests and employees as grenades exploded nearby. Later that evening, with his wife and children trapped on the sixth floor, he risked his life to lead heavily armed commandos around the building in search of terrorists. His family would eventually perish in a fire set by the terrorists. Nevertheless, he remained on-site, doing everything he could to help. As he told me, he felt responsible for the hotel, and like a sea captain, he was determined to go down with his ship if it came to that. As the late Ratan Tata, chairman of Tata Sons Ltd., which owns the Taj Mahal Palace, remarked, "There were no manuals, there were no instructions for what should be done in these circumstances. So what seems to have happened is individuals from the waiters to the managers of the restaurants all had this goal of 'let's get the guests to safety.'"

In most cases, the staff succeeded. Out of over 1,500 people on the premises at the time of the attack, thirty-one were killed, including both guests and staff—a terrible tragedy, but small compared to what might have been. As a guest in Mallika's group would later remember, "The level of calm and composure the staff displayed was amazing, absolutely amazing. . . . I don't think we would have made it out of the hotel without the support, the assurance, the constant service orientation that the staff provided. Without doubt."

We've seen many examples in this book of courageous individuals and teams, but how is it that an *entire organization* of hotel employees, managers, and leaders would be so willing to risk their lives for their guests? These individuals weren't especially prone to bravery—they weren't former Navy SEALs, first responders, or others who are inclined toward courage. The company made no special effort to hire brave people, seeking out instead employees from rural areas who seemed comfortable serving guests, who had "traditional Indian values," and who showed high levels of integrity. Mallika, the phone operators, general manager Kang, the team of chefs who were killed—these weren't people who had signed up to willfully risk their lives. They were ordinary people who found themselves in extraordinary danger, and who rose to the occasion. As Mallika confided, "I was scared, but there was something more important to be done."

As my field research suggests, leaders can design large organizations to make bold action on the part of individual team members more likely. To understand how, let's step back and consider what an organization actually is. Economists have analyzed organizations as a set of contracts or agreements that exist between individuals. To motivate people to perform well, they have argued, leaders simply need to adjust the contracts by crafting the right financial and nonfinancial incentives. In contrast, organizational scholars have analyzed organizations as administrative entities that coordinate people's efforts and enable them to work productively together. By putting in place the right structures and processes, leaders can delegate workflows effectively so that the organization can accomplish difficult or complex tasks.

But not everyone agrees that organizations are strictly contractual or coordinating entities. Organizations have a symbolic dimension to them too. In addition to their economic and administrative functions, they are systems of meaning, bringing people together around commonly held values, beliefs, norms, and practices—what people loosely speak of as *culture.* This culture in turn shapes what people believe and how they behave within the organization. We can find collectives operating in these ways throughout time, from small tribes to multinational corporations. Individuals might care about their own contractual obligations and rewards, this school of thought holds, but the cultural dimension motivates them as well to pursue the organization's interests. Think of the jobs you've had. Were you motivated solely by your desire to make money or get a corner office? Or was your behavior also informed by the meaning your work had, the elevated goals you were pursuing, the beliefs the organization embodied, or the sense that you and the organization were part of something bigger?

Intuitively understanding their organizations as systems of meaning, leaders often try to shape or design the culture to encourage certain behaviors. They attempt to make their people bolder, for example, by creating a "courageous culture," taking steps like formally adopting boldness as a cultural value, lauding it in speeches, and bringing in experts to teach it in trainings. They also embrace traditional tactics like hiring, promoting, and orienting people. These actions aren't necessarily wrong, but they stay at a superficial level and usually fail, on their own, to motivate much courageous behavior.

Leaders at organizations like the Taj Mahal Palace go further, taking steps validated by science to embed courage deeply into an organization's meaning system. They start with a more sophisticated and expansive sense of what a system of meaning encompasses—not just attitudes people have, but also practices and beliefs. As my research revealed, they pursue three key interventions to build courage into the cultural system of the firm. They establish courage as a behavioral norm (attitudes); create more space for brave conduct (practices); and make courage part of the organization's ethos (beliefs). In organizations that design culture in this more thoughtful way, team members become more inclined to see themselves as brave. They feel responsible for taking risky action for the organization's benefit and also empowered to step up and take action when it truly counts.

CULTURE INTERVENTION #1: ESTABLISH COURAGE AS A BEHAVIORAL NORM

Treating an organization strictly as a contractual or administrative system can foster timidity. An organization conceived as only an economic entity lacks the rich layers of meaning that can motivate people to want to take risks and make sacrifices.

As an employee, you'll see your connection to the organization in transactional terms—as "just a job." Meanwhile, administrative systems can mire people in excessive bureaucracy, making it difficult for team members to take action and inspiring a mentality of passivity and operating within the system. Leaders and organizations increase confusion by sending mixed messages, often actively discouraging risk-taking even as they try to promote courage as a behavioral norm. In any situation, they tend to place attention on the downside (avoiding loss), not on the potential upside (benefiting from gain).

Sports coaches often describe such prescribed timidity as "playing not to lose," a risk-averse mindset that prioritizes staving off a loss, even if it costs you a chance at winning.

By contrast, leaders can instill a more ambitious, "playing to win" mindset deep into their organizations. Rather than focusing primarily on limiting risk, they can push the organization to concentrate on the upside of winning and to commit to doing what it takes to emerge victorious. This doesn't mean ignoring risk—as we saw in Chapter 1, anticipating and mitigating dangers helps to boost people's confidence and in turn their courage. But it does mean ensuring that you don't become too oriented around or even obsessed with managing risk. Groups that play to win adopt what we might call realistic optimism: they do what they must to account for risk, while still remaining utterly obsessed with victory. As the legendary football coach Vince Lombardi famously remarked, "Winning is not a sometime thing; it's an all the time thing. You don't win once in a while; you don't do things right once in a while; you do them right all of the time. Winning is a habit."

Scholars have suggested that leaders who model a play-to-win mentality do so in good times and bad. Shifting the organization to a more aggressive stance translates into stronger financial performance, particularly during times of disruption or crisis when our natural reaction is to react timidly and try to conserve what we have. In the introduction to this book, I described my own research showing that companies that do best during recessions tend to play to win, boldly pursuing future growth, confident that good times will eventually return. They don't go overboard on risk-taking, of course. They try their best to protect against short-term risks, choosing tactics thoughtfully so as not to hinder future growth. Such realistic optimism pays off. These play-to-win companies were significantly more likely to outperform their peers in both revenue and profit growth once the economy recovered.

Infusing a winning mindset as a behavioral norm requires more than just easy sloganeering on leaders' part. They must adopt aggressive strategies and execute them diligently. Consider BlackBerry, a leading maker of smartphones during the early 2000s. The company's devices were popular in corporate settings, so addictive that many called them "Crackberries." By the early 2010s, however, competition from Apple's iPhone and Google's Android phones left the company reeling, its market share plummeting to a fraction of what it once was. Although the company brought in a new CEO, he failed to make the company more competitive. By 2013, the company was taking steep losses and its viability as an independent phone manufacturer was in question.

Enter new CEO John Chen, who had previously turned around the ailing software company Sybase. Temperamentally, Chen sought to embrace new challenges and pursue positive goals for the future rather than to sit back and protect what already existed. He began a bold strategy of reinventing BlackBerry's business. As he saw it, the company could no longer hope to compete and win in the device market—profit margins were too low, and competing with the leading players would require vast amounts of capital that BlackBerry didn't have. The best shot at success, Chen thought, was to pivot to software. BlackBerry's devices had long been known for an underlying software architecture that made them more secure than their peers. Perhaps there was something here to be leveraged for future growth. If the company used its expertise to create innovative software that helped companies keep their IT infrastructure safe, Chen believed it could become a leading player in the cybersecurity market.

Unlike his predecessors, Chen was focused squarely on a winning strategy, recognizing that he needed to "re-architect the whole company" if BlackBerry were to reverse its fortunes and thrive once again. The company underwent many wrenching changes, from the way it developed new products to the way its sales force worked. It also made a number of bold moves, including the acquisitions of key companies and the sale of patents to fund growth investments. Yet it had no choice. "I knew the pivot was necessary," Chen later said, "but it took courage. We were walking away from what we knew best. I didn't want the hardware era to end in my hands, on my watch, but I also knew that if we didn't do so, we would take the entire company down."

For the turnaround to succeed, it wasn't enough for Chen and his leadership team to embrace bold risk-taking in their strategy-making. The entire organization had to embrace a forward-looking, risk-taking mindset as a central aspect of their group identity. "A turnaround culture must be positive," Chen says. "Employees need to have the hunger—and confidence—to get things done. Everyone needs the same single-minded desire to win."

Chen set the tone by establishing early on that he was taking aggressive action to secure BlackBerry's future, including by fighting hard when he needed to against external threats. As Mark Wilson, the company's chief marketing officer, recalled, T-Mobile publicly clashed with the company on an issue soon after Chen's arrival. "John went right back to T-Mobile and fought back. That was good for employees to see. He was not just here to sell the company, he was here to fight." Chen also promoted a forceful, play-to-win mentality by emphasizing the importance of long-term growth and innovation. The company wouldn't wait for the market to force it to change—it would pursue innovation proactively. Soon after he became CEO, he established an innovation lab to drive new business opportunities while at the same time cutting back on research oriented around the company's traditional hardware products. This sent a message: the company was focused on building for the future, not protecting its past successes.

Chen sent a powerful signal about the importance of embracing change through his people strategies too. Sensing that some existing members of the company's leadership team might not be eager or equipped to execute on the new strategy, he replaced virtually every member of the team, bringing in those who possessed not only expertise in software but a bent toward transforming the organization. He drove personnel changes deep into the organization with an eye toward boldly advancing the company's transformation. According to his strategy, a full third of the workforce would be new hires who would bring new thinking and enthusiasm. Another third would be existing employees that the company would retain in their previous roles so as to benefit from their deep knowledge of the business. Yet another third would comprise existing employees who would take on new roles inside the company, serving to promote change to an organization that they already knew well. Regarding the latter, Chen instructed managers to promote employees who embraced change and would galvanize others to do so as well. "One trick I have learned from turnarounds," he said, "is that you need to promote some people from inside who may *not* have the right level of experience, but who have the right *attitudes*. Because of their positive attitudes, they become de facto people leaders."

Chen's efforts to infuse BlackBerry with a play-to-win mindset paid off, albeit slowly. The company notched $1 billion in software-related revenues in 2020, with strong profits. While as of this writing BlackBerry's comeback remains ongoing, it still represents an extraordinary accomplishment. There aren't many companies out there that have survived by completely changing their business models midstream, but BlackBerry did by transforming from a hardware to a software company. The fact that the company continues to exist at all is extraordinary, owing to Chen's bold business strategy as well as the organization's courage in leaving behind a familiar business and boldly reinventing itself.

CULTURE INTERVENTION #2: CREATE MORE SPACE FOR BRAVE CONDUCT

A winning mentality won't foster much courage unless people inside an organization have the ability to enact it. If they lack sufficient autonomy, their efforts will become bogged down, and winning will seem like an empty, meaningless ideal. In many large organizations, stifling bureaucracies shrink the space for autonomous action, creating tensions between individual employees and the organization. Rank-and-file employees seeking to take risks are forced to run a bureaucratic gauntlet, obtaining endless sign-offs from their managers and wasting time and energy adhering to established processes and policies. The experience is so frustrating that it typically leaves employees feeling disempowered, disillusioned, and reluctant to behave courageously. As Gary Hamel and Michele Zanini have observed, excessive bureaucracy costs US companies $2.6 *trillion* each year. A significant part of the problem is the tendency of bureaucracy to impede risk-taking. Surveying employees of large companies, the two researchers found that nearly all—95 percent—reported difficulty innovating, while three-quarters claimed that "new ideas in their organization are met with indifference, skepticism, or outright resistance."

I first became focused on the problems posed by bureaucracy while writing an article about the almost magical soulfulness that seems to exist in some startups but that fades as companies grow and mature. As I discovered, employees at larger companies tended to feel stifled by a culture defined by bureaucracy and rules—what the sociologist Max Weber famously called an "iron cage." What these employees specifically lacked, I found, was what we might call *voice* and *choice*: the ability to speak up and express potentially controversial or nonconformist ideas, and the ability to make meaningful decisions about their work, including the decision to take risks. Without sufficient voice and choice, employees felt disempowered, disengaged, and alienated at work. Cowardice reigns as everyone focuses on playing it safe and not getting themselves into trouble.

You can nurture more collective courage by protecting the exercise of personal agency. You can instill in employees a sense of ownership, a perception that the company's future is in their hands and that they're responsible for taking courageous action when necessary to ensure that it thrives. Successful startup companies often do this, creating environments that become legendary for their boldness. But they don't do this arbitrarily or to excess. Rather, they encourage employees to speak up and to exercise discretion within certain guidelines or boundaries that leaders define. Leaders of companies large and small can allow ample room for the exercise of voice and choice, for example by asking employees for feedback, asking managers to listen to employee ideas, consulting employees on important decisions, or celebrating people who behave boldly. Just as important, they can refrain from punishing employees when they broach sensitive topics or when bold ideas for which they advocated fail, thus enhancing a sense of psychological safety. When leaders take these steps, they create the potential for more collective courage by instilling the notion that the organization is a community of valued contributors. Team members understand that acting on your own initiative and taking risks for the organization's benefit is a normal, expected, and celebrated feature of work.

Employees at the Taj Mahal Palace didn't put their lives on the line for their guests because they received training in how to behave courageously (indeed, the company didn't explicitly teach courage; rather, it cultivated a capacity for bold action indirectly). They did so, in the first place, because they understood the organization's cherished values, which centered on providing exceptional service to guests, and because they identified personally with this mission. But importantly, the organization didn't direct them on *how* to provide this service. Rather, it granted them an unusual degree of workplace autonomy to bring those values alive. The Taj Mahal Palace trained its employees not merely to dress appropriately or speak to guests respectfully, but also to think of themselves as ambassadors for the guests, not the company. If employees spotted opportunities in the course of their daily work to please individual guests, the hotel expected them to seize them and act immediately, without seeking approval from a manager. During training, the hotel impressed upon employees that, as one account puts it, "the company's leadership, right up to the CEO, will support any employee decision that puts guests front and center and that shows that employees did everything possible to delight them."

Think of how motivating it must have been for employees to know that they could use their discretion to ensure that guests have a wonderful experience, that management supported them, and that the organization would celebrate and reward them for doing it. But think too of the sense of duty to the organization employees must have felt because they had that autonomy. It was employees' duty to ensure that guests had a wonderful time. They personally "owned" what happened at the hotel. During the terrorist attack, that strong sense of ownership came into play, impelling Mallika and her hundreds of colleagues to overcome their fears and put their guests' safety first.

A number of sizable companies I've studied carved out protected space for employee voice and choice, encouraging employees to behave boldly and innovate not just in crisis situations, but at all times. Netflix, for instance, is well known as an organization where employees take bold risks to innovate and disrupt. Although the company embraces courage as a core value, its willingness to carve out space for employees to exercise voice and choice is an important factor in bringing this to life.

As discussed in the company's so-called culture memo, a document presenting the organization's key operating principles and philosophies, managers at Netflix don't just tolerate dissenting views—they seek them out, what the company calls "farming for dissent." Before a significant project gets underway, team members submit their ideas to colleagues across the organization and ask for feedback. Whether they choose not to listen to what they hear, that's their prerogative, but they must give others the opportunity to weigh in. Managers and employees at the company also provide performance feedback whenever they feel moved to do it, not just in infrequent formal reviews as at most companies. As the culture memo explains it, "It takes courage and vulnerability to ask someone how you could do better, or to seek alternative opinions, and integrity only to say things about a colleague you're willing to share with them directly. . . . But extraordinary candor helps us improve faster as individuals and a company."

As for the exercise of autonomy, this is pronounced at Netflix but hardly unlimited. Leaders lay out general guidelines for employees to follow, most notably basic rules intended to "prevent irrevocable disaster" or keep employees from running into "moral, ethical, or legal issues." So long as employees play by these guidelines, and so long as their actions were informed by their understanding of the company's broader goals and priorities, they can exercise their own judgment. Netflix in the past has called this concept "freedom and responsibility," and today regards it as its "(almost) no rules rule." Ultimately, the company seeks to provide a context for employees to make decisions, but not to control their actions. As some employees find, taking responsibility for your own actions can be scary; they can't blame the organization if something goes wrong. But it also yields a strong sense of agency, a sense that employees are empowered rather than the organization's passive drones. As they take responsibility, the sense of empowerment can infuse their identities. They start to think of themselves as *doers,* people who can make change inside the system. And they in turn take more bold action.

According to the culture memo, allowing ample space for individual agency has figured prominently in the company's success. "In entertainment and technology, our biggest threat is a lack of creativity, adaptability and innovation. It's why trying to minimize rules and processes (rather than errors)—while giving people the freedom to use their own judgment and learn from their mistakes—is a far superior recipe for long-term success." Employees at Netflix have the license to take risks, knowing that they bear responsibility for their actions and their outcomes. As a result, people actually do step up more at work, displaying the courage to challenge convention. To date, Netflix's emphasis on autonomy has allowed it to make any number of bold business moves, including shifting to video streaming in 2007, overcoming competitive challenges from Google and Apple, and transforming itself into a major creator of content.

It's not enough to set out operating principles and philosophies that allow for autonomy. You must also take steps to allow for a supportive culture. As mentioned earlier, my colleague Amy Edmondson has argued, you must act to ensure that people feel psychologically safe to exercise the autonomy that the organization formally grants them. Among other actions, you should explicitly invite employees to exercise their voice and choice, emphasizing that you as leaders don't have all the answers and that you are eager to learn from others in the organization. You should also be sure to respond productively when failures occur, for instance by changing processes or procedures to improve the organization or by celebrating failures as pathways to novel ideas or solutions. When employees perceive that they won't be punished for saying something controversial or taking a risk and failing, they're more inclined to exercise voice and choice going forward.

CULTURE INTERVENTION #3: BUILD COURAGE INTO THE ORGANIZATION'S IDENTITY

To fully nurture a capacity for collective courage, leaders must go further in their organizational design efforts, considering the company's core beliefs about itself—its identity. As we've seen throughout this book, our sense of personal identity—who we are—is fundamental to how we experience and give meaning to the world; it serves, as some scholars have observed, "as a deeply held guide for [our] thoughts, motivations, and behaviors . . ." Organizations, too, have identities, shared ideas about what makes them unique and special—what we previously called collective identities. Such identities might reflect beliefs about the group that employees, customers, and other stakeholders hold in common, while also being enshrined in the organization's own communications efforts. These identities usually contain some aspirational components, messages about what each organization *hopes to become*. The Taj Mahal Palace, for instance, evolved an identity as an iconic Indian destination since its founding in 1903. Known as the country's first luxury hotel, the hotel has become associated in the public mind with its rich heritage as well as its exceptional customer service. The Taj itself affirms this dimension of its identity on its website, noting that the hotel "epitomises the enduring commitment to excellence, heritage, and service."

Some organizations seek to bolster collective courage by positioning it as an aspirational part of their identities. They sometimes do this as part of culture-building efforts that, self-consciously or not, can veer into statements about the organization's deeper identity. The pharmaceutical company Pfizer, in adopting courage as a core part of its identity, has proclaimed it to be "central to the way that we work . . . a mantra that we hold ourselves to every day across our business, wherever we are in the world, and whatever our role." The insurance company Progressive presents courage as closely linked to the organization's core beliefs, with leaders promoting brave behavior through an initiative called "Courage at Our Core." This included a series of seminars in which employees discussed how to be bold at work, "deciding when and how to raise a concern, welcoming disagreement, [and] disclosing bad news." Other organizations implicitly associate themselves with courage by identifying themselves with a higher purpose and portraying the organization as embarked on a heroic quest to realize it. The food manufacturer Danone under former CEO Emmanuel Faber adopted as its purpose "bringing health through food to as many people as possible," and Faber rallied stakeholders and society more broadly to take bold action to bring about a "food revolution."

Although linking courage to organizational identity certainly helps to foster more bravery, leaders can take additional steps. When people belong to organizations, they tend to want to connect their own individual sense of identity with the organizational identity. Further, they want to do this without perceiving that the organization is subsuming their sense of self. This isn't always an easy task. As scholars have shown, the multiple identities we have can conflict with one another. When they do, motivation and performance at work tends to decline. To overcome this challenge, leaders can take steps to reconcile individual and organizational identities, enabling us to identify more closely with the organization and its courageous character. A powerful way of doing this is by embracing a psychological phenomenon we've already encountered: identity fusion.

As we saw in Chapter 7, leaders can build courageous teams by *fusing* personal and group identity. You might wonder whether identity fusion can take root in large organizations, where people don't know most of their colleagues personally. How can you come to develop close, familial ties with colleagues, feeling a responsibility to take risky action on their behalf, when you've never met them and in fact might be separated culturally and geographically from them?

It turns out that you can. In a phenomenon known as "extended fusion," you can feel closely bound to members of large organizations, seeing them *as if they were* members of a small, intimate team. This happens, researchers have found, when organizations spotlight commonalities that people might have with other group members whom they have never met. When people understand that they share a background in common with other members of a large group, or even that they simply share an ideology (core beliefs or values), they feel more connected to them and more inclined to take personal risks on the group's behalf. In one study, researchers found that alerting people to values they shared in common with their fellow countrymen made them more inclined to perceive them as akin to family, and also more likely to endorse "extreme pro-group behavior," including sacrificing their lives for the country.

Employees at the Taj Mahal Palace certainly displayed a family-like sense of connection to the organization, one that contributed to their heroic deeds. When I asked general manager Kang why he had showed such courage that night at the Taj, he mentioned not only his determination to protect his family, but the deep loyalty he felt to the hotel. "You just felt a sense of responsibility, that you cannot abandon the guests of the hotel or the staff. And I mean, everyone on our staff were deeply committed in this way." Elaborating on this spirit of responsibility to one another and the organization, assistant banquet manager Mallika Jagad remarked that it was "just like in a war zone, you don't leave any soldier behind," a concept that she applied not just to guests and colleagues but the physical space of the Taj Hotel itself. The organization wasn't an ordinary commercial enterprise in her mind. It was a tightly knit community, even a family that defined her sense of self. "If your family is in trouble, you're not going to abandon them. You are going to be there with them, in whatever capacity you can. That sense of belonging is very strong at the Taj. In my twenty-odd years of life, it's very rare that I feel like I belong somewhere. The Taj was one place where I did."

To enable extended fusion, courageous organizations I studied drastically overhaul the classic cultural levers of recruiting, onboarding, and branding. In the process, they create the shared beliefs and values upon which fusion relies, as well as a shared identity. For instance, some organizations revamp their onboarding programs to balance skill-building with a heavy dose of history and storytelling to add depth and meaning to infuse extended identity. The US Marine Corps, which we discussed in Chapter 7, doesn't just foster fusion at the team or unit level, but organizationally, too. Even before new recruits arrive at boot camp, they learn that the Marines are an exclusive, elite branch of the military—think of famous advertising taglines like "The Few. The Proud. The Marines." The recruiting process affirms this meaning, requiring that prospective soldiers meet higher standards to join the service and emphasizing what the Corps has to offer individuals who enlist: a chance to become transformed into a person of character. As Major General William J. Bowers, who oversees recruiting for the Marines, explained to me, other military services in the US try to attract new recruits by highlighting benefits like college scholarships, valuable skills they'll learn, and so on. By contrast, "the Marine Corps emphasizes what we call the intangibles, the values, the core values, the honor, courage, commitment, the special feeling you get from being part of something bigger than yourself."

Once recruits reach boot camp, the intense, shared experience they undergo inculcates shared values that define the Marine Corps. Recruits have the opportunity to embark on a fresh start, taking responsibility for mistakes they've made and jettisoning those parts of their identity that conflict with the Corps's values. Recruits also learn in detail about the USMC's history, including glorious battles and instances of individual valor that reflect the organization's core values.

"In our institutional DNA, is the heroism of former battles," Bowers said, "and the realization that every marine we join in the Corps has to be able to go and do this to fight and win on future battlefields. I think the best Marines are also kind of amateur historians, because we connect the present to the past to provide context for the future." The intense physical and mental challenges recruits undergo during boot camp connect them with this proud heritage, imbuing them with the sense that they are now part of something bigger.

Exposure to the values and beliefs that underlie the Marine Corps identity doesn't end with boot camp. As marines deploy to their units overseas, they put their training to work, aware that others around them are judging their actions and whether they measure up to the Marine Corps ethos. They behave boldly because they don't want to let their teams down, but also because they don't want to let the larger organization down. At each step in their careers, they undergo additional training offered by Marine Corps University. They learn new professional skills required to advance while reconnecting with the Marine Corps ethos. "You're getting reinjected with our core values," Bowers said, "and the importance of sustaining that personal transformation. Every great education is continuous. All the way through."

If you lead a large company, you can adapt the USMC's identity-building tactics to increase your organization's courage muscle. At the Taj, new employees went through a rigorous, eighteen-month training program that, like Marine boot camp, allowed close, familial bonds to form. "You go through thick and thin together," Mallika Jagad said, "and you have to have each other's backs, there is a sense of trust in each other." But this training also deeply embeds the organization's core mission, values, and identity, presenting them as not just deeply meaningful, but unique and even sacred. As employees learn about how precisely to deliver the exceptional customer service for which the Taj is famous, they feel a sense of commonality that enables extended fusion.

Managers, not consultants, conduct the training, which enables them to pass on "the tacit knowledge, values, and elements of organizational culture that differentiate it from the competition." Employees emerged with a special connection to the organization and each other, a sense that they collectively belonged to an iconic Indian institution with a long legacy of providing world-class hospitality. Inculcated in the ideology of the Taj Mahal Palace, they feel a common *duty* to live up to its values, which they take as a part of their own individual identity as well.

You might already work hard to attract and retain employees who are a good fit for your organization, but are you focusing at every point on creating an organizational identity rooted in courage? Have you gone back to basics, defining your organization's identity and purpose—*who are we, and why are we here?* If you were to take an inventory of the organization, are any elements—including processes, cultural norms, or leadership behaviors—at odds with the purpose and values-based identity you seek to instill? Although no organization is perfect, designing for courage means doing our best to create a workplace experience where courage isn't some lofty ideal, but a defining reality.

A SPECIAL RESPONSIBILITY

As leaders, we might not expect our team members to willingly risk their lives in defending their workplace, as those at the Taj did, but we do want them to take action from a place of ownership and responsibility. Would our team members rise to the occasion in challenging times? Would they at least feel attached and committed enough to the organization to overcome their fears and behave boldly in more ordinary times? For most leaders, the answer is sadly no. Inside large companies, cowardice appears to be the norm.

You might shrug your shoulders and presume that there's nothing much you can do—team members are what they are. But that doesn't have to be the case; it's possible to design large organizations for courage, as organizations like the Taj Mahal Palace, the US Marine Corps, and Netflix do. That's not to say it's simple or straightforward. Each of the principles I've developed here has its own limitations or downsides. As potent as it is to adopt a bold, "play-to-win" mentality, investors and even customers don't have patience for infinite experimentation and risk-taking. They like stability too. While carving out space for voice and choice might leave employees feeling empowered and personally responsible for taking action, that's not enough: as a leader, you also must hold them accountable for results, or else performance will lag. As for identity fusion, it might unleash tremendous dedication and self-sacrifice, but critics have long been wary of companies that seem to have too much psychological influence over their employees.

It's worth it to tackle these complexities and take steps to foster more organizational courage by delving deeper into the realm of meaning and culture than companies usually do. Unleashing courage at the organizational level is, ultimately, a lever that enhances the ability of people to *execute*. It can unlock higher levels of experimentation, innovation, and fresh thinking inside organizations, not to mention organizational commitment and customer service. It can dramatically improve the level of discourse in workplaces, allowing for more honesty and sharper decision-making at all levels. It can allow organizations to adapt in times of disruption or other crisis rather than freeze up fearfully in the face of uncertainty. And it can allow organizations to foster better, more fulfilling work environments for employees. Courage, after all, isn't just good for business. As we saw at the beginning of this book, it's the cornerstone for a fuller, more vibrant, more fulfilling life.

Most of us can choose which organizations we wish to work for or affiliate with, and we should select those whose cultures will help us to behave more boldly. If we lead others, we have a special responsibility to help enable team members to set aside their fears and take risks on behalf of a noble cause. Of course, when we do so we might not always like how they choose to exercise their voice and choice. Perhaps they'll confront *us* with an inconvenient truth, or invest in an idea that we consider unattractive, or take a risk with a customer or a product that we wouldn't have done ourselves. When leaders design for courage, they make a tacit decision to *trust* their people. In this respect, designing for courage takes us back to the beginning of this book and the strategies we've developed for building our own individual courage muscles. By flexing these muscles inside our organizations, we can build a broader legacy of courageous behavior, with an impact beyond anything we ever could have accomplished on our own.

EPILOGUE

On the evening of June 11, 1891, a group of friends met in a London restaurant to enjoy a celebratory dinner. A young Indian man who had come to the city to study law had been admitted to the bar, and after three years it was now time for him to return home. During his tenure in the city, the man had tried his best to fit into English society. He had bought new outfits for himself and even spent some of his paltry funds on dancing, violin, and elocution lessons. A fellow Indian who had encountered him on the street the previous year described him as "wearing a high silk top hat, burnished bright; a Gladstonian collar, stiff and starched; a rather flashy tie displaying almost all the colours of the rainbow, under which was a fine striped silk shirt."

Despite such stylistic flourishes, this young man was hardly the rambunctious, vivacious, outgoing type. On the contrary, he appears to have been unusually quiet and shy, even among his friends and colleagues. He'd tried on occasion to speak in public, but each time his shyness had overcome him, leading him to bumble through a few words before sitting back down. This evening, it seemed, was no different. As he would later recount, "When my turn for speaking came, I stood up to make a speech. I had with great care thought out one which would consist of a very few sentences. But I could not proceed beyond the first sentence." He apparently attempted to start out with a joke, but couldn't quite get it out, uttering, "I thank you, gentlemen, for having kindly responded to my invitation," and then sitting back down.

This man would continue to struggle with shyness and a fear of public speaking in the coming years as he began his legal career. Once back in India, he suffered the embarrassment of losing his first case after standing up before a judge and finding that the words wouldn't come out. On another occasion, when he was slated to address a sizable group, he had to give notes for the speech he had prepared to someone else to deliver, so fearful was he. Observing such behavior, a bystander might have presumed that this young man was doomed to live a modest and unhappy life, one circumscribed by a fear that he just couldn't shake.

That prediction would have been wrong. This young man would go on to make his mark as an attorney and political activist. He would create a political movement that would lead to the demise of British colonial rule in India and the creation of an independent Indian state. He would shed his need to appear British and boldly adopt Indian clothing and customs, contesting what the French thinker Frantz Fanon called the "colonization" of the mind. In what would perhaps be his most famous act of defiance, one that would land him in prison for seven months, this man would organize a 240-mile trek called the Salt March to protest the colonial practice of making Indians buy their heavily taxed salt from the British. At one point, in front of a sizable audience, he reportedly held up a piece of salt and announced, "With this, I am shaking the foundations of the British Empire." Quite a shift from that young law student who was so timid that he could barely stand up and address his friends.

As you might have guessed, this shy and fearful young man was none other than Mahatma Gandhi, one of the most courageous and impactful individuals of the twentieth century, and a man who inspired figures like Martin Luther King Jr. and Cesar Chavez. In his prime, Gandhi wielded tremendous mastery over his fears, stubbornly continuing his political activism despite multiple attempts on his life. Eventually, an assassin did do him in. Just two days before being shot by a Hindu extremist in 1948, he apparently said, "If I'm to die by the bullet of a madman, I must do so smiling. God must be in my heart and on my lips. And if anything happens, you are not to shed a single tear."

Gandhi also inspired enormous courage in others around him, including many who have largely been ignored by history. One of these was a poet, activist, and mother of five named Sarojini Naidu. When the British imprisoned Gandhi, he assigned her in his absence to lead the ongoing resistance against oppressive British salt policies, a controversial move at the time which challenged societal norms, particularly at a time when women were often relegated to less visible roles. In accepting, Naidu indicated her willingness to risk her own wellbeing, knowing that she might be beaten, imprisoned, or even killed. "I shall actively participate in this campaign for liberty as though I were a man," she said, affirming that "neither jail nor death shall hold any terrors for me." Naidu was arrested during a march at a salt depot at which police brutally attacked peaceful volunteers. Taking "full moral responsibility" for the protest action, she was sentenced to nine months in jail. In the years that followed, she continued to work alongside Gandhi as a leader of the Indian independence movement and became governor of the state of Uttar Pradesh after India gained independence in 1947.

Like so many of the individuals whom we've met in this book, Gandhi wasn't born courageous. He had deep-seated fears that threatened to derail him and prevent him from achieving his objectives. But he *became* more courageous, thanks to his own efforts. He appears to have worked at developing a courageous mindset during the 1900s and early 1910s, when he had left India and was practicing law in South Africa. As one legal historian relates, Gandhi's law practice required him to become comfortable engaging in public and private settings with judges, other attorneys, and clients. Day after day, he put himself in a position where he had to confront his fears of public speaking. Over time, "he grew, he rose to the occasion, and he changed. Before he leaves South Africa, before he gives up the practice of law, he's on his feet giving speeches that last two and more hours. This is how much he changed."

This book has delved into the mental patterns that sustain and support courage, deriving science-based strategies—the 9 C's—that any of us can use to overcome our fears. We've seen that we can significantly enhance our ability to take risks, and lead others to do so as well, by consciously shifting how we view our situations and ourselves. Taking control of the stories we tell ourselves and nurturing our sense of identity and belonging, we can build our courage muscles, manage our fears better in the moment, and inspire others around us to set aside their fears and act.

But even with the 9 C's in hand, we can't expect to become perfectly brave and bold right away, or even ever. As I've found in my own life, developing a capacity for courage, both at the individual and collective levels, is an ongoing process, something we bring forth from within. Understanding and mobilizing these strategies can speed things up and keep us moving forward, but we still must be prepared to work on our courage muscles over an extended period and to see gradual progress. Gandhi chipped away at his fears year after year, and so must we.

We also must be prepared for unanticipated turns in our journeys, moments when we must step back in order to move forward. The gymnast Simone Biles, regarded as the greatest of all time in her sport, knows a thing about cultivating courage over the long term. She has confronted intense anxiety throughout her career, even experiencing panic attacks at times. Yet she's consistently pushed through these negative emotions, winning twenty-three gold medals at World Championships competitions and seven Olympic medals as of 2023. Today, in fact, she teaches an online course titled Overcoming Fear.

But Biles didn't push through fear blindly. In 2021, she shocked fans around the world by pulling herself out of the 2020 Tokyo Olympic Games (held in 2021 on account of the COVID pandemic), citing mental health issues. She had developed what gymnasts call "the twisties," a mental condition where gymnasts lose a sense of their body's physical location in space. She felt doubtful and anxious—in fact, downright terrified. In withdrawing, Biles knew full well that she would be violating the expectations that others had of her, and she was correct: some criticized her decision, accusing her of weakness and calling her a "national embarrassment."

In this instance, *not* pushing through fear was the most courageous choice. And it was one that ultimately allowed her to make progress with her mental health and come back to her sport stronger and bolder than ever. After taking a year off of training, she began competing again in 2023 and in 2024 returned to the Olympics to win four more medals. As she remarked afterward, "I've accomplished way more than my wildest dreams. . . . A couple of years ago I didn't think I'd be back here at an Olympic game." A journey toward more courage might not be a straight line. But if we stick with it, making tough and sometimes counterintuitive decisions, we can continue to progress over the long term.

In closing this book, I'd like to invite you to embark on your own journey toward becoming more courageous. Be forewarned: executing on the 9 C's will require that you muster a variety of additional resources and skills. As you take steps like steeling yourself against uncertainty, building self-efficacy, forming support squads, and adopting a heroic quest, and as you foster identity fusion, exercise charismatic leadership, and redesign your organizations for courage, you will need considerable diligence, persistence, commitment, and strength. You'll need moral clarity, making sure that you don't cultivate valiance on behalf of an immoral cause. And you'll need a sense of balance and perspective, making sure your courageous action doesn't veer into recklessness. Above all, you'll need creativity and mental flexibility, an ability to discard established ways of viewing the world and yourself in favor of new understandings and identities.

In mustering these inner resources, I hope you'll keep in mind the enormous rewards that come with nurturing a capacity for courage. These include not just the ability to influence others and bring about change in the world, but also personal happiness and fulfillment, the ability to exercise agency, realize your full potential, and live a life that you feel to be authentic. Courage doesn't just make the world better—it makes you a better person. I also hope you'll draw strength from the exemplars of courage described in this book, many of whom harbored significant fear but found ways to surmount it. Harriet Tubman, Patrick Awuah, Brandon Tsay, the workers at the Fukushima power plant and the Taj Mahal Palace, Frances Haugen, the soldiers on the front lines in Ukraine: these individuals accomplished extraordinary feats, but a closer look reveals them as ordinary people who in one way or another managed to bring boldness out from within. If they can do it, so can you.

We also can take comfort in remembering that many important figures haven't magically become heroic all of a sudden but rather have done so gradually. Gandhi is one, but Eleanor Roosevelt also was shy and reserved early in life only to make her mark as a public servant, and eventually, as first lady. Celebrities and artists like the reality TV star Joanna Gaines or the actress Jessica Alba recall early struggles with insecurity, shyness, or lack of confidence. In the world of fiction, we find that figures like Harry Potter or Frodo Baggins in *The Lord of the Rings* become braver over the course of their respective stories, achieving an ability to surmount ever greater challenges. And who can forget the cowardly lion in *The Wizard of Oz*, who behaves more boldly as the story proceeds, only to learn at the end that he had been brave all along, without even knowing it.

Courage might be a work in progress, a capacity that arises in us over years or even decades, but there is one thing that all of us can and must do right now: take action. It can help to read a book like this, and perhaps to reread it. Eventually, though, we all must swallow hard and *move*. Boldness, you see, begets more boldness. Just as small actions can serve us as a pathway to knowing, as in Karl Weick's theory of sensemaking, so they also can serve us as a pathway toward developing a courageous mindset. I think here of Nelson Mandela's account of how he found his way into political activism. "I had no epiphany, no singular revelation, no moment of truth," Mandela recalls, "but a steady accumulation of a thousand slights, a thousand indignities, a thousand unremembered moments, produced in me an anger, a rebelliousness, a desire to fight the system that imprisoned my people. There was no particular day on which I said, From henceforth I will devote myself to the liberation of my people; instead, I simply found myself doing so, and could not do otherwise."

Mandela is right: there is no magical moment of epiphany that signals the beginning of a courage journey. You simply start moving toward your goals, as daunting or frightening as that might seem, having faith that your strength and courage will increase over time. It's okay to feel afraid, as I have been on countless occasions. And it's okay to start slow. If you feel wary of raising your hand in a meeting to share a crazy idea you had, pull a colleague aside and try it on them first. If you can't bring yourself to quit your job and start your own company, try getting an initial client and moonlighting on the side. Again, just take a small, tentative, first step. Once you've done that, draw on the 9 C's to take still others. This is *your* hero's story, the one you always knew you could write. I can't wait to see how it turns out.

ACKNOWLEDGMENTS

Writing this book was an intense, twelve-year journey, and I could not have completed it without guidance, encouragement, and support from many people. To Kirby Sandmeyer and Hollis Heimbouch, my editors at HarperCollins: thank you for believing in this project. You asked the right questions, read multiple drafts, and provided invaluable feedback. To Richard Pine, my literary agent: thank you for believing in this book when it was just a loose set of ideas, and for pushing me hard to refine my thinking. Your support during our many conversations meant more than you know.

I also wish to thank the research associates, colleagues, and friends who helped refine these ideas. David Shin spent countless hours collecting and collating a large volume of research I had accumulated over a decade and offering his sharp insights on numerous issues small and large. My former doctoral student Luciana Silvestri provided multiple rounds of feedback on every part of the book, challenging me to explore more deeply the motives and goals of brave individuals. I am grateful to her for her detailed inputs across multiple iterations that were critical in shaping just about every single chapter in this book. Others who made critical contributions included Jennifer Beauregard, Allison Ciechanover, Jennifer Daniels, Caroline de Lacvivier, Patrick Healy, Jeff Huizinga, Akhil Iyer, Kanika Jain, Samir Junnarkar, Charlotte Krontiris, Terrence McMullen, Joseph Mesfin, Eppa Rixey, Rachna Tahilyani, and Evan Terwilliger. I am immensely grateful to Seth Schulman for his superb editorial help. His commitment to excellence and passion for simplicity inspired me to keep pushing forward even when I sometimes felt I was done. Finally, thank you to my dear friends and colleagues Nikhil Bhojwani, Bruce Carruthers, Frank Cooper, Rakesh Khurana, Lakshmi Ramarajan, Jenny Taylor, Maxim Sytch, Mark Wiedman, and Ting Zhang, who did me the great favor of reading this book in its earlier stages. I am deeply indebted to you for plodding through pages and pages of rough, verbose text and for providing intensive feedback that dramatically improved it.

To Heather Kreidler, the guru of fact-checking, thank you for meticulously drilling into every last one of my 900-odd endnotes, making sure that I recorded accurate page numbers and much more. My publicist, Jessica Krakoski, as well as Jessica Gilo and the whole team at Harper Business worked extraordinarily hard to bring attention to this book, doing so with grace, humor, and great competence. Likewise, Danny Stern and his very capable team tirelessly sought out opportunities for me to share my ideas through talks, panel discussions, and more.

I feel blessed to have a supportive and loving circle of close friends in my adopted hometown of Boston. They are all more family than friends to me. I can't thank you enough for your love and for tolerating my incessant ramblings about this book. You reminded me, sometimes with a raised eyebrow, that boldness isn't always found in words, but in the simple act of showing up. You were a grounding influence when the writing got messy, and a source of light when doubts crept in.

My family too has been immensely supportive, not just during the writing of this book but well before it. Sadhana and Ashok, my adopted elder siblings, took me under their wing over forty years ago when I first arrived in the United States. My cousin-sisters Meera, Neera, and Kiran have showered me with love and unconditional support ever since I can remember. I feel tremendously lucky as well for my nephews and nieces Arjun, Monisha, Poonam, Sachin, Sanjay, and Sooraj—you are an important part of my life.

My wife, Anuradha, and children, Varoun and Shivani, patiently listened during our evening meals as I excitedly recounted many stories of courageous people. Invariably, their feedback helped me to decide which I would actually include in this book. Anuradha, you have long inspired me with your principled way of looking at the world, your moral courage, and your instinctive empathy for others. Varoun and Shivani, you amaze me with your intense curiosity and desire to make the world a better place. I hope that you will continue to courageously pursue lives of purpose in the years ahead.

Given how long this book took to write, I might have inadvertently missed some names. If so, I humbly beg forgiveness from those I have omitted. Please know that I'm grateful to each of you beyond words. Coming from someone who just wrote a whole book, and not a particularly short one, that's saying something.

THE COURAGE PLAYBOOK

INTRODUCTION

- Courage is not the absence of fear. Courageous people are those who willfully take bold, risky action to serve a purpose that they perceive to be worthy, usually in the face of an abiding fear.

- We often think of courage as an innate virtue, but personality isn't the whole answer for why some people behave more courageously than others. Any of us can learn to become more courageous.

- The 9 C's are a science-backed playbook for becoming bolder at work and throughout your life, and for inspiring courage in others. When we follow these strategies to prepare in advance for courageous action and to maximize boldness in the moment, we position ourselves and others to take bold action when it really counts.

ON COWARDICE

- Cowardice—an inability to behave bravely, take risks, and, ultimately, to realize one's own potential—is a fundamental human tendency rooted in our biological need for safety and survival. Elements of our social environments nudge us toward cowardice, both by magnifying the fear we feel and by making it easier for us to give in to fear and shrink back from taking action. Social factors that lead to cowardice include:

PEER PRESSURE. Taking action that might jeopardize our social relationships feels scary and dangerous, which is why we frequently opt to stay quiet and passive.

THE BYSTANDER EFFECT. People often feel less of a sense of ownership in group settings, leading to less courage.

CULTURE. Cultural norms such as an aversion to risk can discourage courageous behavior.

PART 1: BUILDING YOUR COURAGE MUSCLES

Chapter 1: Coping

- Uncertainty and a closely related experience—loss of control—arouse an emotional response that can make courage difficult, sparking doubt and fear. To bolster our courage muscles, we must not only mitigate risk but also cope better with uncertainty and the loss of control that comes with it.

- Two strategies can mask the reality of uncertainty, allowing individuals to manage their fear and act: leaning into the power of faith, or so-called magical thinking, and risk-hunting.

- By putting our faith in external, nonrational forces that we believe will intervene and protect us against unforeseen threats, we create a comforting and agency-boosting mini-narrative in our minds that says, "I have encountered adversity, but I'm not entirely powerless. I can appeal to God (or fate, or luck, or the universe), and I will probably emerge victorious."

- Risk-hunting involves obsessively identifying and mitigating risks, thereby creating an illusion of certainty. This process frames the world as orderly and enhances our ability to act courageously, as we believe that we only face manageable dangers. To make risk-hunting easier and more practicable in everyday situations, we can modify it by:

  1. **LIMITING OUR ASSESSMENT OF RISK.** Make risk-hunting easier by identifying and actively reducing only those risks that could result in significant harm.
  2. **NARROWING THE SCOPE.** By deciding in advance which actions you will and won't take, you can place upper limits on the actual uncertainty you face.
  3. **IMPROVING YOUR ABILITY TO IMPROVISE.** Limit your need for risk-hunting by equipping yourself to handle unpredictable threats as they arise. Recognizing that you can arrive at solutions in real time, you'll feel more comfortable facing some measure of uncertainty. Two tactics can help you improve your improvisational ability: adopting shortcuts and keeping your options open.

Chapter 2: Confidence

- When we possess confidence or "self-efficacy," we feel a greater sense of control, leaving us more empowered to take risks and more likely to keep fear in check.
- The key to enhancing confidence is *building our actual skills* in ways that support our own internal narratives about our competency in

complex, real-life settings. Two kinds of skill-building are important here:

1. SPECIFIC. If we want to feel confident and in control, we need training in specific skills we need to perform a given task.

2. GENERAL. We also need training that leaves us with a sense that we possess a broad capability to obtain results across a variety of situations—that we're resilient, adaptive, and committed to excellence no matter what.

- As helpful as skill-building can be to boost self-efficacy and hence courage, we must do more to truly internalize self-confidence. We must take steps to change or influence the situations we're in, understanding that our ability to feel in control of a situation lies at least in part in our capacity to shape it. Three strategies for turning situations to our advantage and boosting confidence are:

    1. GO SMALL TO GO BIG. If you're feeling overwhelmed by a challenge, break it down into smaller parts. Celebrate small wins to boost your confidence, and then take on larger tasks that challenge you further.

    2. SEE YOUR STRENGTHS THROUGH OTHERS' EYES. Rely on the support of those around you. When others praise us, it feels good and inspires us to be even better. This "social persuasion" helps us further develop our skills and increase our self-efficacy.

    3. GET TOOLS YOU CAN USE. We need to feel properly equipped for success—dependable devices, trustworthy partners, or practiced strategies for dealing with challenges can all inspire a boost of self-confidence. When we feel prepared with the tools and abilities to improvise solutions, we will more likely take risks and act despite our fears.

- Building confidence can help us perform brave acts, but we should do our best to avoid becoming overly inflated in our self-perception. Overconfidence might hinder our ability to face real limitations and lead to reckless behavior, ultimately harming our performance.

Chapter 3: Commitment

- The stories we tell ourselves or communicate to others about our lives and goals have an enormous influence on our sense of self, our understanding of the wider world, and our ability to behave courageously. To build our courage muscles, we can tell stories that shape how we and others around us think about our endeavors, conveying them as morally resonant heroic quests.

- To narrate a quest, two aspects are important:

    1. **CONTENT: ADOPTING A QUEST THAT IS DECIDEDLY MORAL UNLOCKS TREMENDOUS EMOTIONAL POWER.** All of us have moral values that we hold dear, concepts such as truthfulness, justice, or compassion. These values often inform our deepest sense of identity and purpose. To be bolder, imagine yourself as a vanquisher of evil, taking risks to make a positive impact in the world.

    2. **FORM: THE MOST EMOTIONALLY RESONANT STORIES ARE THOSE THAT POSSESS A NARRATIVE ARC.** Rely on three core narrative elements: a vision of a desired future, an elaboration of the obstacles or challenges, and the outlining of practical steps we could or will take to make our vision real.

- We can be quite frightened yet still manage to transcend our emotions, simply by crafting an epic narrative in our minds, shaping our identities and giving our lives meaning. This process allows us to gain a sense of power and control over our destinies, making us feel truly courageous at our core.

Chapter 4: Connection

- When we discuss courageous people, we often portray the brave individuals as "great heroes" who single-handedly bring glory to themselves and others. What we don't often recognize is that heroes seldom act alone. Behind every hero, we usually find other, less visible supporters.

- To behave more courageously, we can assemble support squads for ourselves—groups of close confidants who can deliver multiple kinds of support: giving us an emotional lift; providing us with information we need to succeed; offering us tangible resources; and presenting useful feedback on how we're doing.

- Our social relationships also enable boldness in another way: by helping us internalize our own view of ourselves as *courageous people*. When we have a strong support crew behind us, our sense of who we are shifts. Above and beyond our perceived self-efficacy when facing a specific task, with a support crew we begin to think of ourselves *in general* as bigger, stronger, and more capable of taking action.

- Don't wait for a challenge to arise to forge connections. After all, you never know when you might need to lean on your network. Ensure that you have a diverse group of people on your team who can provide the range of support you may need—whenever that time arrives.

Chapter 5: Comprehension

- Sudden threats can destabilize, confuse, or overload us. Our minds might freeze, and thereby our physical bodies. Even more prolonged crises might cause our minds to become frazzled and disoriented as we experience overwhelming uncertainty and loss of control.

- A simple strategy called sensemaking can help us to avoid freezing up in these situations. Although conventional wisdom holds that you should think first and then act, the essence of sensemaking is to build your comprehension of an uncertain situation by thinking and acting at the same time. If we view action as a pathway to comprehension rather than just a means to achieve a goal, we can take small steps that will help us see things more clearly. This clarity will help us act more effectively, continuously moving forward rather than getting stuck.

- As an ongoing process, sensemaking is comprised of three basic steps:

  1. **STAY MINDFUL AND ALERT FOR A SENSEMAKING TRIGGER.** If we make a habit of looking for relatively minor disruptions of our normal reality and regarding them as triggers for a sensemaking process, we can increase the odds that any unusual events we encounter will prompt us to try to act our way toward knowledge.

  2. **NOTICE AND INTERPRET CUES.** Observe cues in the unfamiliar environment and form an initial interpretation or story about them. With just a few tantalizing scraps of knowledge, you can try to create a set of hypotheses about your reality, choosing the one that seems most plausible. This preliminary assessment addresses what happened, why it occurred, and the possible consequences.

  3. **TAKE ACTION.** Take action based on the imperfect meaning you have gleaned, then learn as you notice new cues. A balanced approach is most effective: act decisively while acknowledging that your actions may be incorrect, requiring you to adapt as new information arises.

- More than just a strategy, sensemaking is a comprehensive way of approaching the world, one that fuses action with a posture of humility, openness, and curiosity. Adopting a beginner's mind, we release the need for a perfect plan and open ourselves to possibilities, trusting that the path will become clearer as we proceed.

Chapter 6: Calm

- Strategies described in previous chapters will help us minimize fears far in advance of adverse situations, but we can reinforce those preventative efforts by taking additional steps in the moment. Shaping our emotional response, we can calm ourselves and find new meaning in otherwise negatively charged situations, allowing us to take more action.

- You can reduce fear quickly in the moment by addressing it early, allowing yourself to be better prepared for bold action. Three mental moves can help you do so:

  1. **RETURN TO A RITUAL.** Rituals subtly alter the situations we're in, normalizing what's going on in our minds. Through rituals, we inject an element of familiarity and predictability into our lives that allows us to perceive these circumstances as less threatening.

  2. **PAY SELECTIVE ATTENTION.** Faced with a perilous situation, you can selectively direct your attention in ways that alter your experience of the situation so that it appears less frightening. On the one hand, you can distract yourself so that you don't ruminate on dangers that might otherwise wear on your psyche. On the other hand, you can selectively focus on specific parts of a situation that tend to reassure you by affirming your own agency.

  3. **REINTERPRET A SITUATION IN YOUR MIND.** You can preempt or limit your fear response by directly reframing what a situation in its

totality *means* to you. With this technique, you can acknowledge fully the dangers that you face but reassess the situation in ways that shift how it affects you emotionally, in particular making it seem less frightening and more familiar.

PART 2: LEADING FOR COURAGE

Chapter 7: Clan

- To build a team capable of collective courage, a powerful strategy is to nurture loyalty to the group. Our collective identities—those we have by virtue of belonging to organizations, social movements, teams, religions, and other kinds of groups—enable courage by motivating us to take risks on others' behalf. When we link our sense of self to a larger collective, we feel a duty to promote the common good.

- To build collective identity, we can cultivate what scholars call identity fusion. People with fused identities feel a particularly intense connection that encompasses both a strong sense of belonging to a group *and also* a feeling that they are a unique and valued member of that group.

- Successful military organizations, sports teams, startups, and other successful programs promote identity fusion in three key ways:

    1. **THEY MOBILIZE THE POWER OF SHARED ADVERSITY.** Overcoming a shared challenge is often more effective than traditional team-building for fostering relationships.

    2. **THEY MAKE COLLECTIVE IDENTITY MORE SPACIOUS.** To strengthen collective identity, it's important to also foster an environment where each team member feels understood and valued for their

uniqueness. Achieving this balance—between strong group identity and a sense of individual self and agency—is essential.

   3. **THEY KEEP THE GROUP FUSED OVER TIME.** To sustain fusion, we must take proactive steps to renew our collective identity before any group erosion can occur. Purpose and values play a crucial role here. As team members transition out and new ones join, we can keep our collective identity vibrant by ensuring that everyone understands the team's core mission and the values that underpin it.

- In your capacity as a team member, you also can draw on the power of identity fusion to become more courageous, and in many cases, happier too. Seek out teams whose goals and values align firmly with your own, inspiring your intense loyalty and commitment.

Chapter 8: Charisma

- The most inspiring leaders seem to possess a force of personality that others find motivational—what we typically call "charisma." Charisma, like bravery itself, isn't a matter of personality but rather a result of underlying *behaviors* that any of us might cultivate. Great, charismatic leaders, in other words, aren't just born; they're also made through the right training.

- Leaders deploy three specific strategies for projecting their charisma. First, they craft and communicate a heroic quest in ways that followers will find clear and compelling. Second, they show a deep personal devotion to the quest, modeling it and making their example accessible and relevant to followers. And third, once the quest is underway, they convey strength in the face of hardship, inspiring followers with their extraordinary sense of calm and encouraging them to stay committed. These strategies then inspire followers to become heroes themselves, a stance that leads them to surmount their fears and take more risk on behalf of the shared mission.

- You can boost your own, individual capacity for courage by seeking out inspiring leaders to follow. Look beyond the stereotypes to see if leaders exhibit the three behavioral strategies outlined in this chapter.

Chapter 9: Culture

- Leaders can design large organizations to make bold action on the part of individual team members more likely, shaping the culture to encourage certain courageous behaviors. You can do so by taking three steps validated by science to embed courage deeply into your organization's meaning system:

    1. **ESTABLISH COURAGE AS A BEHAVIORAL NORM.** Instill an ambitious, "playing to win" mindset deep into your organization. Rather than focusing primarily on limiting risk, push the organization to concentrate on the upside of winning. This doesn't mean ignoring risk, but it does mean ensuring that you don't become too oriented around or even obsessed with managing risk.

    2. **CREATE MORE SPACE FOR BRAVE CONDUCT.** Nurture more collective courage by instilling in employees a sense of ownership, a perception that the company's future is in their hands and that they're responsible for taking courageous action when necessary to ensure that it thrives. Encourage employees to speak up and to exercise discretion within certain guidelines or boundaries that leaders define—what I call voice and choice.

    3. **BUILD COURAGE INTO THE ORGANIZATION'S IDENTITY.** The phenomenon known as "extended fusion" allows individuals to feel

a close connection to large organizations, as if they were part of a small, intimate team. This sense of connection occurs when organizations highlight shared values and beliefs. Courageous organizations drastically overhaul the classic cultural levers of recruiting, onboarding, and branding, creating the shared beliefs and values upon which fusion relies, as well as a shared identity.

EPILOGUE

- Even with the 9 C's in hand, we can't expect to become perfectly brave and bold right away, or even ever. Developing a capacity for courage, both at the individual and collective levels, is an ongoing process, something we bring forth from within.

- Executing on the 9 C's will require that you muster a variety of additional resources and skills, including diligence, persistence, commitment, strength, moral clarity, and balance. Above all, you'll need creativity and mental flexibility, an ability to discard established ways of viewing the world and yourself in favor of new understandings and identities.

NOTES

INTRODUCTION

xix courageous mindset: Sean T. Hannah, Patrick J. Sweeney, and Paul B. Lester, "Toward a Courageous Mindset: The Subjective Act and Experience of Courage," *Journal of Positive Psychology* 2, no. 2 (2007): 129–35; Melissa L. McKinlay and Peter J. Norton, "The Role of Courage in Predicting Behavior: Replication in a Public-Speaking Fearful Sample," *Motivation and Emotion* 47 (2023): 1–6.

xxi *"courageous disposition"*: Pauline Schilpzand, David R. Hekman, and Terence R. Mitchell, "An Inductively Generated Typology and Process Model of Workplace Courage," *Organization Science* 26, no. 1 (2015): 52–77, esp. 54. See also Aristotle's *Nicomachean Ethics*, trans. W. D. Ross (Kirchener: Bathoche Books, 1999), Plato's *Protogoras, in Complete Works,* ed. John M. Cooper and D. S. Hutchinson (Indianapolis: Hackett, 1997), and Mencius, *Mencius,* trans. Irene Bloom, ed. Philip J. Ivanhoe (New York: Columbia University Press, 2003).

xxi *"quality of a warrior"*: Carl von Clausewitz, *On War*, Book I: "On the Nature of War," chap. 3, "The Genius for War," trans. Col. James John Graham (London: N. Trübner, 1873), https://clausewitzstudies.org/readings/OnWar1873/BK1ch03.html.

xxii *explain their actions*: My initial hypothesis about the origins of courage grew out of a tradition within sociology called symbolic interactionism (SI). Many sociological theories focus on large-scale phenomena like social classes or institutions, but SI considers social life from the individual's perspective. As first formally articulated by the scholar Herbert Blumer, SI argues that we humans create meaning about the outside world and form our behavior based on these interpretations. But we don't do this in splendid isolation. Others around us come to their own interpretations, and their sense of reality colors the meanings that we create in our own minds, and vice versa. In other words, social life is generative, a venue for creating meaning both shared and individual. Interactions between people influence the individual's creation of meaning—hence the theory's name. As Blumer puts it, "symbolic interactionism sees meanings as social products, as creations that are formed in and through the defining activities of people as they interact." Herbert Blumer, *Symbolic Interactionism: Perspective and Method* (Englewood Cliffs, NJ: Prentice-Hall, Inc., 1969), 5. Relatedly, the meanings we create can change as we live our lives and engage with others—they're not fixed. Meaning-making, ultimately, is a messy, uneven *process* of social interaction, one that is central to how we experience the world. Although we can't fully control this process, we do still retain quite a bit of agency in shaping how we perceive the world in our own minds, and in turn, how we act. *How to Be Bold* proposes that we take advantage of our capacity as meaning creators to help ourselves take more courageous action. By becoming more aware of our interpretations of the world and by learning to think differently, we can induce ourselves to act more boldly in service to our ideals. See Blumer, *Symbolic Interactionism: Perspective and Method*. For a summary of how this tradition has evolved, see Michael J. Carter and Celene Fuller, "Symbols, Meaning, and Action: The Past, Present, and Future of Symbolic Interactionism," *Current Sociology Review* 64, no. 6 (2016): 931–61.

xxii *an abiding fear:* I base this definition on the more precise notion of courage presented in Christopher R. Rate, Jennifer A. Clarke, Douglas R. Lindsay, and Robert J. Sternberg, "Implicit Theories of Courage," *Journal of Positive Psychology* 2, no. 2 (2007): 80–98. They write: "[W]e might best describe or conceptualize courage as: (a) a willful, intentional act, (b) executed after mindful deliberation, (c) involving objective substantial risk to the actor, (d) primarily motivated to bring about a noble good or worthy end, (e) despite, *perhaps,* the presence of the emotion of fear" (95). Another relevant definition that emphasizes the subjective experience of courage is: "we define true courage as a subjective experience where an actor perceives risk, experiences fear, and overcomes those fears to act." Sean T. Hannah, Patrick J. Sweeney, and Paul B. Lester, "Toward a Courageous Mindset: The Subjective Act and Experience of Courage," *Journal of Positive Psychology* 2, no. 2 (April 2007): 129–35, esp. 129.

xxiv *"can be protected":* Suma Jain, "Reflections on the Past 2½ Years and Inspiration for the Future," *Ochsner Journal* 22, no. 4 (2022): 290–91.

xxv *"felt that responsibility":* Suma Jain (pulmonary critical care specialist at Ochsner Medical Center), interview with the author, July 25, 2023.

xxvi *full human potential:* Adam Grant, *Hidden Potential: The Science of Achieving Greater Things* (New York: Viking, 2023).

xxvi *an innate virtue:* Academic researchers have reinforced this notion that courage isn't just a matter of innate disposition. R. S. Hallam and S. J. Rachman suggest that individual acts of courage spawn from both personality and external forces. See "Courageous Acts or Courageous Actors." See also Monica C. Worline, "Courage in Organizations: An Integrative Review of the 'Difficult Virtue,'" in Gretchen M. Spreitzer and Kim S. Cameron, eds., *The Oxford Handbook of Positive Organizational Scholarship* (Oxford: Oxford University Press, 2012), 305–315. Worline writes: "organizational research has moved away from a dispositional approach to the study of courage and moved toward research that emphasizes courage as an emergent pattern of action in context. Working from this definition emphasizes the fact that anyone in an organization can undertake courageous action when the right combination of opportunity and resources presents itself" (306–307); also James R. Detert and Evan A. Bruno, "Workplace Courage: Review, Synthesis, and Future Agenda for a Complex Construct," *Academy of Management Annals* 11, no. 2 (2017): 593–639; Pauline Schilpzand, David R. Hekman, and Terence R. Mitchel, "An Inductively Generated Typology and Process Model of Workplace Courage," *Organization Science* 26, no. 1 (2015): 52–77; "Our findings . . . challenge the conventional wisdom that courage is an individual dispositionally motivated action, largely isolated from the broader social context" (71).

xxvii *"break corporate America":* Fredric M. Jablin, "Courage and Courageous Communication Among Leaders and Followers in Groups, Organizations, and Communities," *Management Communication Quarterly* 20, no. 1 (2006): 94–110, esp. 102.

ON COWARDICE

xxx *"end of the world was coming":* Fan Meizhong blog posting, accessed and translated February 12, 2024, http://cache.tianya.cn/publicforum/content/books/1/106727.shtml (link no longer active).

xxx *"only care about my own life":* Fan Meizhong blog posting, accessed and translated February 12, 2024, http://cache.tianya.cn/publicforum/content/books/1/106727.shtml (link no longer active).

xxx *"no point in me dying with you":* Fan Meizhong blog posting, accessed and translated February 12, 2024, http://cache.tianya.cn/publicforum/content/books/1/106727.shtml (link no longer active).

xxx *7.9 on the Richter scale:* John R. Rafferty and Kenneth Pletcher, "Sichuan Earthquake of 2008," *Britannica,* https://www.britannica.com/event/Sichuan-earthquake-of-2008.

xxx *students and teachers perished:* Xu Weichao and Li Rongde, "Teacher Who Left Students Behind in Sichuan Earthquake Looks Back," Caixin Global, May 15, 2018, https://www.caixinglobal.com/2018-05-15/teacher-who-left-students-behind-in-sichuan-earthquake-looks-back-101250246.html.

xxxi *"can't see any 'person' here":* "Teacher Fired for Running from Quake School," Reuters, June 17, 2008, https://www.reuters.com/article/lifestyle/teacher-fired-for-running-from-quake-school-idUSN17355527/.

xxxi *denounced him as "shameless":* Louisa Lim, "China's 'Biggest Coward' Finds Sympathy," NPR, July 14, 2008, https://www.npr.org/2008/07/14/92517549/chinas-biggest-coward-finds-sympathy.

xxxi coward *derives from:* Chris Walsh, *Cowardice: A Brief History* (Princeton, NJ: Princeton University Press, 2014).

xxxi *court-martialed for cowardice:* "General Orders, 7 July 1775," *Founders Online,* National Archives, https://founders.archives.gov/documents/Washington/03-01-02-0040. [Original source: *The Papers of George Washington,* Revolutionary War Series, vol. 1, *16 June 1775–15 September 1775,* Philander D. Chase, ed. (Charlottesville: University Press of Virginia, 1985), 71–75.]

xxxi *hobbled the efforts of Allied forces:* Jonathan Fennell, "Courage and Cowardice in the North African Campaign: The Eighth Army and Defeat in the Summer of 1942," *War in History* 20, no. 1 (2013): 99–122; Chris Walsh, "The Coward's Guide to History: Why We Really Fight Wars," *Foreign Affairs,* June 17, 2015, https://www.foreignaffairs.com/world/cowards-guide-history.

xxxi *deserting his fellow soldiers:* Conor Kostick, "Courage and Cowardice on the First Crusade, 1096–1099," *War in History* 20, no. 1 (2013): 32–49.

xxxi *during World War I:* Some have more recently called for posthumous pardons for these soldiers: "Call to Rethink Cases of French WWI 'Coward' Soldiers," BBC, October 1, 2013, https://www.bbc.com/news/world-europe-24356041.

xxxi *"cowardly conduct":* Jeffrey Gettleman, "Soldier Accused as Coward Says He Is Guilty Only of Panic Attack," *New York Times,* November 6, 2003, https://www.nytimes.com/2003/11/06/us/soldier-accused-as-coward-says-he-is-guilty-only-of-panic-attack.html; Joint Service Committee on Military Justice, *Manual for Courts-Martial United States* (2024 Edition), https://jsc.defense.gov/military-law/current-publications-and-updates/.

xxxi *Following the 9/11 attacks:* "Terror Attacks Spark Cowardly Debate," *ABC News,* September 26, 2001, https://abcnews.go.com/Politics/story?id=121312&page=1.

xxvii *a billboard went up:* Celestine Bohlen, "Defining Cowardice," *New York Times,* September 16, 2001, https://www.nytimes.com/2001/09/16/weekinreview/defining-cowardice.html; Katie Kindelan, "'Cowards' Billboard Lights Up Boston Skyline in Wake of Blasts," *ABC News,* April 18, 2013, https://abcnews.go.com/blogs/headlines/2013/04/cowards-billboard-lights-up-boston-skyline-in-wake-of-blasts.

xxxii *prison time for manslaughter:* "Costa Concordia captain's sentence upheld by Italy court," *BBC News,* May 12, 2017, https://www.bbc.com/news/world-europe-39903968.

xxxii *failed to go inside the building to confront:* Lisa J. Huriash, "Police Say More Deputies Waited Outside School During Stoneman Douglas Shooting," *SunSentinel,* December 15, 2018, https://www.sun-sentinel.com/local/broward/parkland/florida-school-shooting/fl-florida-school-shooting-response-fail-20180223-story.html.

xxxii *waited for over an hour to engage:* Terri Langford, "'If There's Kids in There, We Need to Go In': Officers in Uvalde Were Ready with Guns, Shields and Tools—But Not Clear Orders," *Texas Tribune,* June 20, 2022, https://www.texastribune.org/2022/06/20/uvalde-police-shooting-response-records/.

xxxii *dream of becoming entrepreneurs:* "Expectations vs. Reality: What's It Really like to Go It Alone?," Vistaprint, January 15, 2018, https://www.vistaprint.com/news/expectations-vs-reality.

xxxiii *15 percent in 2023:* "2023 Policy Roadmap," Global Entrepreneurship Monitor, https://www.gemconsortium.org/economy-profiles/united-states-2.

xxxiii *express ourselves honestly:* Courageous leaders, Brown argues, are those who can stand the discomfort of making themselves vulnerable so that they can have the tough conversations and take bold action. They "lean into vulnerability" (10) and are willing to own up to their own flaws and to admit the possibility of failure. They're honest with themselves and others, even if it frightens them. Cowardly leaders, by implication, aren't. They hide behind an "armor" of perfectionism, cynicism, criticism, domination, and control. Brené Brown, *Dare to Lead: Brave Work, Tough Conversations, Whole Hearts* (New York: Random House, 2018), esp. 78–117.

xxxiii *hadn't spoken up to raise the alarm:* "The State of Workplace Safety 2021," *AllVoices*, August 11, 2021, https://www.allvoices.co/blog/the-state-of-workplace-safety-2021.

xxxiv *"neither earthquakes nor the waves":* Allan V. Horwitz, *What's Normal: Reconciling Biology and Culture* (Oxford: Oxford University Press, 2016), 77.

xxxiv *lack a sense of certainty and control:* Aaron C. Kay, Jennifer A. Whitson, Danielle Gaucher, and Adam D. Galinsky, "Compensatory Control: Achieving Order Through the Mind, Our Institutions, and the Heavens," *Current Directions in Psychological Science* 18, no. 5 (2009): 164–68.

xxxiv *Neuroscience teaches us:* Kimberly Holland, "Amygdala Hijack: When Emotion Takes Over," *Healthline*, March 16, 2023, https://www.healthline.com/health/stress/amygdala-hijack. The journalist Daniel Goleman is credited with the notion of "amygdala hijacking." Jeremy Sutton, "The Fight-or-Flight Response: Everything You Need to Know," *Positive Psychology*, January 9, 2022, https://positivepsychology.com/fight-or-flight-response/.

xxxv *in harm's way:* Jim Detert, *Choosing Courage: The Everyday Guide to Being Brave at Work* (Boston: Harvard Business Review Press, 2021), 5.

xxxv *"strive to avoid dangers":* Allan V. Horwitz, *What's Normal: Reconciling Biology and Culture* (New York: Oxford University Press, 2016), 73.

xxxv *Scholars have linked courage:* James R. Detert and Ethan R. Burris, "Leadership Behavior and Employee Voice: Is the Door Really Open?," *Academy of Management Journal* 50, no. 4 (2007): 869–84; Sarai Garcia, Sergio Lopez, Kaitlyn Longo, and Glenn Geher, "Are We Evolved to Be Courageous? A Study of the Psychological Correlates of Courage," presentation at the annual meeting of the NorthEastern Evolutionary Psychology Society, April 2023, New Paltz, New York; Matt C. Howard and Kent K. Alipour, "Does the Courage Measure Really Measure Courage? A Theoretical and Empirical Evaluation," *Journal of Positive Psychology* 9, no. 5 (2014): 449–59.

xxxv *cowardly people appear to possess:* Chad T. Brinsfield, "Employee Silence Motives: Investigation of Dimensionality and Development of Measures," *Journal of Organizational Behavior* 34, no 5 (2013): 671–97; Lewis R. Goldberg, "An Alternative 'Description of Personality': The Big-Five Factor Structure," *Journal of Personality and Social Psychology* 59, no. 6 (1990): 1216–29.

xxxv *the experience of fear:* Jennifer S. Lerner and Dacher Keltner, "Fear, Anger, and Risk," *Journal of Personality and Social Psychology* 81, no. 1 (2001): 146–59.

xxxvi *change in our circumstances:* Olga Khazan, "The Best Headspace for Making Decisions," *Atlantic*, September 19, 2016, https://www.theatlantic.com/science/archive/2016/09/the-best-headspace-for-making-decisions/500423/.

xxxvi *officers might refrain from reporting:* For research on the willingness of police officers to report on officer misconduct, see Carl B. Klockars, Sanja Kutnjak Ivkovich, William E. Harver, and Maria R. Haberfeld, "The Measurement of Police Integrity," National Institute of Justice Research in Brief, U.S. Department of Justice, May 2000.

xxxvi *wired to value our relationships:* Richard M. Ryan and Edward L. Deci, *Self-Determination Theory: Basic Psychological Needs in Motivation, Development, and Wellness* (New York: Guilford Press, 2017).

xxxvii *majority had made:* Solomon E. Asch, "Effects of Group Pressure upon the Modification and Distortion of Judgments," in *Groups, Leadership, and Men: Research in Human Relations*, Harold Guetzkow, ed., (Pittsburgh, PA: Carnegie Press, 1951), 177–90. See also Monica C. Worline, "Understanding the Role of Courage in Social Life," in *The Psychology of Courage: Modern Research on an Ancient Virtue*, Cynthia L.S. Pury and Shane J. Lopez, eds. (Washington, DC: American Psychological Association, 2010), 209–226.

xxxvii *seemingly painful electric shocks:* Stanley Milgram, "Behavioral Study of Obedience," *Journal of Abnormal and Social Psychology* 67, no. 4 (1963): 371–78.

xxxvii *boldly telling the bullies to stop:* Bailee Hill, "Fox News Meteorologist Adam Klotz Attacked on NYC Subway After Stopping Teens from Assaulting Older Man," *Fox News*, January 23, 2023, https://www.foxnews.com/media/fox-news-meteorologist-adam-klotz-attacked-nyc-subway-stopping-teens-assaulting-older-man.

xxxviii *"no one wanted to step in":* Fox 5 Atlanta Digital Team, "Former Fox 5 Meteorologist Attacked by Teens on New York Subway," *Fox 5*, January 23, 2023, https://www.foxnews.com/media/fox-news-meteorologist-adam-klotz-attacked-nyc-subway-stopping-teens-assaulting-older-man.

xxxviii *"bystander effect":* Peter Fischer, Joachim I. Krueger, Tobias Greitemeyer, Claudia Vogrincic, Andreas Kastenmüller, Dieter Frey, Moritz Heene, Magdalena Wicher, and Martina Kainbacher, "The Bystander-Effect: A Meta-Analytic Review on Bystander Intervention in Dangerous and Non-Dangerous Emergencies," *Psychological Bulletin* 137, no. 4 (2011): 517–37.

xxxix *lack of what my colleague:* Amy Gallo, "What Is Psychological Safety?," *Harvard Business Review*, February 15, 2023, https://hbr.org/2023/02/what-is-psychological-safety. This concept originates in the work of Amy Edmondson, described in detail in Amy Edmondson, *The Fearless Organization: Creating Psychological Safety in the Workplace for Learning, Innovation, and Growth* (New York: Wiley, 2018).

xxxix *institutional cowardice:* Laura S. Brown, "Institutional Cowardice: A Powerful,

Often Invisible Manifestation of Institutional Betrayal," *Journal of Trauma & Dissociation* 22, no. 3 (2021): 241–48. Brown defines institutional cowardice as a form of institutional betrayal—"a knowing or consciously motivated act, an intentional decision to go in a particular direction and allow a vulnerable person or persons to be harmed" (242).

xxxix *in which they're operating:* Brown, "Institutional Cowardice."

xxxix *"trained to obey":* G. M. Gilbert, *The Psychology of Dictatorship* (New York: Ronald Press Co., 1950), 255.

xl *can throw at us:* Chris Walsh, *Cowardice: A Brief History* (Princeton, NJ: Princeton University Press, 2014), 2.

xli *good coward:* William Ian Miller, *The Mystery of Courage* (Cambridge, MA: Harvard University Press, 2000), 1.

xli *"What is a coward":* Miller, *Mystery of Courage*, 3.

xlii *propaganda out of the earthquake:* Linjun Fan, "Fan Meizhong: Why I Challenged the Chinese Public on Ethics," *China Digital Times*, June 19, 2008.

xlii *poor building construction that contributed:* Xu Weichao and Li Rongde, "Teacher Who Left Students Behind in Sichuan Earthquake Looks Back," *Caixin Global*, May 15, 2018, https://www.caixinglobal.com/2018-05-15/teacher-who-left-students-behind-in-sichuan-earthquake-looks-back-101250246.html.

xlii *"dissatisfied with the narrative":* Louisa Lim, "China's 'Biggest Coward' Finds Sympathy," NPR, July 14, 2008, https://www.npr.org/2008/07/14/92517549/chinas-biggest-coward-finds-sympathy.

xlii *"possible consequences of my actions":* Lim, "China's 'Biggest Coward.'"

CHAPTER 1: COPING

3 *a perilous trek:* Sydney Page, "Why These Women Just Walked Harriet Tubman's 116-mile Journey from the Underground Railroad," *Washington Post*, October 27, 2020, https://www.washingtonpost.com/lifestyle/2020/10/27/why-these-women-just-walked-harriet-tubmans-116-mile-journey-underground-railroad/; Martha S. Jones, "Finding Traces of Harriet Tubman on Maryland's Eastern Shore," *New York Times*, June 21, 2022, https://www.nytimes.com/2022/06/21/travel/harriet-tubman-maryland.html.

3 *Fugitive Slave Act:* "The Underground Railroad," *PBS American Experience*, https://www.pbs.org/wgbh/americanexperience/features/lincolns-underground-railroad/.

4 *"die just for one coward":* Jean McMahon Humez, *Harriet Tubman: The Life and the Life Stories* (Madison: University of Wisconsin Press, 2003), 235–37. See also William Still, *The Underground Railroad: A Record of Facts, Authentic Narratives, Letters, &c., Narrating the Hardships, Hair-Breadth Escapes, and Death Struggles of the Slaves in Their Efforts for Freedom, as Related by Themselves and Others or Witnessed by the* Author: *Together with Sketches of Some of the Largest Stockholders*

and Most Liberal Aiders and Advisers of the Road (Oxfordshire, UK: Benediction Classics, 2008), 297.

4   *throwing her enemies off:* Catherine Clinton, *Harriet Tubman: The Road to Freedom* (New York: Little, Brown and Company, 2004), 89.

5   *fellow believers:* Clinton, *Harriet Tubman*, 88–89.

5   *gave them opium:* Sarah H. Bradford, *Harriet Tubman, the Moses of Her People* (New York: G.R. Lockwood & Son, 1886), 35 and 119.

5   *critical head start:* Clinton, *Harriet Tubman*, 89–90.

5   *slave catchers and unfriendly locals:* Clinton, *Harriet Tubman*, 85.

5   *"Promised Land":* "Underground Railroad Codes," African American Museum of Iowa, https://blackiowa.org/wp-content/uploads/2020/08/Underground-Railroad-Worksheets.pdf.

5   *"Canaan":* "Underground Railroad Codes," African American Museum of Iowa, https://blackiowa.org/wp-content/uploads/2020/08/Underground-Railroad-Worksheets.pdf.

6   *"calculated risk-taking":* Kathleen K. Reardon, "Courage as a Skill," *Harvard Business Review*, January 2007, https://hbr.org/2007/01/courage-as-a-skill.

6   *"probabilities that disguised uncertainty":* John Kay and Mervyn King, *Radical Uncertainty: Decision-Making Beyond the Numbers* (New York: W. W. Norton & Company, 2020), 8–9.

7   *Economists have posited a basic distinction:* In his classic book first published in 1921, *Risk, Uncertainty, and Profit*, the economist Frank Knight distinguished between risks, or dangers whose odds of occurring we can measure, and uncertainty, which describes situations that carry risks unbeknownst to us. Frank H. Knight, *Risk, Uncertainty, and Profit* (Boston and New York: Houghton Mifflin Company, 1921). Building on this distinction, the economists John Kay and Mervyn King distinguish between two kinds of uncertainty that we typically confront, resolvable and radical. Kay and King, *Radical Uncertainty*.

7   *"unknown unknowns":* Dan Zak, "'Nothing Ever Ends': Sorting Through Rumsfeld's Knowns and Unknowns," *Washington Post*, July 1, 2021, https://www.washingtonpost.com/lifestyle/style/rumsfeld-dead-words-known-unknowns/2021/07/01/831175c2-d9df-11eb-bb9e-70fda8c37057_story.html.

8   *mercy of outside forces:* Jennifer S. Lerner et al., "Emotion and Decision-Making," *Annual Review of Psychology* 66 (2015): 799–823.

8   *one-two punch of uncertainty:* For an analysis of the concept of uncertainty that emphasizes doubt, please see Amar Bhidé, *Uncertainty and Enterprise: Venturing Beyond the Known* (New York: Oxford University Press, 2024).

8   *uncertainty and loss of control:* In one study of 182 students, researchers asked participants to describe situations in which they experienced different emotions, including fear. They then asked them to rate the underlying factors that they felt that contributed to the emotion. As the researchers found, participants strongly

associated lack of control and uncertainty with fear. Ira J. Roseman, "Appraisal Determinants of Emotions: Constructing a More Accurate and Comprehensive Theory," *Cognition & Emotion* 10, no. 3 (1996): 241–78.

8   *quite brave:* The "fear equation" was inspired by Jennifer Lerner's research on appraisal tendencies, or "goal-directed processes through which emotions exert effects on judgement and choice." In papers derived from her dissertation, Lerner hypothesized that the experience of fear was closely associated with appraisals of low certainty and low control. In this book, I argue that these appraisals also have the effect of *eliciting* fear. See Jennifer S. Lerner and Dacher Keltner, "Beyond Valence: Toward a Model of Emotion-Specific Influences on Judgement and Choice," *Cognition and Emotion* 14 (2000): 473–93, esp. 478–79, and their paper "Fear, Anger, and Risk," p. 147, for additional context.

8   *"to see the world as structured, orderly":* Justin P. Friesen, Aaron C. Kay, Richard P. Eibach, and Adam D. Galinsky, "Seeking Structure in Social Organization: Compensatory Control and the Psychological Advantages of Hierarchy," *Journal of Personality and Social Psychology* 106, no. 4 (2014): 590–609, esp. 591.

10 *only in truly dire situations:* I draw this story from John Shaughnessy, "Firefighter's Trust in God Is Forged by Fire and Faith," *Gulf Coast Catholic,* September 7, 2022, https://gulfcoastcatholic.org/firefighters-trust-god-forged-fire-and-faith.

10 *"26 hours away":* Shaughnessy, "Firefighter's Trust in God Is Forged by Fire and Faith."

11 *magical thinking:* "Magical Thinking," *Psychology Today,* https://www.psychologytoday.com/us/basics/magical-thinking.

11 *physical laws of nature:* "Any explanation of a behavior or an experience that contradicts the laws of nature may be considered magical thinking," the scholar Gloria Keinan has written. "Such an explanation usually refers to powers, principles, or entities that lack empirical evidence or scientific foundation." Giora Keinan, "Effects of Stress and Tolerance of Ambiguity on Magical Thinking," *Journal of Personality and Social Psychology* 67 (1994): 48–55.

11 *frames reality:* Eugene Subbotsky, "Magical Thinking—Reality or Illusion?," *The Psychologist* 17, no. 6 (June 2004): 336–39.

11 *create a mini-narrative:* As the courage researcher Robert Biswas-Diener has remarked, "magical thinking is as common as black cats," or rather, the belief that a black cat crossing our path will bring bad luck. Robert Biswas-Diener, *The Courage Quotient: How Science Can Make You Braver* (San Francisco: Jossey-Bass, 2012), 68. Biswas-Diener suggests that magical thinking might even include certain heuristics or "thinking tricks" that we use to make life more comprehensible, even if they defy logic. For instance, we might regard two events as connected to one another, even if there is no basis for thinking of them as anything other than a coincidence.

12 *passing on our genes:* Biswas-Diener, *Courage Quotient,* 72. Also see D. Thomas Markle, "The Magic That Binds Us: Magical Thinking and Inclusive Fitness," *Journal of Social, Evolutionary, and Cultural Psychology* 4, no. 1 (2010): 18–33.

12 *"faith gives him the necessary courage":* Émile Durkheim, *The Elementary Forms of the Religious Life,* trans. Joseph Ward Swain (London: George Allan and Unwin, Ltd., 1915), 159. Other scholars have come to similar conclusions about magical thinking and its relationship to courage. As Robert Biswas-Diener has observed, magical beliefs foster a sense of personal control, boosting our confidence, helping us stay in the game, and emboldening us to take risks. We perform better under pressure, and we're better able to handle it when we fail. Biswas-Diener, *Courage Quotient,* 76.

12 *"a helpful hand in circumstances":* Subbotsky, "Magical Thinking," 339.

12 *crossing your fingers:* Lysann Damisch, Barbara Stoberock, and Thomas Mussweiler, "Keep Your Fingers Crossed: How Superstition Improves Performance," *Psychological Science* 21, no. 7 (2010): 1014–20.

12 *belief that we have good luck:* Maia J. Young, Ning Chen, and Michael W. Morris, "Belief in Stable and Fleeting Luck and Achievement Motivation," *Personality and Individual Differences* 47 (2009): 150–54. See also Nicholas M. Hobson, Juliana Schroeder, Jane L. Risen, Dimitris Xygalatas, and Michael Inzlicht, "The Psychology of Rituals: An Integrative Review and Process-Based Framework," *Personality and Social Psychology Review* 22, no. 3 (2018): 260–84.

12 *enact our beliefs:* Nicholas M. Hobson et al., "The Psychology of Rituals: An Integrative Review and Process-Based Framework," 260–84.

12 *"a sense of control":* Dimitris Xygalatas, "Culture, Cognition, and Ritual," in *Handbook of Advances in Culture and Psychology,* ed. M. J. Gelfand, C.-Y. Chiu, and Y.-Y. Hong (Oxford: Oxford University Press, 2023), 118–54, esp. 129–30.

13 *"lucky cat" on her hand:* Hounche Chung, "Lucky Charms: The Rituals and Superstitions of Olympic Athletes," Olympics.com, January 31, 2022, https://olympics.com/en/news/lucky-charms-the-rituals-and-superstitions-of-olympic-athletes.

13 *slap his face:* Will Thomas, "John Henderson—Face Slap," YouTube video, May 21, 2013, https://www.youtube.com/watch?v=mIIbj6mYJLU.

13 *"then I'll lose":* Serena Williams, "Superstitions That Serve Me Well," *The Standard,* April 12, 2012, https://www.standard.co.uk/hp/front/superstitions-that-serve-me-well-by-serena-williams-6594813.html.

13 *"down in battle":* Andrew E. Kramer, "In an Epic Battle of Tanks, Russia Was Routed, Repeating Earlier Mistakes," *New York Times,* March 1, 2023, https://www.nytimes.com/2023/03/01/world/europe/ukraine-russia-tanks.html.

13 *"closer to God":* Mitchell J. Neubert, "Entrepreneurs Feel Closer to God Than the Rest of Us Do," *Harvard Business Review,* October 2013, https://hbr.org/2013/10/entrepreneurs-feel-closer-to-god-than-the-rest-of-us-do.

13 *perceive that God sees them individually*: Kevin D. Dougherty, Jenna Griebel, Mitchell J. Neubert, and Jerry Z. Park, "A Religious Profile of American Entrepreneurs," *Journal for the Scientific Study of Religion* 52, no. 2 (2013): 401–409.

14	*"always talking to the Lord"*: Bradford, *Harriet Tubman*, 24.
14	*Lord asked her three times:* Bradford, *Harriet Tubman*, 260.
14	*Thomas Garrett, recounted:* Bradford, *Harriet Tubman*, 84.
14	*"consulted" God, who told her to pass:* Bradford, *Harriet Tubman*, 83–88.
14	*"don't desert me in the seventh!":* Bradford, *Harriet Tubman*, 57–60.
15	*"fear of being arrested":* Bradford, *Harriet Tubman*, 84.
15	*"I was ready to go":* Bradford, *Harriet Tubman*, 61.
17	*"in a state of question mark":* Scott Simon, host, "Philippe Petit: The 'Man on Wire,'" *Weekend Edition*, NPR, February 28, 2009, https://www.npr.org/transcripts/101298523.
17	*eleven years collecting data:* Calvin Tomkins, "The Man Who Walks on Air," *The New Yorker*, March 29, 1999, https://www.newyorker.com/magazine/1999/04/05/the-man-who-walks-on-air.
18	*"will pay for it with my life":* Tomkins, "The Man Who Walks on Air."
18	*"follow with specifics":* Philippe Petit, "In Search of Fear," *Lapham's Quarterly* 10, no. 3 (Summer 2017).
18	*"a star to a jerk":* Larry Fink, quoted in *BlackRock: 25th Anniversary Video*, cited in Ranjay Gulati, Jan W. Rivkin, and Kelly McNamara, "BlackRock (A): Selling the Systems?," Harvard Business School Case Study 9-717-014, October 2016 (revised January 2018), 2.
18	*"tools to understand [the risk involved]":* Suzanna Andrews, "Larry Fink's $12 Trillion Shadow," *Vanity Fair*, April 2010, https://www.vanityfair.com/news/2010/04/fink-201004.
19	*$11 trillion of assets:* Arasu Kannagi Basil and Davide Barbuscia, "BlackRock's Assets Hit Record $11.5 Trillion Amid Private Market Push," Reuters, October 11, 2024, https://www.reuters.com/business/finance/blackrock-hits-record-high-115-trillion-assets-market-rally-etf-boost-2024-10-11/.
20	*Algorithms are never perfect representations:* See John Kay and Mervyn King, *Radical Uncertainty: Decision-Making Beyond the Numbers* (New York: W. W. Norton, 2020), 248. As they write: "Radical uncertainty precludes optimising behaviour. In the world as it is, we cope rather than optimise. The numbers which were used in these calculations are invented. Or they are derived from historic data series and assume a non-existent stationarity in the world. Struggling to cope with a large world which they could only imperfectly understand, the proponents of these calculations invented a small world which gave them the satisfaction of clear-cut answers" (248).
20	*risks that are under our control:* That is, they allow us to cover nonsystematic risks, the ones that affect us uniquely, not the systematic risks that affect everyone in a market and that are beyond our control.
20	*shifts the sense of reality:* As Amar Bhidé suggests, we find a similar example in the

pitches entrepreneurs make about their startups to secure funding. Entrepreneurs often make elaborate arguments accounting for and mitigating risk to investors, a presentation that can often perpetuate the fiction that they've mitigated uncertainty too. Bhidé, *Uncertainty and Enterprise.*

21 *satisficing:* Herbert A. Simon, "Rational Choice and the Structure of the Environment," *Psychological Review* 63, no. 2 (1956): 129–38; Herbert A. Simon, "A Behavioral Model of Rational Choice," *Quarterly Journal of Economics* 69, no. 1 (February 1955): 99–118.

22 *seek out and aggressively mitigate:* Kay and King, *Radical Uncertainty,* 299.

22 *laddering up boldness:* See, for instance, Jim Detert's courage ladder concept. Jim Detert, *Choosing Courage: The Everyday Guide to Being Brave at Work* (Boston, MA: Harvard Business Review Press, 2021), chapter 4.

23 *"going off a risk cliff":* Terry Virts, interview with the author, March 8, 2023.

23 *"solo in the vacuum of space":* Terry Virts, *How to Astronaut: An Insider's Guide to Leaving Planet Earth* (New York: Workman Publishing, 2020), 206.

23 *"don't fly by the seat of your pants":* Virts, *How to Astronaut,* 206.

24 *ability to improvise on the spot:* Peter Felsman, Colleen M. Seifer, Brandy Sinco, and Joseph A. Himle, "Reducing Social Anxiety and Intolerance of Uncertainty in Adolescents with Improvisational Theater," *Arts in Psychotherapy* 82 (February 2023): 101985; Raymond A. R. MacDonald and Graeme B. Wilson, "Musical Improvisation and Health: A Review," *Psychology of Well-Being* 4 (2014): 20.

24 *common heuristics or mental shortcuts:* Amos Tversky and Daniel Kahneman, "Judgment under Uncertainty: Heuristics and Biases," *Science* 185, no. 4157 (1974): 1124–31.

25 *speed and ease:* For more on how heuristics make decision-making cognitively easier, see Anuj K. Shah and Daniel M. Oppenheimer, "Heuristics Made Easy: An Effort-Reduction Framework," *Psychological Bulletin* 134, no. 2 (2008): 207–222; Benjamin Frimodig, "Heuristics: Definition, Examples, and How They Work," *Simply Psychology,* updated October 24, 2023, https://www.simplypsychology.org/what-is-a-heuristic.html.

25 *study of experienced firefighters:* Gary Klein, Roberta Calderwood, and Anne Clinton-Cirocco, "Rapid Decision Making on the Fire Ground: The Original Study Plus a Postscript," *Journal of Cognitive Engineering and Decision Making* 4, no. 3 (2010): 186–209.

25 *seasoned entrepreneurs:* Robert A. Baron and Michael D. Ensley, "Opportunity Recognition as the Detection of Meaningful Patterns: Evidence from Comparisons of Novice and Experienced Entrepreneurs," *Management Science* 52, no. 9 (2006): 1331–44.

26 *"potential evolution of understanding and action":* Fabrizio Ferraro, Dror Etzion, and Joel Gehman, "Tackling Grand Challenges Pragmatically: Robust Action Revisited," *Organization Studies* 36, no. 3 (2015): 363–90, esp. 390.

CHAPTER 2: CONFIDENCE

29   *keep infestations under control:* "Corn Snake," Reptilia, https://reptilia.org/corn-snake/.

29   *"phobic dread":* Albert Bandura, Linda Reese, and Nancy E. Adams, "Microanalysis of Action and Fear Arousal as a Function of Differential Levels of Perceived Self-Efficacy," *Journal of Personality and Social Psychology* 43, no. 1 (1982): 5–21, esp. 7.

29   *previous one:* Bandura, Reese, and Adams, "Microanalysis of Action and Fear Arousal as a Function of Differential Levels of Perceived Self-Efficacy."

31   *"self-efficacy":* In Bandura's words, "perceived self-efficacy refers to beliefs in one's capabilities to organize and execute the courses of action required to produce given attainments." See Albert Bandura, *Self-Efficacy: The Exercise of Control* (New York: W. H. Freeman and Company, 1997), 3. Psychologists and sociologists tend to differ slightly in how they think about self-efficacy. Psychologists conceive of self-efficacy as a belief shaped by various psychological factors, such as how positive our attitude is, how motivated we feel, and so on. Sociologists tend to see self-efficacy in social terms, regarding it as our belief in our ability to exert our will *in particular environments*. Social factors, including those that are beyond our conscious awareness, can also shape our beliefs about our ability to take action. Nancy J. Burke, Joyce A. Bird, Melissa A. Clark, William Rakowski, Claudia Guerra, Judith C. Barker, and Rena J. Pasick, "Social and Cultural Meanings of Self-Efficacy," *Health Education & Behavior* 36, no. 5 (2009): 111S–28S. Although some scholars take a cognitive approach to self-efficacy, conceiving of it in terms of beliefs we have about our own competency, others take a motivational approach, emphasizing the *experience* of having agency and dealing competently with the outside world—something that we all as humans need to feel. See Viktor Gecas, "The Social Psychology of Self-Efficacy," *Annual Review of Sociology* 15 (1989): 291–316.

31   *tend to underestimate our abilities:* Don A. Moore and Deborah A. Small, "Error and Bias in Comparative Judgment: On Being Both Better and Worse Than We Think We Are," *Journal of Personality and Social Psychology* 92, no. 6 (2007): 972–89.

31   *think that others are* always *better suited:* Isabelle Engeler and Gerald Häubl, "Miscalibration in Predicting One's Performance: Disentangling Misplacement and Misestimation," *Journal of Personality and Social Psychology* 120, no. 4 (2021): 940–55; Elizabeth R. Tenney, Nathan L. Meikle, David Hunsaker, Don A. Moore, and Cameron Anderson, "Is Overconfidence a Social Liability? The Effect of Verbal versus Nonverbal Expressions of Confidence," *Journal of Personality and Social Psychology* 116, no. 3 (2019): 396–415.

32   *brave people:* Sean T. Hannah, Patrick J. Sweeney, and Paul B. Lester, "Toward a Courageous Mindset: The Subjective Act and Experience of Courage," *Journal*

	of Positive Psychology 2, no. 2 (2007): 129–35; Melissa L. McKinlay and Peter J. Norton, "The Role of Courage in Predicting Behavior: Replication in a Public-Speaking Fearful Sample," *Motivation and Emotion* 47 (2023): 1–6.
32	*"variety of circumstances":* Bandura, *Self-Efficacy,* 36–37.
33	*recruits in a paratrooper unit:* T. M. McMillan and S. J. Rachman, "Fearlessness and Courage in Paratroopers Undergoing Training," *Personality and Individual Differences* 9, no. 2 (1988): 373–78.
33	*increasing confidence leads to such a reduction:* Stanley Rachman, "Fear and Courage," *Behavior Therapy* 15, no. 1 (1984): 109–120.
34	*"completely routine and unremarkable":* Captain Sully's Minute-by-Minute Description of The Miracle On The Hudson	*Inc.*, YouTube video, 12:22, posted by Inc., March 6, 2019, https://www.youtube.com/watch?v=w6EblErBJqw, timestamp 0:14.
34	*"as if it were a Hitchcock film":* Captain Sully's Minute-by-Minute Description, timestamp 0:44.
34	*"bottom had fallen out of our world":* Captain Sully's Minute-by-Minute Description, timestamp 1:47.
34	*pilots don't even train for this specific scenario:* Ella Rhoades, "TEAM COVERAGE: Pilot Discusses Engine Failure Reported in I-75 Plane Crash," *Fox 4 Now*, February 9, 2024, https://www.fox4now.com/naples/double-engine-failure-boeing-777-pilot-gives-perspective-on-deadly-naples-plane-crash.
34	*"make all these things happen simultaneously":* Katie Couric, interview with Captain Chesley "Sully" Sullenberger, *60 Minutes*, CBS, February 8, 2009, timestamp 7:32.
35	*"sure that I could do it":* Katie Couric, interview with Captain Chesley "Sully" Sullenberger, *60 Minutes*, CBS, February 8, 2009, timestamp 9:35 and 9:54.
35	*lives he arguably could have saved:* This account and the quotes in the next few paragraphs come from Jamie Thompson, "To Stop a Shooter," *The Atlantic*, January 29, 2024, https://www.theatlantic.com/magazine/archive/2024/03/parkland-shooter-scot-peterson-coward-broward/677170/.
36	*"It's a farce":* Thompson, "To Stop a Shooter."
36	*"better to hold":* "Broward County Sheriff's Office Training Materials Say First One or Two Officers on Scene Should 'Confront the Shooter,'" Judicial Watch, March 15, 2018, https://www.judicialwatch.org/judicial-watch-broward-county-sheriffs-office-training-materials-say-first-one-two-officers-scene-confront-shooter/.
37	*"Officer Snuggles":* Thompson, "To Stop a Shooter."
37	*Two kinds of skill-building:* On the difference between general and specific self-efficacy, see, for example, Ralf Schwarzer and Matthias Jerusalem, "General Self-Efficacy Scale (GSE)," in *Measures in Health Psychology: A User's Portfolio. Causal and Control Beliefs*, ed. John Weinman, Stephen Wright, and Marie Johnston

(1995), 35–37. Also Laura Galiana, Javier Sánchez-Ruiz, Juan Gómez-Salgado, Philip J. Larkin, and Noemí Sansó, "Validation of the Spanish Version of the Five-Item General Self-Efficacy (GSE) Scale in a Sample of Nursing Students: Evidence of Validity, Reliability, Longitudinal Invariance and Changes in General Self-Efficacy and Resilience in a Two-Wave Cross-Lagged Panel Model," *Nurse Education in Practice,* 74 (2024): 103865. Galiana et al. write: "Although Bandura (1977) originally described self-efficacy as situation-specific, that is, being related to specific competencies and skills, other theories and definitions of self-efficacy have addressed it as a general construct (Schwarzer et al., 1997; Sherer et al., 1982). For example, Schwarzer et al. (1997) raised the concept of general self-efficacy, as one's overall self-confidence when dealing with challenges in different environments. That is, general self-efficacy refers to a relatively stable and generalized belief that an individual can marshal the resources needed to deal with challenges (Scherbaum et al., 2006)."

37 *"deliberate practice":* K. Anders Ericsson, Michael J. Prietula, and Edward T. Cokely, "The Making of an Expert," *Harvard Business Review,* July–August 2007, https://hbr.org/2007/07/the-making-of-an-expert.

38 *"thank goodness crooks don't know":* Thompson, "To Stop a Shooter."

38 *struggle to access the specialized skills:* Bandura presents a four-part model of how to build self-efficacy, which includes practicing and mastering a skill yourself, experiencing skills performance vicariously (having people show you how to do it), receiving feedback and encouragement from others, and attending to your emotional and physiological response to the task at hand (for instance, reducing your body's stress response). See Bandura, *Self-Efficacy,* chapter 3.

39 *"what I thought":* Interview with Terry Virts, March 8, 2023.

39 *"pushed to our physical and mental limits":* Virts, *How to Astronaut,* 30.

40 *"didn't promise you a rose garden":* Lance Cpl. Ed Galo, "We Didn't Promise You a Rose Garden," *Marine Corps Training and Education Command,* March 22, 2010, https://www.tecom.marines.mil/In-the-News/Stories/News-Article-Display/Article/528225/we-didnt-promise-you-a-rose-garden/.

41 *"foot-in-the-door" dynamic:* Schilpzand quotes the politician and war hero John McCain: "Courage is like a muscle. The more we exercise it, the stronger it gets." See Pauline Schilpzand, "Personal Courage: A Measure Creation Study," Ph.D. dissertation, University of Florida, 2008, esp. 16–20. McCain's quote appears on p. 17. See also, John McCain, "In Search of Courage," *Fast Company,* September 1, 2004, https://www.fastcompany.com/50692/search-courage.

42 *"one play at a time":* Ranjay Gulati and Eppa Rixey, "Nick Saban: Embracing 'The Process' of Sustaining Success," Harvard Business School Case Study N9-423-033, December 20, 2022, 5. I base my account of Saban and the University of Alabama football program in this and the following paragraphs on this case. All quotes originally appeared there.

43 *"not being so outcome-oriented":* Gulati and Rixey, "Nick Saban," 5.

43 *unlock adaptive, on-the-fly thinking:* Alexandra M. Freund and Marie Hennecke,

"On Means and Ends: The Role of Goal Focus in Successful Goal Pursuit," *Current Directions in Psychological Science* 24, no. 2 (2015): 149–53; Cynthia L. S. Pury and Charles B. Starkey, "Is Courage an Accolade or a Process? A Fundamental Question for Courage Research," in *The Psychology of Courage: Modern Research on an Ancient Virtue*, ed. C. L. S. Pury and S. J. Lopez (American Psychological Association, 2010): 67–87.

43 *"you are process oriented":* Gulati and Rixey, "Nick Saban," 8.

43 *"I want to be a complete player at my position":* Gulati and Rixey, "Nick Saban," 9.

43 *"most consistent, process-driven person":* Gulati and Rixey, "Nick Saban," 9.

44 *"trust the process:"* Gulati and Rixey, "Nick Saban," 10. Others in sports have talked about the virtues of emphasizing process over a results-orientation. As the legendary basketball coach Phil Jackson has said, "At the start of every season I always encouraged players to focus on the journey rather than the goal." Phil Jackson and Hugh Delehanty, *Eleven Rings: The Soul of Success* (New York: Penguin Books, 2014), 24.

44 *"social persuasion":* Bandura, *Self-Efficacy*, 101.

45 *"a constant nightmare":* Andrew E. Kramer, "Trading Books for a Rifle: The Teacher Who Volunteered in Ukraine," *New York Times*, February 18, 2023, https://www.nytimes.com/2023/02/18/world/europe/ukraine-teacher-combat.html.

45 *"am an infantry soldier now":* Kramer, "Trading Books for a Rifle."

46 *securing the tools we need to perform:* As one group of scholars has written, "Means efficacy, an individual's belief in the quality and utility of the tools available for task performance, will also reduce perceived fear and heighten confidence towards inspiring courageous action." Sean T. Hannah, Patrick J. Sweeney, and Paul B. Lester, "Toward A Courageous Mindset: The Subjective Act and Experience of Courage," *Journal of Positive Psychology* 2, no. 2 (2007): 129–35, esp. 132.

46 *get the job done:* My account of Danaher in this section draws heavily on Bharat Anand et al., "Danaher Corporation," Harvard Business School Case Study 9–79-708–48-445, November 30, 2015.

47 *Between 2007 and 2018*: Yahoo Finance (2009, January). DHR: Danaher Corporation. Retrieved February 4, 2025, from https://finance.yahoo.com/quote/DHR/; Yahoo Finance (2015, December). DHR: Danaher Corporation. Retrieved February 4, 2025, from https://finance.yahoo.com/quote/DHR/.

47 *helped make Danaher a more innovative company:* Larry Culp, interview with the author, January 28, 2018.

47 *produce extraordinary results:* Interview with Larry Culp, January 28, 2018.

48 *confident individuals:* Don A. Moore and Derek Schatz, "The Three Faces of Overconfidence," *Social and Personality Psychology Compass* 11, no. 8 (2017): e12331.

48 *overconfidence doesn't necessarily help:* For instance, in one study, medical students who did better academically were less prone to be overconfident. Raúl A.

Borracci and Eduardo B. Arribalzaga, "The Incidence of Overconfidence and Underconfidence Effects in Medical Student Examinations," *Journal of Surgical Education* 75, no. 5 (2018): 1223–29.

49 *take bolder action:* Viktor Gecas, "The Social Psychology of Self-Efficacy," *Annual Review of Sociology* 15 (1989): 291–316.

CHAPTER 3: COMMITMENT

50 *his continent was on fire:* My account of the founding of Ashesi University draws heavily on Ranjay Gulati and Caroline de Lacvivier, "Ashesi University: The Journey from Vision to Reality," Harvard Business School Case Study N9-418-085, January 16, 2016, 6, as well as follow-up interviews with Patrick Awuah and Nina Marini.

51 *"neither fixing problems nor creating solutions":* Patrick Awuah, "Path to a New Africa," *Stanford Social Innovation Review*, Summer 2012, https://ssir.org/articles/entry/path_to_a_new_africa.

51 *help fuel Africa's transformation:* Patrick Awuah, "How to Educate Leaders? Liberal Arts," *TEDGlobal 2007*, June 2007, https://www.ted.com/talks/patrick_awuah_how_to_educate_leaders_liberal_arts?subtitle=en.

51 *think carefully through ethical dilemmas:* Awuah, "How to Educate Leaders?"

52 *named after the word for "beginning":* "Our History," Ashesi University, https://ashesi.edu.gh/our-story-history/.

52 *"as difficult as climbing Mount Everest":* Patrick Awuah, "Patrick Awuah's Olin College Commencement Speech," Ashesi University Foundation, accessed June 2, 2017, https://www.ashesi.org/blog/patrick-awuahs-olin-college-commencement-speech/.

52 *"uncharted territory for me":* Nina Marini (cofounder of Ashesi University), interview with the author, September 25, 2019.

53 *"like we were taking on a quest":* Nina Marini (cofounder of Ashesi University), interview with the author, September 25, 2019.

53 *oxytocin at work:* Paul J. Zak, "How Stories Change the Brain," *Greater Good Magazine*, December 17, 2013, https://greatergood.berkeley.edu/article/item/how_stories_change_brain.

53 *leads people to take positive actions:* Paul J. Zak, "Why Inspiring Stories Make Us React: The Neuroscience of Narrative," *Cerebrum* 2 (2015): 2.

54 *"very easy to believe":* Nina Marini (cofounder of Ashesi University), interview with the author, September 25, 2019.

54 *shared identity and a sense of common fate:* Anselm L. Strauss, *Mirrors and Masks: The Search for Identity* (London: Martin Robertson, 1977), 41–45.

54 *"'no Plan B'":* Gulati and de Lacvivier, "Ashesi University," 11.

54 *"not somebody who is just making up a story":* Ken Maguire, "A New Model of

Leadership for Africa," *Swarthmore College Bulletin*, January 2010, https://www.swarthmore.edu/bulletin/archive/wp/january-2010_a-new-model-of-leadership-for-africa.html.

56 *make a difference:* Linda J. Skitka and Daniel C. Wisneski, "Moral Conviction and Emotion," *Emotion Review* 3, no. 3 (July 2011): 328–30.

56 *"felt responsibility":* Pauline Schilpzand, David R. Hekman, and Terence R. Mitchell, "An Inductively Generated Typology and Process Model of Workplace Courage," *Organization Science* 26, no. 1 (2015): 52–77.

56 *"moral potency":* Sean T. Hannah and Bruce J. Avolio, "Moral Potency: Building the Capacity for Character-Based Leadership," *Consulting Psychology Journal: Practice and Research* 62, no. 4 (2010): 291–310, esp. 291.

56 *sense of meaning and self-worth:* Michelle Dugas, Jocelyn J. Bélanger, Manuel Moyano, Birga M. Schumpe, Arie W. Kruglanski, Michele J. Gelfand, Kate Touchton-Leonard, and Noëmie Nociti, "The Quest for Significance Motivates Self-Sacrifice," *Motivation Science* 2, no. 2 (2016): 15–32.

57 *engineer quests they think are good:* Scholars call this "bad courage." Cynthia L. S. Pury, Charles B. Starkey, Renee E. Kulik, Karen L. Skjerning, and Emily A. Sullivan, "Is Courage Always a Virtue? Suicide, Killing, and Bad Courage," *Journal of Positive Psychology* 10, no. 5 (2015): 383–88.

57 *"narrative arc":* Paul J. Zak, "Why Inspiring Stories Make Us React: The Neuroscience of Narrative," 2.

57 *classic "hero's journey":* Paul J. Zak, "How Stories Change the Brain."

57 *complex ways:* The literary theorist Joseph Campbell famously saw such epic stories as a sequence of seventeen different phases, starting with a depiction of ordinary life, proceeding with a series of plot twists and adventures, and ending with the hero's triumphant return to normality. Joseph H. Campbell, *The Hero with a Thousand Faces* (Princeton, NJ: Bollingen Foundation, 1949).

58 *dream a reality:* In thinking of this three-part structure, I was inspired in part by the work of the psychologist Gabriele Oettingen. She proposes a visualization technique in which we contemplate a desired future, the obstacles that prevent us from achieving it, and a plan for overcoming the obstacles. Gabriele Oettingen, *Rethinking Positive Thinking: Inside the New Science of Motivation* (New York: Current, 2014).

58 *Novichok:* Richard Stone, "How German Military Scientists Likely Identified the Nerve Agent Used to Attack Alexei Navalny," *Science*, September 8, 2020, https://www.science.org/content/article/how-german-military-scientists-likely-identified-nerve-agent-used-attack-alexei-navalny.

58 *"but he's taking a risk":* RFE/RL, "One Year After His Arrest, Russia's Opposition Asks: Was Navalny's Return a Mistake?," Radio Free Europe/Radio Liberty, January 17, 2022, https://www.rferl.org/a/navalny-return-anniversary-mistake/31658323.html.

58 *remote Siberian penal colony:* Oleg Boldyrev and Laura Gozzi, "Alexei Navalny's

Life in 'Polar Wolf' Remote Arctic Penal Colony," *BBC News*, February 16, 2024, https://www.bbc.com/news/world-europe-68322113.

59   *"beautiful Russia of the future"*: Sarah Rainsford, "Alexei Navalny Was Often Asked: 'Do You Fear for Your Life?,'" *BBC News*, February 16, 2024, https://www.bbc.com/news/world-europe-68320268.

59   *"I want to live"*: Lucian Kim, "Banned From Election, Putin Foe Navalny Pursues Politics by Other Means," NPR, February 8, 2018, https://www.npr.org/sections/parallels/2018/02/08/584369719/banned-from-election-putin-foe-navalny-pursues-politics-by-other-means.

59   *"should be sacred concepts"*: "Read Excerpts From Navalny's Interview With The Times," *New York Times*, August 25, 2021, https://www.nytimes.com/2021/08/25/world/europe/navalny-interview-excerpts.html.

59   *"party of crooks and thieves"*: David M. Herszenhorn, "Alexey Navalny Never Wanted to Be a Dissident," *Politico*, October 31, 2023, https://www.politico.com/news/magazine/2023/10/31/alexey-navalny-russian-dissident-book-excerpt-00123792.

59   *"basis of Putin's regime"*: Lucian Kim, "Banned from Election, Putin Foe Navalny Pursues Politics by Other Means."

60   *sought to work within the system:* Herszenhorn, "Alexey Navalny Never Wanted to Be a Dissident."

60   *"smart voting" scheme:* Daria Litvinova and Kelvin Chan, "Apple, Google Remove Opposition App as Russian Voting Begins," AP News, September 17, 2021, https://apnews.com/article/europe-russia-elections-voting-vladimir-putin-a6e00789816f93b224a69074d3999568; Daria Litvinova, "EXPLAINER: How Navalny Election Tool Challenges the Kremlin," AP News, September 14, 2021, https://apnews.com/article/europe-russia-elections-media-voting-cec43110142e7ce362b2d4f9acd9b1f0.

60   *confront brutal truths:* Jim Collins, *Good to Great: Why Some Companies Make the Leap . . . and Others Don't* (New York: Harper Business, 2001).

61   *plan for overcoming the obstacles they identified:* Gabriele Oettingen, *Rethinking Positive Thinking*. Oettingen frames her mental contrasting exercises as a four-step process called WOOP. You first envision a wish and an outcome from the realization of that wish, then you envision the obstacles, and finally you form a plan via a quick "if-then" statement (i.e., If your obstacle materializes, then you'll take a designated action).

61   *"continue to fight that unscrupulous evil"*: "Alexei Navalny, In His Own Words," *Journal of Democracy*, https://www.journalofdemocracy.org/news-and-updates/alexei-navalny-in-his-own-words/.

61   *"new, free, rich country"*: Navalny, "In His Own Words."

61   *unimaginable acts of courage:* Neil MacFarquhar, "With Prison Certain and Death Likely, Why Did Navalny Return?," *New York Times*, February 17, 2024, https://www.nytimes.com/2024/02/17/world/europe/why-navalny-returned-to-russia.html.

62   *pursue grand ideals:* Ranjay Gulati, "Why Today's Startups Pursue Both Ideas and Ideals," *Harvard Business Review,* May 13, 2021, https://hbr.org/2021/05/why-todays-startups-pursue-both-ideas-and-ideals.

62   *rideshare company Lyft:* I base this account of Lyft on Ranjay Gulati and Jeff Huizinga, "Lyft 2023: Roads to Growth and Differentiation," Harvard Business School Case Study, February 26, 2024, draft.

63   *market changed in their favor:* Gulati and Huizinga, "Lyft 2023."

63   *"world's best transportation":* U.S. Securities and Exchange Commission, Form S-1 Registration Statement for Lyft, Inc., "Our Life's Work: A Letter from Our Co-Founders," 109–111, esp. 109, https://www.sec.gov/Archives/edgar/data/1759509/000119312519059849/d633517ds1.htm#toc633517_13.

63   *"core purpose that lit a fire under us":* Logan Green (cofounder of Lyft), interview with the author, November 1, 2023.

64   *"a source of resilience":* Gulati and Huizinga, "Lyft 2023."

64   *front and center and in big, bold print:* U.S. Securities and Exchange Commission, Form S-1 Registration Statement for Lyft, Inc., "Our Life's Work," 3.

64   *"Imagine for a minute":* U.S. Securities and Exchange Commission, Form S-1 Registration Statement for Lyft, Inc., "Our Life's Work," 109.

64   *"Mass car ownership":* U.S. Securities and Exchange Commission, Form S-1 Registration Statement for Lyft, Inc., "Our Life's Work," 109.

65   *"one of the most significant shifts to society":* U.S. Securities and Exchange Commission, Form S-1 Registration Statement for Lyft, Inc., "Our Life's Work," 111.

65   *"heroes of our own stories":* Christina Radish, "George R. R. Martin Interview: Game of Thrones," *Collider,* April 17, 2011, https://collider.com/george-r-r-martin-interview-game-of-thrones/.

66   *"the motivation for everything":* Patrick Awuah (founder of Ashesi University), interview with the author, September 19, 2019.

66   *"courage to imagine something new":* "Ashesi's President: Babson College Commencement 2013 Address," Ashesi University, May 18, 2013, accessed June 2, 2024, https://www.ashesi.edu.gh/about/ashesi-s-leadership/ashesi-s-president/presidents-selected-speeches/1674-babson-college-commencement-2013.html.

66   *Awuah has tried to build that courage:* Patrick Awuah, "Courage Is the Cornerstone of Progress," in *Practicing Development: Upending Assumptions for Positive Change,* ed. Susan H. Holcombe and Marion Howard (Boulder, CO: Kumarian Press, 2019), 95–108.

CHAPTER 4: CONNECTION

67   *"most remote corners of the planet":* Sarah Reid, "What It's Like to Cross Antarctica's Weddell Sea," *National Geographic,* February 5, 2024, https://www.nationalgeographic.com/travel/article/voyage-antarctica-weddell-sea.

68 "*half the party were insane*": Kieran Mulvaney, "The Stunning Survival Story of Ernest Shackleton and His *Endurance* Crew," *History*, last updated May 2, 2024, https://www.history.com/news/shackleton-endurance-survival.

68 *damaged beyond repair:* "The Remarkable Expedition of Shackleton and His Crew," *Arctic Kingdom*, https://resources.arctickingdom.com/the-remarkable-expedition-of-shackleton-and-his-crew.

68 "*marooned at least 1,500 miles*": Michael Smith, "Shackleton's Imperial Trans-Antarctic Expedition," *Shackleton*, August 9, 2021, https://shackleton.com/en-us/blogs/articles/shackleton-imperial-trans-antarctic-expedition.

69 "*from moment to moment*": Frank Hurley, *Argonauts of the South* (New York and London: G. P. Putnam's Sons, 1925), 242.

69 *torturous 1910 expedition:* Michael Smith, *Tom Crean: Unsung Hero of the Scott and Shackleton Antarctic Expeditions* (Seattle, WA: Mountaineers Books, 2001).

69 *later receiving a medal:* "The Scott Expedition," *West Coast Times*, July 31, 1913, 3, https://paperspast.natlib.govt.nz/newspapers/WCT19130731.2.18.6.

70 "*not afraid to speak his mind*": Smith, *Tom Crean*, 170.

70 *reassured Shackleton:* Hurley, *Argonauts of the South*, 242.

70 *Roald Amundsen: Log Entry for 8 February 1997*, Irish South Arís Shackleton's Boat Journey Expedition, accessed April 1, 2025, https://www.pelagic.co.uk/logbooks/log97ind/970208.html.

70 *basic psychological need:* Joseph H. Campbell, *The Hero with a Thousand Faces* (Princeton, NJ: Bollingen Foundation, 1949), 30.

70 *motivate us with their force of personality:* Scott T. Allison and George R. Goethals, "Hero Worship: The Elevation of the Human Spirit," *Journal for the Theory of Social Behaviour* 46, no. 2 (2016): 187–210. For more on the functions that hero-worship serves, also see Elaine L. Kinsella, Timothy D. Ritchie, and Eric R. Igou, "Perspectives on the Social and Psychological Functions of Heroes," *Frontiers in Psychology* 6 (2015): 130; Aulona Ulqinaku, Gülen Sarial-Abi, and Elaine L. Kinsella, "Benefits of Heroes to Coping with Mortality Threats by Providing Perceptions of Personal Power and Reducing Unhealthy Compensatory Consumption," *Psychology & Marketing* 37, no. 10 (2020): 1433–45.

70 *knew he could count on Crean:* Alfred Lansing, *Endurance: Shackleton's Incredible Voyage* (New York: Basic Books, 2014); Smith, *Tom Crean*, 249.

70 "*first class seaman and navigator*": John Thomson, *Frank Worsley: Shackleton's Fearless Captain* (Nelson, New Zealand: Craig Potton Publishing, 2014), 42.

71 *something of a kindred spirit:* Thomson, *Frank Worsley*, 43–44.

71 "*happy knack of saying nothing*": "Meet Shackleton's Team," *NOVA*, PBS, https://www.pbs.org/wgbh/nova/shackleton/1914/team.html.

71 "*utterly, utterly reliable*": "Tending Sir Ernest's Legacy: An Interview with Alexandra Shackleton, Part 2," *NOVA*, PBS, https://www.pbs.org/wgbh/nova/shackleton/1914/alexandra2.html.

71   *"right-hand man":* Jo Woolf, "Frank Wild: The Call of the 'White Unknown,'" *Royal Scottish Geographical Society*, April 13, 2023, https://www.rsgs.org/blog/frank-wild-the-call-of-the-white-unknown.

71   *talked it through with Wild:* Roland Huntford, *Shackleton* (New York: Atheneum, 1986), 473.

71   *prevailed on Shackleton to bring a third boat:* Smith, *Tom Crean*, 195.

71   *navigator Hubert Hudson:* Smith, *Tom Crean*, 200–201.

72   *seek it out the least:* Edward Bishop Smith et al., "Status Differences in the Cognitive Activation of Social Networks," *Organization Science* 23, no. 1 (2012): 67–82.

72   *not adept at handling adversity alone:* Scholars of courage haven't focused very much on the social forces that might nurture it—a consequence, perhaps, of the enduring myth of the Great Hero. But a few broad academic areas *have* considered the benefits of having social support: the health sciences, as well as fields like sociology, psychology, medicine, and criminology. Here we find compelling evidence of the power of social support. Matt C. Howard and Joshua E. Cogswell, "The Left Side of Courage: Three Exploratory Studies on the Antecedents of Social Courage," *Journal of Positive Psychology* 14, no. 3 (2019): 324–40.

72   *"adequate social relationships":* Julianne Holt-Lunstad, Timothy B. Smith, and J. Bradley Layton, "Social Relationships and Mortality Risk: A Meta-analytic Review," *PLOS Medicine* 7, no. 7 (2010): e1000316. A wealth of research also shows that social support can help people reduce stress and burnout, overcome illnesses, and stay out of trouble with the law, among many other positive outcomes. For research on the health benefits of various forms of social support, see, for example, Kimberly S. Bowen, Bert N. Uchino, Wendy Birmingham, McKenzie Carlisle, Timothy W. Smith, and Kathleen C. Light, "The Stress-Buffering Effects of Functional Social Support on Ambulatory Blood Pressure," *Health Psychology* 33, no. 11 (2014): 1440–43; Chris Hartley and Pete Coffee, "Perceived and Received Dimensional Support: Effects on Dimensions of Burnout," *Frontiers in Psychology* 10 (2019): 1724; Francis T. Cullen, "Social Support as an Organizing Concept for Criminology: Presidential Address to the Academy of Criminal Justice Sciences," *Justice Quarterly* 11, no. 4 (1994): 527–59; Jane Leserman, Eric D. Jackson, John M. Petitto, Robert N. Golden, Susan G. Silva, Diana O. Perkins, Jianwen Cai, James D. Folds, and Dwight L. Evans, "Progression to AIDS: The Effects of Stress, Depressive Symptoms, and Social Support," *Psychosomatic Medicine* 61, no. 3 (1999): 397–406.

73   *act with courage:* I have adapted the first four elements of support from the work of James House. In his 1981 book *Work Stress and Social Support*, he described four specific ways that others can help us cope when times get tough, speaking of instrumental, emotional, informational, and appraisal support. James S. House, *Work Stress and Social Support* (Reading, MA: Addison-Wesley Publishing Company, 1981). For a brief summary of these four forms, please see Catherine P. Hinson Langford, Juanita Bowsher, Joseph P. Maloney, and Patricia P. Lillis,

"Social Support: A Conceptual Analysis," *Journal of Advanced Nursing* 25, no. 1 (1997): 95–100.

73 *how we're doing:* Research suggests that these four kinds of behaviors might help us to ease the stress we feel in tough situations and also improve our well-being generally, thus increasing our resilience. Scholars have since elaborated on these four distinct types of helping behaviors, studying how they helped people struggling with domestic violence, incarceration, and medical emergencies. Miguel Muñoz-Laboy, Nicolette Severson, Ashley Perry, and Vincent Guilamo-Ramos, "Differential Impact of Types of Social Support in the Mental Health of Formerly Incarcerated Latino Men," *American Journal of Men's Health* 8, no. 3 (2014): 226–39; Judy King, Brenda O'Neill, Pam Ramsay, Mark A. Linden, A. Darweish Medniuk, Joanne Outtrim, and Bronagh Blackwood, "Identifying Patients' Support Needs Following Critical Illness: A Scoping Review of the Qualitative Literature," *Critical Care* 23 (2019): 187; Pedro Henrique Ribeiro Santiago, Lisa Gaye Smithers, Rachel Roberts, and Lisa Jamieson, "Psychometric Properties of the Social Support Scale (SSS) in Two Aboriginal Samples," *PLOS ONE* 18, no. 1 (2023): e0279954.

73 *perhaps most important form of support:* Yik Kiu Leung, Jinia Mukerjee, and Roy Thurik, "The Role of Family Support in Work-Family Balance and Subjective Well-Being of SME Owners," *Journal of Small Business Management* 58, no. 1 (2020): 130–63.

74 *validation of our feelings:* Cinthia Benitez, Kristen P. Howard, and Jennifer S. Cheavens, "The Effect of Validation and Invalidation on Positive and Negative Affective Experiences," *Journal of Positive Psychology* 17, no. 1 (2022): 46–58.

74 *"chose to ignore them and move forward":* Interviews with Meera Devi conducted by the author's research team, September 13, 2022, and February 27, 2023.

75 *As a lower-caste woman:* Rina Chandran, "Report Like a Dalit Girl: One Indian Publication Shows How," Reuters, January 24, 2017, accessed January 6, 2025, https://web.archive.org/web/20171219161934/https://in.reuters.com/article/india-women-dalit/report-like-a-dalit-girl-one-indian-publication-shows-how-idINKBN1581E4. See also *Hidden Apartheid: Caste Discrimination Against India's "Untouchables,"* Human Rights Watch, vol. 19, no. 3 (Human Rights Watch, 2007).

75 *"not just a job for me":* Benu Joshi Routh, "Kavita Devi and Meera Devi: Giving Voice to Marginalised with Khabar Lahariya," *Forbes India*, December 12, 2022, https://www.forbesindia.com/article/leadership/kavita-devi-and-meera-devi-giving-voice-to-marginalised-with-khabar-lahariya/81839/1.

75 *"either ridiculed or chose not to speak to us":* Interviews with Meera Devi conducted by the author's research team, September 13, 2022, and February 27, 2023.

75 *defaming the village:* Interviews with Meera Devi conducted by the author's research team, September 13, 2022, and February 27, 2023.

75 *Government press liaisons:* Interviews with Meera Devi conducted by the author's research team, September 13, 2022, and February 27, 2023.

NOTES

75   *"consider my colleagues as family":* Interviews with Meera Devi conducted by the author's research team, September 13, 2022, and February 27, 2023.

76   *"draw strength and courage from them":* Interview conducted by HBS research staff members Kanika Jain and Kairavi Dey on October 11, 2022.

76   *"My story is not unique":* Interviews with Meera Devi conducted by the author's research team, September 13, 2022, and February 27, 2023.

77   *experimental, solar-powered airplane:* Guinness World Records, "First Circumnavigation in a Solar-Powered Aeroplane (FAI-Approved)," https://www.guinnessworldrecords.com/world-records/459403-first-circumnavigation-in-a-solar-powered-aeroplane-fai-approved.

77   *The two became media celebrities:* Alan Taylor, "Flying Around the World in a Solar Powered Plane," *The Atlantic*, July 26, 2016, accessed July 1, 2024, https://www.theatlantic.com/photo/2016/07/flying-around-the-world-in-a-solar-powered-plane/493085/; Neil Shea, "Solar Plane Takes Off on Round-the-World Quest," *National Geographic*, March 8, 2015, https://www.nationalgeographic.com/adventure/article/150308-solar-impulse-flight-pilot-circumnavigate-world-piccard-swiss; Sabrina Toppa, "The First Solar-Powered Round-the-World Flight Has Begun," *Time*, March 9, 2015, https://time.com/3736858/fueless-flight-bertrand-piccard-solar-impulse-2-andre-borschberg/.

77   *relied on a team of dozens of specialists:* Celina Lafuente de Lavotha, "Solar Impulse Pioneer Pilots & Their Team Celebrated with Prince Albert the Completion of First Round-the-World Flight with Zero Fuel," *Monaco Reporter*, August 8, 2016, https://monacoreporter.com/2016/08/08/solar-impulse-pioneer-pilots-their-team-celebrated-with-prince-albert-the-completion-of-first-round-the-world-flight/.

77   *an engineering marvel:* Solar Impulse Foundation, "Pilots & Team," https://aroundtheworld.solarimpulse.com/pilots-team.

77   *"most energy efficient airplane ever built":* Solar Impulse Foundation, "Pilots & Team."

79   *save the company from almost certain bankruptcy:* "Xerox Back from the Brink," *Forbes*, November 6, 2002, https://www.forbes.com/2002/11/06/1106soapbox.html.

79   *"intense on-the-job learning":* Lisa Vollmer, "Anne Mulcahy: The Keys to Turnaround at Xerox," Stanford Graduate School of Business, December 1, 2004, https://www.gsb.stanford.edu/insights/anne-mulcahy-keys-turnaround-xerox.

79   *"prepared to answer all the ugly, tough questions":* Bill George and Andrew N. McLean, "Anne Mulcahy: Leading Xerox through the Perfect Storm (A)," Harvard Business School Case Study 9-405-050, January 2005, revised July 22, 2010, 8.

79   *stock price rose 75 percent:* Knowledge at Wharton Staff, "The Cow in the Ditch: How Anne Mulcahy Rescued Xerox," *Knowledge at Wharton*, November 16, 2005, https://knowledge.wharton.upenn.edu/article/the-cow-in-the-ditch-how-anne-mulcahy-rescued-xerox/.

80 *talk through with others the contradictory signals:* Audrey J. Murrell, Stacy Blake-Beard, and David M. Porter Jr., "The Importance of Peer Mentoring, Identity Work and Holding Environments: A Study of African American Leadership Development," *International Journal of Environmental Research and Public Health* 18, no. 9 (2021): 4920.

80 *improving our sense of self-worth:* Noelle M. Hurd, Jamie Albright, Audrey Wittrup, Andrea Negrete, and Janelle Billingsley, "Appraisal Support from Natural Mentors, Self-Worth, and Psychological Distress: Examining the Experiences of Underrepresented Students Transitioning Through College," *Journal of Youth and Adolescence* 47, no. 5 (2018): 1100–12.

80 *information that pertains to us:* House, *Work Stress and Social Support*, 25–26.

80 *study of youth swimmers:* J. Douglas Coatsworth and David E. Conroy, "The Effects of Autonomy-supportive Coaching, Need Satisfaction and Self-Perceptions on Initiative and Identity in Youth Swimmers," *Developmental Psychology* 45, no. 2 (2009): 320–28.

81 *bring entourages with them:* John Branch, "Pets Are the Portable Part of a Tennis Player's Entourage," *New York Times*, August 30, 2009, https://www.nytimes.com/2009/08/31/sports/tennis/31tennisdogs.html.

81 *"analyse everything Novak does":* Charlie Eccleshare, "The Rise and Rise of the Tennis Entourage: Revealing the Secrets behind a Top Player's Team," *The Telegraph*, June 28, 2019, https://www.telegraph.co.uk/tennis/2019/06/28/rise-rise-tennis-entourage-revealing-secrets-behind-top-players/.

81 *real-time evaluations:* Christopher Clarey, "The Quiet Coaching Revolution in Tennis That Can Feel Like 'Cheating,'" *New York Times*, January 28, 2023, https://www.nytimes.com/2023/01/28/sports/tennis/coaching-analytics-australian-open.html.

82 *"social identity":* For a general theory of the social formation of identity, see Sheldon Stryker, "Identity Salience and Role Performance: The Relevance of Symbolic Interaction Theory for Family Research," *Journal of Marriage and Family* 30, no. 4 (1968): 558–64. For social identity theory, see Henri Tajfel, ed., *Differentiation Between Social Groups: Studies in the Social Psychology of Intergroup Relations* (London: Academic Press, 1978).

82 *early development of children:* John Bowlby, *Attachment and Loss: Vol. 1. Attachment*, 2nd ed. (New York: Basic Books, 1982).

82 *take root and grow as others validate:* Kaitlyn Atkins, Bryan M. Dougan, Michelle S. Dromgold-Sermen, Hannah Potter, Viji Sathy, and A. T. Panter, "'Looking at Myself in the Future': How Mentoring Shapes Scientific Identity for STEM Students from Underrepresented Groups," *International Journal of STEM Education* 7 (2020): 42.

83 *situations impact:* Melissa M. Koerner, "Courage as Identity Work: Accounts of Workplace Courage," *Academy of Management Journal* 57, no. 1 (2014): 79.

83 *sense of self-worth or self-esteem:* Anna Riley and Peter J. Burke, "Identities and

Self-Verification in the Small Group," *Social Psychology Quarterly* 58, no. 2 (1995): 61–73.

83 *competent, adventurous, or important:* Jane E. Dutton, "Pathways for Positive Identity Construction at Work: Four Types of Positive Identity and the Building of Social Resources," *Academy of Management Review* 35, no. 2 (2010): 265–93.

83 *One-on-one coaching and mentoring relationships:* Frank L. Smoll, Ronald E. Smith, Nancy P. Barnett, and John J. Everett, "Enhancement of Children's Self-Esteem Through Social Support Training for Youth Sport Coaches," *Journal of Applied Psychology* 78, no. 4 (1993): 602–610; Kathy E. Kram and Lynn A. Isabella, "Mentoring Alternatives: The Role of Peer Relationships in Career Development," *Academy of Management Journal* 28, no. 1 (1985): 110–32.

83 *in the world:* Murrell et al., "The Importance of Peer Mentoring, Identity Work and Holding Environments."

84 *our potential future:* Atkins et al., "'Looking at Myself in the Future.'"

85 *blacklist whistleblowers in the industry:* Whitelaw Reid, "Q&A: Professor's Long-Held Contentions Confirmed by Facebook Whistleblower," *UVA Today*, October 5, 2021, https://news.virginia.edu/content/qa-facebook-whistleblower-confirms-professors-long-held-contentions.

85 *the problem of misinformation on Facebook:* Frances Haugen, *The Power of One* (New York: Little, Brown and Company, 2023), 150–52.

85 *"failed to warn the public":* Haugen, *The Power of One*, 3.

86 *"fight the institutional decay":* Haugen, *The Power of One*, 184.

86 *"the ultimate amenity":* Billy Perrigo, "Inside Frances Haugen's Decision to Take on Facebook," *Time*, November 22, 2021, https://time.com/6121931/frances-haugen-facebook-whistleblower-profile/.

86 *"gave me a cadence":* Frances Haugen, interview with the author, June 4, 2024.

86 *intangible knowledge and expertise:* Frances Haugen, interview with the author, June 4, 2024.

87 *"that destroys people":* Frances Haugen, interview with the author, June 4, 2024.

CHAPTER 5: COMPREHENSION

89 *"faculty-lounge atmosphere":* J. Oliver Conry, "Blood and Terror: Witnesses Tell of Attack on Salman Rushdie at Literary Festival," *The Guardian*, August 12, 2022, https://www.theguardian.com/books/2022/aug/12/rushdie-attack-book-festival-scene-chautauqua-ny.

89 "Here you are": Salman Rushdie, *Knife: Meditations After an Attempted Murder* (New York: Random House, 2024), 6.

89 *"stabbing wildly":* Rushdie, *Knife*, 13.

90 *"keeping writers safe from harm":* Rushdie, *Knife*, 3.

90 *wrestle with the attacker:* See the account in Seth Abramovitch, "Salman Rushdie Attack Witnesses: 'There Were Many Screams of Terror,'" *Hollywood Reporter*, August 13, 2022, https://www.hollywoodreporter.com/news/general-news/salman-rushdie-attack-witness-screams-of-terror-1235198594/. See also Rushdie, *Knife*.

90 *Shakespearean sonnet:* Rushdie, *Knife*, 14–15.

90 *"pure heroism":* Rushdie, *Knife*, 14.

90 *"empathetic community":* Henry Reese, "I Was Onstage with Salman Rushdie That Day, and What I Saw Was Remarkable," *New York Times*, September 2, 2022, https://www.nytimes.com/2022/09/02/opinion/salman-rushdie-free-speech-writers.html.

90 *fight back or take flight:* W. B. Cannon, *The Wisdom of the Body* (New York: W. W. Norton, 1932); B. Cannon, "Walter Bradford Cannon: Reflections on the Man and His Contributions," *International Journal of Stress Management* 1 (1994): 145–58; R. McCarty, "The Fight-or-Flight Response: A Cornerstone of Stress Research," in *Stress: Concepts, Cognition, Emotion, and Behavior,* ed. George Fink, volume 1 (London: Academic Press, 2016): 33–37.

90 *people freeze up:* Karin Roelofs, Muriel A. Hagenaars, and John Stins, "Facing Freeze: Social Threat Induces Bodily Freeze in Humans," *Psychological Science* 21, no. 11 (2010): 1575–81.

91 *"like a rabbit-in-the-headlights":* Rushdie, *Knife*, 6.

91 *"and I fall":* Rushdie, *Knife*, 3–4.

91 *"Reality dissolves":* Rushdie, *Knife*, 11–12.

92 *minds might freeze:* Norman B. Schmidt, J. Anthony Richey, Michael J. Zvolensky, and Jon K. Maner, "Exploring Human Freeze Responses to a Threat Stressor," *Journal of Behavior Therapy and Experimental Psychiatry* 39, no. 3 (2008): 292–304.

93 *"temporary paralysis":* Anthony F. C. Wallace, "Mazeway Disintegration: The Individual's Perception of Socio-Cultural Disorganization," *Human Organization* 16, no. 2 (1957): 23–27.

93 *"status quo bias":* Daniel Kahneman, Jack L. Knetsch, and Richard H. Thaler, "The Endowment Effect, Loss Aversion, and Status Quo Bias," *Journal of Economic Perspectives* 5, no. 1 (1991): 192–206.

93 *When hurricanes strike:* Many people die each year—hundreds in the case of some storms—because they ignore evacuation orders by state and local governments. See for example Jon Schuppe, Elizabeth Chuck, Melissa Chan, Lewis Kamb, and Nigel Chiwaya, "Ian Was One of the Most Lethal Hurricanes in Decades. Many of the Deaths Were Preventable," *NBC News*, November 22, 2022, https://www.nbcnews.com/news/us-news/hurricane-ian-florida-death-toll-rcna54069.

93 *status quo:* William Samuelson and Richard Zeckhauser, "Status Quo Bias in Decision-Making," *Journal of Risk and Uncertainty* 1 (1988): 7–59.

94 *bias tires:* Michelin, "Radial or Bias Tires?" https://www.michelinman.com/motorcycle/tips-and-advice/how-to-choose-the-right-motorcycle-tire/radial-or-bias.

94 *"active inertia":* Donald N. Sull, "The Dynamics of Standing Still: Firestone Tire & Rubber and the Radial Revolution," *Business History Review* 73, no. 3 (1999): 430–64, esp. 459–60.

94 *8.7 million tires:* Sull, "The Dynamics of Standing Still," 443.

95 *ultimately sold off:* Jonathan P. Hicks, "Bridgestone in Deal for Firestone," *New York Times*, March 18, 1988, https://www.nytimes.com/1988/03/18/business/bridgestone-in-deal-for-firestone.html.

96 *forced authorities to evacuate:* Carol Smith, "Radiation from Fukushima Disaster Still Affects 32 Million Japanese," *Our World*, March 12, 2015, https://ourworld.unu.edu/en/radiation-from-fukushima-disaster-still-affects-32-million-japanese.

96 *nuclear disaster:* The Editors of *Encyclopaedia Britannica*, "Fukushima Accident," last updated December 25, 2024, https://www.britannica.com/event/Fukushima-accident; World Nuclear Association, "Fukushima Daiichi Accident," updated April 29, 2024, accessed January 7, 2025, https://world-nuclear.org/information-library/safety-and-security/safety-of-plants/fukushima-daiichi-accident#radioactive-releases-to-air.

96 *my research into the response to this extraordinary crisis:* I base my account of the Fukushima disaster and my analysis of its handling by workers and leaders on Ranjay Gulati, Charles Castro, and Charlotte Krontiris, "How the *Other* Fukushima Plant Survived," *Harvard Business Review*, July–August 2014. I also draw on an earlier, unpublished draft of this article as well as a subsequent interview I performed with site superintendent Naohiro Masuda on February 21, 2019.

96 *workers had to enter:* Naohiro Masuda (site superintendent at the Fukushima Daini plant), interview with the author, April 17, 2019.

99 *process called "sensemaking":* Karl E. Weick, *Sensemaking in Organizations* (Thousand Oaks, CA: Sage Publications, 1995).

99 *three basic steps:* Since Weick presented his original concept, other scholars have identified various forms of sensemaking and elaborated on nuances in the sensemaking process, although there is no consensus on a precise description of the sensemaking process. On the evolution of sensemaking theory since Weick, see Sally Maitlis and Marlys Christianson, "Sensemaking in Organizations: Taking Stock and Moving Forward," *Academy of Management Annals* 8, no. 1 (2014): 57–125. In the absence of a consensus definition of sensemaking, Maitlis and Christianson draw on the literature to distill four common features of sensemaking: its ongoing nature; the importance of cues that trigger and shape sensemaking; its social character; and the fact that it unfolds through action. Their resulting definition of sensemaking is as follows: "A process,

prompted by violated expectations, that involves attending to and bracketing cues in the environment, creating intersubjective meaning through cycles of interpretation and action, and thereby enacting a more ordered environment from which further cues can be drawn" (67). See also Karl E. Weick, Kathleen M. Sutcliffe, and David Obstfeld, "Organizing and the Process of Sensemaking," *Organization Science* 16, no. 4 (2005): 409–421.

100 *9.0 on the Richter scale:* The Editors of *Encyclopaedia Britannica*, "Japan Earthquake and Tsunami of 2011," last updated December 16, 2024, https://www.britannica.com/event/Japan-earthquake-and-tsunami-of-2011.

100 *"had never done that before":* This quote appeared in an earlier, unpublished draft of Gulati et al., "the *Other* Fukushima Plant." It reflects an interview with Masuda conducted by my coauthor Charles Castro on April 11, 2019.

100 *protocols to shut down:* Naohiro Masuda interview with Yoichi Funabashi, translation via Akiko Kanno at JRC. This appeared in an earlier, unpublished draft of Gulati et al., "the *Other* Fukushima Plant."

101 *to those emotions:* Sally Maitlis, Timothy J. Vogus, and Thomas B. Lawrence, "Sensemaking and Emotion in Organizations," *Organizational Psychology Review* 3, no. 3 (2013): 222–24.

101 *recognize events as triggers:* Maitlis and Christianson, "Sensemaking in Organizations."

102 *"seeds from which people develop":* Weick, *Sensemaking in Organizations*, 50.

103 *"continued redrafting of an emerging story":* Weick et al., "Organizing and the Process of Sensemaking," 415.

104 *how precisely you notice small cues:* Weick, *Sensemaking in Organizations*, 18–24.

104 *what to do:* Gary Klein, "An Introduction to the World of Naturalistic Decision Making," transcribed from a talk for the virtual NDMA Open House on May 9, 2022, Naturalistic Decision Making Association, January 24, 2023, https://naturalisticdecisionmaking.org/2023/01/24/test-introduction-to-the-world-of-naturalistic-decision-making/. See also Gary Klein, Roberta Calderwood, and Anne Clinton-Cirocco, "Rapid Decision Making on the Fire Ground: The Original Study Plus a Postscript," *Journal of Cognitive Engineering and Decision Making* 4, no. 3 (2010): 186–209.

105 *"knew almost everything about the inside of the plant":* This quote appeared in an earlier, unpublished draft of Gulate et al., "the *Other* Fukushima Plant." It reflects an interview with Masuda conducted by my coauthor Charles Castro on April 11, 2019.

105 *can't act decisively:* On various forms of leader-directed sensemaking, see Sally Maitlis, "The Social Processes of Organizational Sensemaking," *Academy of Management Journal* 48, no. 1 (2005): 21–49.

106 *shifted midstream:* This quote appeared in an earlier, unpublished draft of Gulati, et. al, "the *Other* Fukushima Plant." It reflects an interview with Masuda conducted by my coauthor Charles Castro on April 11, 2019.

107 *contemplating the evacuation of Tokyo:* Amy Goodman, "Ex-Japanese PM on How Fukushima Meltdown Was Worse Than Chernobyl & Why He Now Opposes Nuclear Power," interview with Naoto Kan, *Democracy Now!*, March 11, 2014, https://www.democracynow.org/2014/3/11/ex_japanese_pm_on_how_fukushima.

107 *"engineering hero" for his bold action:* Mariana Barillas, "Engineer Who Saved Nuclear Plant From Meltdown Shares Leadership Lessons," Catholic University of America, June 7, 2023, https://www.catholic.edu/all-stories/engineer-who-saved-nuclear-plant-meltdown-shares-leadership-lessons; see also *Fukushima Daiichi Reflection*, Nuclear Engineering Department, University of California, Berkeley, https://nuc.berkeley.edu/fukushimareflection/.

109 *"beginner's mind":* Leo Babauta, "Approaching Life with Beginner's Mind," *Zen Habits*, https://zenhabits.net/beginner/.

CHAPTER 6: CALM

111 *massive bombing campaign:* Andrian Prokip, "Ukraine Quarterly Digest: October–December 2022," Wilson Center, January 18, 2023, https://www.wilsoncenter.org/blog-post/ukraine-quarterly-digest-october-december-2022.

111 *attacked Ukrainian population centers:* "Ukraine: Russian Attacks on Energy Grid Threaten Civilians," Human Rights Watch, December 6, 2022, https://www.hrw.org/news/2022/12/06/ukraine-russian-attacks-energy-grid-threaten-civilians.

111 *"life-threatening" amid snow:* David L. Stern, Emily Rauhala, and Michael Birnbaum, "Ukrainian Energy Systems on Brink of Collapse After Weeks of Russian Bombing," *Washington Post*, updated November 23, 2022, https://www.washingtonpost.com/world/2022/11/23/ukraine-infrastructure-damage-electricity-water-russia/.

111 *tormented by the wail of air raid sirens:* Mansur Mirovalev, "Ukraine's Harsh Winter a Memory but New Russian Tactics Sow Destruction," *Al Jazeera*, January 18, 2024, https://www.aljazeera.com/news/2024/1/18/ukraine-winter-shelling; Jen Kirby, "Can Ukraine's Infrastructure Survive the Winter?," *Vox*, November 18, 2022, https://www.vox.com/world/2022/11/18/23460933/ukraine-infrastructure-strikes-russia-blackouts-war; Mansur Mirovalev, "How Kyiv Copes with Blackouts," *Al Jazeera*, November 4, 2022, https://www.aljazeera.com/news/2022/11/4/how-kyiv-copes-with-blackouts.

111 *"cynical strategy" on the Russians' part:* Sylvie Corbet, Inna Varenytsia, and John Leicester, "Donors Meet in Paris to Get Ukraine Through Winter, Bombing," *Denver Post*, December 13, 2022, https://www.denverpost.com/2022/12/13/ukraine-winter-russia-war-bombing/.

112 *"never succeed in leaving us without the desire":* Volodymyr Zelenskyy, "No Terrorist Attack Will Stop Our Defenders—Address of the President of Ukraine," Presidential Office of Ukraine, October 22, 2022, https://www

.president.gov.ua/en/news/zhoden-udar-teroristiv-ne-zupinit-nashih-zahisnikiv-zvernenn-78657.

112 *"even if there is no electricity":* Volodymyr Zelenskyy, "We Stand, We Fight and We Will Win. Because We Are United. Ukraine, America and the Entire Free World—Address by Volodymyr Zelenskyy in a Joint Meeting of the US Congress," Presidential Office of Ukraine, December 22, 2022, https://www.president.gov.ua/en/news/mi-stoyimo-boremos-i-vigrayemo-bo-mi-razom-ukrayina-amerika-80017.

112 *"darkness will not prevent us":* Volodymyr Zelenskyy, "The Darkness Will Not Prevent Us from Leading the Occupiers to Their New Defeats—Address by the President of Ukraine," Presidential Office of Ukraine, December 25, 2022, https://www.president.gov.ua/en/news/temryava-ne-zavazhatime-nam-privoditi-okupantiv-do-novih-yih-80077.

112 *"NATO hasn't arrived yet":* Volodymyr Zelenskyy, "The Program of the Famous TV Host David Letterman with the Participation of Volodymyr Zelenskyy Was Published on the Website of the Office of the President and on YouTube," Presidential Office of Ukraine, December 27, 2022, https://www.president.gov.ua/en/news/na-sajti-ofisu-prezidenta-i-v-youtube-oprilyudneno-programu-80085; Anton Gerashchenko, Twitter post, December 14, 2022, 1:22 PM, https://twitter.com/ianbremmer/status/1603093091245858816?lang=en.

113 *well-known comedian:* Since his election he had continued to weave humor into his leadership. In 2020, for instance, joking about the role a phone call between him and President Donald Trump had played the previous year in Trump's impeachment proceedings, he noted that he'd dreamed during his previous career of winning an Oscar and gaining popularity in the United States. "I am now president, and very popular in the USA. . . . That's not the kind of popularity I'd been seeking." "'I Wanted to Be Popular in U.S.': Zelensky Jokes About Trump Phone Call," *UNIAN*, February 15, 2020, https://www.unian.info/politics/10875773-i-wanted-to-be-popular-in-u-s-zelensky-jokes-about-trump-phone-call.html. In March 2022, speaking of the prospect of negotiations with Russian president Vladimir Putin, he indicated that he was ready—"but not at 30 meters." This was a lighthearted reference to the ridiculously long table that Putin used to keep foreign dignitaries with whom he was meeting at an extreme distance. Jessica Riga, "Volodymyr Zelenskyy Jokes He's Open for Talks with Vladimir Putin About Ukraine-Russia Conflict, but Not at That '30-Metre' Table," *ABC News*, March 3, 2022, https://www.abc.net.au/news/2022-03-04/ukraines-zelenskyy-challenges-russias-putin-sit-down-for-talks/100881038.

113 *comedy actually became a feature of everyday life:* "Ukrainian Stand-Up Comedy Has Seen a Renaissance During the War," *The Economist*, January 6, 2024, https://www.economist.com/europe/2024/01/06/ukrainian-stand-up-comedy-has-seen-a-renaissance-during-the-war; Kim Barker, "Jokes and Offbeat Auctions for the Troops: Standup Comedy Sweeps Ukraine," *New York Times*, October 13, 2024, https://www.nytimes.com/2024/10/13/world/europe/stand-up-comedy-ukraine.html.

113   *city's funniest jokes:* Sasha Kurovska, "How Humor Helps Ukrainians Cope with the War," *Le Monde*, January 2, 2024, https://www.lemonde.fr/en/international/article/2024/01/02/how-humor-helps-ukrainians-cope-with-the-war_6394622_4.html.

113   *circulated funny memes:* "Ukrainian Jokes: War Memes That Became Hits," *Visit Ukraine*, https://visitukraine.today/blog/1855/ukrainian-jokes-war-memes-that-became-hits; Sofiya Maksymiv, "How Humor Helps Ukrainians Withstand War Atrocities," *UkraineWorld*, July 21, 2022, https://ukraineworld.org/en/articles/analysis/how-humor-helps-ukrainians.

113   *suggesting that errant cigarettes:* Judith Matloff, "Ukraine's Latest Weapon in the War: Jokes," *Al Jazeera*, September 6, 2022, https://www.aljazeera.com/features/2022/9/6/ukraine-latest-weapon-in-the-war-jokes.

113   *soldiers developed a black humor:* Tim Mak, "The Dark Art of Comedy in Ukraine," *The Atlantic*, January 29, 2024, https://www.theatlantic.com/international/archive/2024/01/dark-art-comedy-ukraine/677262/.

114   *"when the comedy really thrives":* Yaroslav Druziuk, "'Maybe I Am Dead': Ukrainian Comedian Serhii Lipko Looks at Stand-Up Differently Now—After a Year and a Half as a Soldier in an Active War Zone," *Vulture*, June 21, 2023, https://www.vulture.com/article/serhii-lipko-ukraine-war-comedy-interview.html.

114   *stabilize themselves emotionally:* A description of one documentary about wartime humor in Ukraine described it as "a balm to injured spirits." *Comedy of War: Laughter in Ukraine*, Tribeca Film Festival, 2023, https://tribecafilm.com/films/comedy-of-war-laughter-in-ukraine-2023.

114   *"an anesthetic for the soul":* Tim Mak and Oksana Ostapchuk, "We Could All Use a Laugh," *Counteroffensive*, February 11, 2024, https://www.counteroffensive.news/p/we-could-all-use-a-laugh.

114   *well-being is compromised:* James J. Gross and Oliver P. John, "Individual Differences in Two Emotional Regulation Processes: Implications for Affect, Relationships, and Well-being," *Journal of Personality and Social Psychology* 85, no. 2 (2003): 348–62. For a critique of positive psychology, please see Barbara S. Held, "The Negative Side of Positive Psychology," *Journal of Humanistic Psychology* 44, no. 1 (2004): 9–46.

115   *"heal what we're all feeling":* Lola Fadulu and Emily Schmall, "Can Climate Cafes Help Ease the Anxiety of Planetary Crisis?," *New York Times*, March 20, 2024, https://www.nytimes.com/2024/03/20/climate/climate-change-anxiety-fear.html.

116   *three mental moves you can make:* I've omitted two of the five emotional regulation strategies Gross references in his model. One of them, avoiding situations that trigger an emotional response, doesn't help us build courage—it's actually what we often do when we're *not* behaving boldly. A second strategy he discusses—suppressing our emotions—doesn't shape the experience of an emotion itself but instead occurs *after* the emotion is generated. Further,

as we've seen, Gross finds suppression to be sub-optimal. See James J. Gross, "The Emerging Field of Emotion Regulation: An Integrative Review," *Review of General Psychology* 2, no. 3 (1998): 271–99. For work that suggests how emotional regulation can entail creating a sense of equilibrium, please see Marco Del Giudice, "The Motivational Architecture of Emotions," in *The Oxford Handbook of Evolution and the Emotions*, ed. Laith Al-Shawaf and Todd K. Shackelford (Oxford: Oxford University Press, 2024), 99–132. See also Cindy S. Bergeman, Jessica Blaxton, and Raquael Joiner, "Dynamic Systems, Contextual Influences, and Multiple Timescales: Emotion Regulation as a Resilience Resource," *The Gerontologist* 61, no. 3 (2021): 304–311.

116 *rears its head:* As scholars have argued, a basic desire of ours is precisely to restore a measure of control and orderliness when we feel those are lacking. Justin P. Friesen et al., "Seeking Structure in Social Organization: Compensatory Control and the Psychological Advantages of Hierarchy," *Journal of Personality and Social Psychology* 106, no. 4 (2014): 590–609; Nicholas M. Hobson et al., "The Psychology of Rituals: An Integrative Review and Process-Based Framework," *Personality and Social Psychology Review* 22, no. 3 (2018): 260–84.

117 *fear she feels before performances:* Carmine Gallo, "How Adele Is Managing Stage Fright," *Forbes*, December 5, 2015, https://www.forbes.com/sites/carminegallo/2015/12/05/how-adele-is-managing-stage-fright.

117 *kissing a photograph:* Giorgina Ramazzotti, "Celine Dion: How Adele Starts Every Concert with Tribute to Her 'Idol' as Canadian Star Battles Health Issues," *Smooth Radio*, August 7, 2023, https://www.smoothradio.com/artists/celine-dion/adele-concert-ritual-tribute.

117 specific meanings *they hold:* To understand how rituals work to help us moderate our emotions, psychologist Nicholas M. Hobson and his colleagues have distinguished between "bottom-up" processing, which has to do with the physical act of partaking in a ritual, and "top-down processing," which has to do with its cognitive meaning. Bottom-up processing "Constrains thinking and blocks out anxious intrusive thoughts by acting as an attentional distraction." It also "Satisfies a fundamental need for order, buffering against negative uncertainty and reestablishing feelings of lost control." Top-down processing "Evokes feelings of agentic control and restores a sense of personal order in the face of anxious uncertainty." It also "Creates feelings of self-transcendence, allowing a person to escape ego-based thoughts and anxieties." Hobson et al., "The Psychology of Rituals," Table 1.

117 *Flight 232:* Patricia Bauer, "United Airlines Flight 232," *Encyclopaedia Britannica*, January 7, 2025, https://www.britannica.com/event/United-Airlines-Flight-232.

117 *no easy way of controlling the plane:* National Transportation Safety Board, *Aircraft Accident Report: United Airlines Flight 232, McDonnell Douglas DC-10-10, Sioux Gateway Airport, Sioux City, Iowa, July 19, 1989*, NTSB/AAR-90/06, PB90-910406 (Washington, DC: National Transportation Safety Board, 1990), https://www.ntsb.gov/investigations/AccidentReports/Reports/AAR-90-06.pdf.

NOTES

118   *Dennis Fitch:* Howard Berkes, "Hero Pilot in 1989 United Crash Dies," NPR, May 10, 2012, https://www.npr.org/sections/thetwo-way/2012/05/10/152402632/hero-pilot-in-1989-united-crash-dies.

118   *"or you will die":* I base my account of this story on Ranjay Gulati and Charlotte Krontiris, "Leadership Study: UA 232," Harvard Business School, 2014.

118   *"sure as hell have one":* Aviation Safety Network, "United Airlines DC-10-10, July 19, 1989: Cockpit Voice Recorder Transcript of July 19, 1989 Emergency Landing of a United Airlines DC-10-10 at Sioux Gateway Airport, IA (SUX), USA," https://tailstrike.com/media/up3bi4qo/190789.pdf.

119   *"let off steam":* Karin Dangermond, Ricardo Weewer, Joachim Duyndam, and Anja Machielse, "'If It Stops, Then I'll Start Worrying.' Humor as Part of the Fire Service Culture, Specifically as Part of Coping with Critical Incidents," *HUMOR* 35, no. 1 (2022): 31–50, esp. 42. See also: Wayne Maxwell, "The Use of Gallows Humor and Dark Humor During Crisis Situations," *International Journal of Emergency Mental Health* 5, no. 2 (2003): 93–98. Humor was big during the American Civil War, for instance. Jon Grinspan, "Laugh During Wartime," *New York Times* (Opinionator blog), January 9, 2012, https://archive.nytimes.com/opinionator.blogs.nytimes.com/2012/01/09/laugh-during-wartime/.

119   *thirty-three drug dealers:* Rashida Powell, "Georgia State University Criminologist Finds Humor Helps Drug Dealers Cope," Georgia State News Hub, June 28, 2018, https://news.gsu.edu/2018/06/28/georgia-state-university-criminologist-finds-humor-helps-drug-dealers-cope/.

120   *"can't laugh and be afraid":* OK! Staff, "Stephen Colbert Gets Serious About His Faith," *OK! Magazine*, September 19, 2007, attributed to *Parade Magazine*, September 23, 2007, https://okmagazine.com/news/stephen-colbert-gets-serious-about-his-faith/.

120   *Focusing on what is right in front of us:* Anne Sugar, "Michael Gervais Shares the First Rule of Mastery: Stop Worrying What Other People Think of You," *Forbes*, November 28, 2023, https://www.forbes.com/sites/annesugar/2023/11/28/michael-gervais-shares-the-first-rule-of-mastery-stop-worrying-what-other-people-think-of-you/.

120   *starting to grow fearful:* Michael Gervais, "How to Stop Worrying about What Other People Think of You," *Harvard Business Review,* May 2, 2019, https://hbr.org/2019/05/how-to-stop-worrying-about-what-other-people-think-of-you.

121   *reassess the situation:* Gross, "The Emerging Field of Emotion Regulation."

122   *We're loss-averse:* See, for instance, Daniel Kahneman, *Thinking, Fast and Slow* (New York: Farrar, Straus and Giroux, 2013).

122   *courses by airlines:* "Flying with Confidence Online Course," https://online.flyingwithconfidence.com/.

122   *large fuel tanks that won't suddenly run out:* Sarah Lyall, "'The Plane Is Fine': An Airline Course Looks to Overcome Fear in the Skies," *New York Times*, April 2,

NOTES [259

2024, https://www.nytimes.com/2024/04/02/travel/fear-of-flying-course-british-airways.html.

123   *"person who continues to inspire me":* Niren Chaudhary, appearance in my class at Harvard Business School, March 23, 2024, and April 1, 2024.

123   *become a motivational speaker:* Aisha Chaudhary, "Being Happy and Living at the Moment: Aisha Chaudhary at TEDxPune," *TEDx Talks,* February 3, 2014, YouTube video, 12:45, https://www.youtube.com/watch?v=ENTf10L1jt0.

123   *"the limited time she had":* In telling Aisha's story, I also draw on Ranjay Gulati and Paul R. Lawrence, "To Succeed with Purpose, Make It Personal: A CEO's Reminder to Lead Authentically," *Inc.,* January 26, 2022, https://www.inc.com/ranjay-gulati/a-ceos-reminder-to-lead-authentically.html.

124   *"clearly a choice one can make":* Aisha Chaudhary, "Finding Happiness," *INKtalks,* November 1, 2013, YouTube video, 10:29, https://www.youtube.com/watch?v=cUkZLttONGM at 6:59.

124   *penned during the last year of her life:* Aisha Chaudhary, *My Little Epiphanies* (New Delhi, India: Bloomsbury Publishing, 2015), Kindle version, 9.

125   *the epic poem* The Aeneid*:* I am grateful to my former research associate Charlotte Krontiris for bringing this poem to my attention.

125   *do the same:* Virgil, *The Aeneid,* trans. A. S. Kline (Moscow, ID: Roman Roads Media, LLC, 2015).

126   *friends of his who had perished:* Virgil, *The Aeneid,* 7.

CHAPTER 7: CLAN

129   *marked by conflict:* Nouran Salahieh, Jeffrey Winter, Casey Tolan, Ralph Ellis, and Scott Glover, "What We Know About the Suspect in the Monterey Park Massacre," CNN, updated January 26, 2023, https://www.cnn.com/2023/01/23/us/huu-can-tran-monterey-park-shooting-what-we-know/index.html.

129   *argued with customers and dance instructors:* "Chinese New Year Shooting: What We Know About California Attack Gunman Huu Can Tran," *Sky News,* January 24, 2023, https://news.sky.com/story/california-shooting-suspect-hostile-gunman-huu-can-tran-was-distrustful-former-dance-teacher-12794082; ABC7.com staff, "Monterey Park Shooting: Here's What We Know About Gunman Huu Can Tran," ABC7, January 23, 2023, https://abc7news.com/monterey-park-shooter-72-year-old-huu-can-tran-shooting/12728677/.

129   *"years accumulating unhappiness":* Ruth Styles, "EXCLUSIVE: Monterey Park Killer Huu Can Tran, 72, Was an 'Unhappy' Man Without 'Family, Money or a Future' Who 'Spent Years Accumulating Disgruntlement Towards People,'" *Daily Mail,* January 23, 2023, updated January 24, 2023, https://www.dailymail.co.uk/news/article-11668991/Monterey-Park-killer-Huu-Tran-72-unhappy-man-without-family-money-future.html.

129   *"evil things about him":* Aditi Sangal, Matt Meyer, Maureen Chowdhury, Veronica

Rocha, Seán Federico O'Murchú, and Meg Wagner, "January 22, 2023, Monterey Park Mass Shooting News," CNN, January 22, 2023, updated January 23, 2023, https://www.cnn.com/us/live-news/los-angeles-mass-shooting-01-22-2023/index.html.

129 *ex-wife of Tran recalled:* Scott Schwebke, "Two Weeks Later: What We Know and Still Don't Know About Monterey Park Shooter," *Mercury News*, February 6, 2023, https://www.mercurynews.com/2023/02/06/two-weeks-later-what-we-know-and-still-dont-know-about-monterey-park-shooter/; Andrea Cavallier and Jack Newman, "Monterey Park Massacre That Left 10 Dead After Gunman's Rampage Inside a Dance Studio Was Triggered by His 'Jealousy' After 'a Domestic Dispute': Shooter Huu Can Tran, 72, Was 'Hostile and Quick to Anger,'" *Daily Mail*, January 23, 2023, updated January 23, 2023, https://www.dailymail.co.uk/news/article-11665473/Monterey-mass-shooter-killed-10-people-California-dance-studio-complained-students.html.

130 *opened fire on a floor of patrons:* "Sheriff: Gunman Didn't Know Monterey Park Dance Hall Victims," NY1, January 26, 2023, https://www.ny1.com/nyc/all-boroughs/public-safety/2023/01/26/sheriff--gunman-didn-t-know-monterey-park-dance-hall-victims; Tim Arango and Jill Cowan, "Authorities Ask Why Gunman Attacked California Ballroom He Once Enjoyed," *New York Times*, January 23, 2023, https://www.nytimes.com/2023/01/23/us/monterey-park-shooting-suspect.html.

130 *Eleven people died:* Nouran Salahieh, Stella Chan, and Eric Levenson, "11 Victims of Monterey Park Mass Shooting Ranged in Age from 57 to 76 Years Old, Coroner Says," CNN, January 25, 2023, https://www.cnn.com/2023/01/24/us/monterey-park-california-mass-shooting-tuesday

130 *Ming Wei Ma:* Mari Uyehara, "Huu Can Tran's American Dream," *The Nation*, February 6, 2023, https://www.thenation.com/article/society/monterey-park-killings-guns/.

130 *Surveillance footage shows:* Julianne McShane and Antonio Planas, "Exclusive Video Captures the Moment Man Disarms Monterey Park Gunman at Second Dance Hall," *NBC News*, January 23, 2023, https://www.nbcnews.com/news/us-news/watch-exclusive-video-captures-moment-man-disarms-monterey-park-shoote-rcna67061.

130 *"I thought, this was the end":* Brandon Tsay, interview with the author, February 20, 2023.

131 *"How can I resist":* Brandon Tsay, interview with the author, February 20, 2023.

131 *Police touted Tsay's courage:* Tina Burnside and Sarah Moon, "Brandon Tsay, the Hero Who Disarmed the Monterey Park Shooting Suspect, Honored with Medal of Courage," CNN, January 29, 2023, https://www.cnn.com/2023/01/29/us/brandon-tsay-monterey-park-shooting-medal-of-courage/index.html.

131 *standing ovation:* "Brandon Tsay Receives Standing Ovation at President Biden's State of the Union Address," KTLA 5, YouTube video, February 7, 2023, https://www.youtube.com/watch?v=VFiW_fR64j0.

131 *"found the courage to act":* Joe Biden, "Remarks by President Biden on Efforts to Reduce Gun Violence," *The White House*, March 14, 2023, https://www.whitehouse.gov/briefing-room/speeches-remarks/2023/03/14/remarks-by-president-biden-on-efforts-to-reduce-gun-violence/.

132 *"so out of character":* Brandon Tsay, interview with the author, February 20, 2023.

132 *affiliations with larger collectives:* Lakshmi Ramarajan, "Past, Present and Future Research on Multiple Identities: Toward an Intrapersonal Network Approach," *Academy of Management Annals* 8, no. 1 (2014): 589–659, esp. 593.

132 *identity as comprising three levels:* Marilynn B. Brewer and Wendi Gardner, "Who Is This 'We'? Levels of Collective Identity and Self Representations," *Journal of Personality and Social Psychology* 71, no. 1 (1996): 83–93.

132 *more salience than others:* Sheldon Stryker, "Identity Salience and Role Performance: The Relevance of Symbolic Interaction Theory for Family Research," *Journal of Marriage and Family* 30, no. 4 (1968): 558–64.

133 *"if I fail to do what I set out to do":* Brandon Tsay, interview with the author, February 20, 2023.

134 *billions on team-building exercises:* Lynnley Browning, "Do Team Games for Employees Really Improve Productivity?" *Newsweek*, October 26, 2014, https://www.newsweek.com/2014/11/07/do-team-games-employees-really-improve-productivity-279804.html.

134 *others around them:* Rebecca Knight, "17 Team-Building Activities for In-Person, Remote, and Hybrid Teams," *Harvard Business Review*, August 7, 2024, https://hbr.org/2024/08/17-team-building-activities-for-in-person-remote-and-hybrid-teams.

134 *collective courage:* Doug McAdam, "Recruitment to High-Risk Activism: The Case of Freedom Summer," *American Journal of Sociology* 92, no. 1 (July 1986): 64–90; David A. Snow, Louis A. Zurcher, and Sheldon Ekland-Olson, "Social Networks and Social Movements: A Microstructural Approach to Differential Recruitment," *American Sociological Review* 45, no. 5 (1980): 787–801.

134 *registered voters:* "Interviewee Information I through M: Robert Moses (1935–)," *Eyes on the Prize Interviews*, Washington University in St. Louis, https://digitalexhibits.library.wustl.edu/s/eyes-1-interviews/page/interviewee-infortmation-i-through-m.

135 *Tensions in the South:* "Freedom Summer," Martin Luther King, Jr. Research and Education Institute, Stanford University, https://kinginstitute.stanford.edu/freedom-summer.

135 *had been kidnapped:* "Freedom Summer," Martin Luther King, Jr. Research and Education Institute, Stanford University, https://kinginstitute.stanford.edu/freedom-summer.

135 *almost a third:* Doug McAdam, "Recruitment to High-Risk Activism: The Case of Freedom Summer," *American Journal of Sociology* 92, no. 1 (1986): 64–90. For more on the power of close social ties to encourage risk-taking, see Damon

Centola and Michael Macy, "Complex Contagions and the Weakness of Long Ties," *American Journal of Sociology* 113, no. 3 (2007): 702–34. We also know that being personally asked to take part in a protest movement plays an outsized role in determining whether someone actually does participate. Alan Schussman and Sarah A. Soule, "Process and Protest: Accounting for Individual Protest Participation," *Social Forces* 84, no. 2 (2005): 1083–1108.

135 *collective dimension of identity:* Doug McAdam and Ronnelle Paulsen, "Specifying the Relationship between Social Ties and Activism," *American Journal of Sociology* 99, no. 3 (1993): 640–67.

136 *"I must act NOW":* McAdam and Paulsen, "Specifying the Relationship between Social Ties and Activism," 656.

136 "All of us in the movement *must join forces":* McAdam and Paulsen, "Specifying the Relationship between Social Ties and Activism," 656.

137 *"People almost never . . . die for the Cause":* Scott Atran, *Talking to the Enemy: Faith, Brotherhood, and the (Un)Making of Terrorists* (New York: HarperCollins, 2010), 33.

137 *"identity fusion" that takes place:* William B. Swann Jr., Jolanda Jetten, Ángel Gómez, Harvey Whitehouse, and Brock Bastian, "When Group Membership Gets Personal: A Theory of Identity Fusion," *Psychological Review* 119, no. 3 (2012): 441.

137 *college students might have risked their life:* McAdam and Paulsen, "Specifying the Relationship between Social Ties and Activism."

138 *feel like a close-knit clan or tribe:* Swann Jr. et al., "When Group Membership Gets Personal"; William B. Swann Jr., Michael D. Buhrmester, Angel Gómez, Jolanda Jetten, Brock Bastian, Alexandra Vázquez, and Amarina Ariyanto, "What Makes a Group Worth Dying For? Identity Fusion Fosters Perception of Familial Ties, Promoting Self-Sacrifice," *Journal of Personality and Social Psychology* 106, no. 6 (2014): 912–26.

138 *intimate families:* Swann Jr. et al., "When Group Membership Gets Personal"; Swann Jr. et al., "What Makes a Group Worth Dying For?," 912–26.

139 *"visceral sense of oneness":* Swann Jr. et al., "What Makes a Group Worth Dying For?," 913.

139 *"construe to be living extensions of themselves":* Swann Jr. et al., "What Makes a Group Worth Dying For?," 925.

139 *"part of my identity for my whole life":* Macy Jenkins and Karla Rendon, "Nearly Year After Monterey Park Mass Shooting, Community Stays Strong and Hosts Remembrance Event," NBC Los Angeles, January 13, 2024, https://www.nbclosangeles.com/news/local/nearly-year-after-monterey-park-mass-shooting-community-stays-strong-and-hosts-remembrance-event-in-honor-of-victims/3311677/.

139 *"kind and nurturing household":* Kimmy Yam, "Monterey Park Ballroom Shooting Hero Says City's 'Golden Bubble' Has Burst, Calls for Gun Control,"

NBC News, January 18, 2024, https://www.nbcnews.com/news/asian-america/monterey-park-shooting-community-brandon-tsay-rcna132147.

140 *help save the family business:* Brandon Tsay, interview with the author, February 20, 2023.

141 *overcoming a shared adversity:* Swann Jr. et al., "When Group Membership Gets Personal."

141 *"no man behind":* George Galdorisi, "Why We Leave No Man Behind," CNN, June 9, 2014, https://www.cnn.com/2014/06/09/opinion/galdorisi-leave-no-man-behind/index.html.

141 Semper Fi: "Semper Fidelis," Marines.com, https://www.marines.com/about-the-marine-corps/who-are-the-marines/semper-fidelis.html.

142 *persevering through a series of tests:* Mark Perna, "The Crucible—Marines Epic 54-Hour Test for Recruits," Marines Boot Camp HQ, June 12, 2022, https://www.marinesbootcamphq.com/the-crucible-marines/.

142 *"your allotted time":* Akhil Iyer (former US marine), interview with the author, August 2, 2024.

143 *"part of something bigger than yourself":* William Bowers, interview with the author, July 29, 2024.

144 *overwhelmed and anguished:* Sheldon Stryker and Anne Statham Macke, "Status Inconsistency and Role Conflict," *Annual Review of Sociology* 4 (1978): 57–90. For more on multiple identities, see Lakshmi Ramarajan, "Past, Present and Future Research on Multiple Identities: Toward an Intrapersonal Network Approach," *Academy of Management Annals* 8 (2014): 589–659.

144 *"important part of the group":* Swann Jr. et al., "When Group Membership Gets Personal," 442.

145 *harmonizing them with that of the group:* Ramarajan, "Past, Present and Future Research on Multiple Identities," 589–659, esp. 616.

145 *function as one unified being:* I base my account of Carroll on Ranjay Gulati, Matthew Breitfelder, and Monte Burke, "Pete Carroll: Building a Winning Organization through Purpose, Caring, and Inclusion," Harvard Business School Case Study 9-421-020, October 2020, revised March 2021.

145 *"whole package of the player that's crucial":* John Boyle, "The Carroll Culture: 'He Focuses On Your Purpose Beyond The Game,'" Seahawks.com, September 10, 2016, https://www.seahawks.com/news/the-carroll-culture-he-focuses-on-your-purpose-beyond-the-game-166611.

146 *"optimal distinctiveness":* Marilynn B. Brewer, "The Social Self: On Being the Same and Different at the Same Time," *Personality and Social Psychology Bulletin* 17, no. 5 (1991): 475–82, esp. 478.

146 *creating relevant experiences:* Gulati et al., "Pete Carroll."

146 *"pretty powerful to be a part of":* Gulati et al., "Pete Carroll."

264] NOTES

147 *"de-fusion":* Swann Jr. et al., "When Group Membership Gets Personal."

148 *priests who broke with the Anglican Church:* Swann Jr. et al., "When Group Membership Gets Personal," 451.

148 *"deep purpose":* Ranjay Gulati, *Deep Purpose: The Heart and Soul of High-Performance Companies* (New York: Harper Business, 2022).

149 *"working without a playbook":* Jeffrey Bussgang, "Are You Suited for a Start-Up?," *Harvard Business Review*, November–December 2017, 151, https://hbr.org/2017/11/are-you-suited-for-a-start-up.

149 *the "soul" of the startup:* Ranjay Gulati, "The Soul of a Startup," *Harvard Business Review* 97, no. 4 (July–August 2019): 85–91.

150 *by 2018 was operating:* Warby Parker, *Impact Report 2018*, https://www.warbyparker.com/assets/img/impact-report/Impact-Report-2018.pdf.

150 *Blue-Footed Booby:* Richard Feloni, "How a Blue-Footed Boobie Helped Create the Warby Parker Brand," *Business Insider*, June 27, 2014, https://www.businessinsider.com/warby-parkers-blue-footed-boobie-2014-6.

150 *system called Warbles:* Oliver Staley, "Warby Parker Is Getting Better Results by Reducing Managers' Control over Workers," *Quartz*, September 15, 2016, https://qz.com/749863/warby-parker-is-getting-better-results-by-reducing-managers-control-over-workers.

151 *"virtual room together":* Ranjay Gulati and Sam Yogi, "Warby Parker: Scaling a Startup," Harvard Business School Case Study 9-419–042, October 3, 2019, 9. My discussion of Warby Parker in this and the preceding paragraphs draws on this case study.

152 *"community is really an integral part of my life":* Brandon Tsay, interview with the author, February 20, 2023.

153 *"do something important with it for the community":* Teresa Liu, "Brandon Tsay Once Shunned the Spotlight; Then He Disarmed a Mass Shooter," *Security Info Watch*, June 14, 2023, https://www.securityinfowatch.com/industry-news/news/53063434/brandon-tsay-once-shunned-the-spotlight-then-he-disarmed-a-mass-shooter.

153 *"epidemic of loneliness":* U.S. Department of Health and Human Services, *Our Epidemic of Loneliness and Isolation*, Surgeon General's Advisory, 2023, https://www.hhs.gov/sites/default/files/surgeon-general-social-connection-advisory.pdf.

153 *collective identification:* Gianpiero Petriglieri et al., "Agony and Ecstasy in the Gig Economy: Cultivating Holding Environments for Precarious and Personalized Work Identities," *Administrative Science Quarterly* 64, no. 1 (2019): 124–70.

CHAPTER 8: CHARISMA

154 *policy of appeasement:* Imperial War Museums, "How Britain Hoped to Avoid War with Germany in the 1930s," https://www.iwm.org.uk/history/how-britain-hoped-to-avoid-war-with-germany-in-the-1930s.

154 *blitzkrieg tactics:* "Blitzkrieg," *History*, last updated December 12, 2022, https://www.history.com/topics/world-war-ii/blitzkrieg.

154 *Dunkirk evacuation:* Imperial War Museums, "What You Need to Know about the Dunkirk Evacuations," https://www.iwm.org.uk/history/what-you-need-to-know-about-the-dunkirk-evacuations.

155 *rally his dispirited countrymen:* Winston Churchill, "Fight Them on the Beaches," International Churchill Society, June 4, 1940, https://winstonchurchill.org/resources/speeches/1940-the-finest-hour/fight-them-on-the-beaches/.

155 *"we shall never surrender":* Winston Churchill, "We Shall Fight on the Beaches," International Churchill Society, June 4, 1940, https://winstonchurchill.org/resources/speeches/1940-the-finest-hour/we-shall-fight-on-the-beaches/.

155 *moved some to tears:* Richard Toye, "'We Shall Fight on the Beaches': 3 Things You Never Knew about Churchill's Most Famous Speech," *History of Government Blog*, December 2, 2013, https://history.blog.gov.uk/2013/12/02/we-shall-fight-on-the-beaches-three-things-you-never-knew-about-churchills-most-famous-speech/.

155 *"magnificent oration that obviously moved the House":* Kristin Hunt, "Winston Churchill's Historic 'Fight Them on the Beaches' Speech Wasn't Heard by the Public Until After WWII," *Smithsonian Magazine*, November 21, 2017, https://www.smithsonianmag.com/history/winston-churchills-historic-fight-them-beaches-speech-wasnt-heard-public-until-after-wwii-180967278/.

155 *"finest speech that I have ever heard":* Hunt, "Winston Churchill's Historic 'Fight Them on the Beaches' Speech Wasn't Heard by the Public Until After WWII."

155 *"dark days and darker nights":* John F. Kennedy, "Remarks Upon Signing Proclamation Conferring Honorary Citizenship on Sir Winston Churchill," April 9, 1963, *The American Presidency Project*, https://www.presidency.ucsb.edu/documents/remarks-upon-signing-proclamation-conferring-honorary-citizenship-sir-winston-churchill, quoted in Tom Vitale, "Winston Churchill's Way with Words," NPR, July 14, 2012, https://www.npr.org/2012/07/14/156720829/winston-churchills-way-with-words.

155 *"Be brave":* John McCain, *Why Courage Matters: The Way to a Braver Life* (New York: Random House, 2004), 39–40.

156 *"supernatural, superhuman, or at least specifically exceptional":* Max Weber, *The Theory of Economic and Social Organization,* trans. A. M. Henderson and Talcott Parsons (Glencoe, IL: The Free Press, 1947), 358.

156 *"bold, colorful, mischievous, and imaginative":* Jasmine Vergauwe, Bart Wille, Joeri Hofmans, Robert B. (Rob) Kaiser, and Filip De Fruyt, "Too Much Charisma Can Make Leaders Look Less Effective," *Harvard Business Review,* September 26, 2017, https://hbr.org/2017/09/too-much-charisma-can-make-leaders-look-less-effective. This article summarizes findings in Jasmine Vergauwe, Bart Wille, Joeri Hofmans, Robert B. Kaiser, and Filip De Fruyt, "The Double-Edged Sword of Leader Charisma: Understanding the Curvilinear Relationship Between Charismatic Personality and Leader Effectiveness," *Journal of Personality and Social Psychology* 114, no. 1 (2018): 110–30.

156 *problem with the notion of charisma:* Some scholars also have disparaged charisma on grounds that it is overly vague as a concept and lacking in scientific validity. For a summary of this criticism, see George C. Banks, Krista N. Engemann, Courtney E. Williams, Janaki Gooty, Kelly Davis McCauley, and Melissa R. Medaugh, "A Meta-Analytic Review and Future Research Agenda of Charismatic Leadership," *Leadership Quarterly* 28, no. 4 (2017): 508–529.

157 *right training:* John Antonakis, Marika Fenley, and Sue Liechti, "Can Charisma Be Taught? Tests of Two Interventions," *Academy of Management Learning & Education* 10, no. 3 (2012): 374–96.

157 *specific behaviors that motivate others:* For more on the scholarship about charisma that focuses on behavior, see John Antonakis, "Using the Power of Charisma for Better Leadership," *The Guardian*, December 3, 2012, https://www.theguardian.com/sustainable-business/blog/learning-charisma-sustainability-leaders.

158 *draw national attention to the civil rights cause:* Anissa Durham, "Remembering Math and Civil Rights Activist Bob Moses," PBS SoCal, August 6, 2021, https://www.pbssocal.org/education/pbs-socal-family-math/remembering-math-and-civil-rights-activist-bob-moses.

158 *"strategist at the core of the civil rights movement":* "Robert 'Bob' Parris Moses," Civil Rights Movement Archive, https://www.crmvet.org/mem/mosesb.htm.

158 *Activists who worked alongside Moses:* Laura Visser-Maessen, *Robert Parris Moses: A Life in Civil Rights and Leadership at the Grassroots* (Chapel Hill: University of North Carolina Press, 2016), 2.

159 *Moses knew this would be a dangerous undertaking:* "Freedom Summer," *History*, last updated April 16, 2021, https://www.history.com/topics/black-history/freedom-summer; Visser-Maessen, *Robert Parris Moses*, 196–97.

159 *"like guerrilla warfare":* John Lewis, "Mississippi Freedom Summer—20 Years Later," *Dissent Magazine*, Winter 1985, https://www.dissentmagazine.org/article/mississippi-freedom-summer-20-years-later/.

159 *unaccounted for after having been arrested:* "Murder in Mississippi," *American Experience*, PBS, accessed January 11, 2025, https://www.pbs.org/wgbh/americanexperience/features/freedomsummer-murder/.

159 *they had been murdered:* My account of Robert Parris Moses in this chapter draws on an unpublished research report I drafted in 2014 in partnership with my research team member Charlotte Krontiris.

160 *"had to tell the students":* Interview with Robert Moses, conducted by Blackside, Inc. on May 19, 1986, for *Eyes on the Prize: America's Civil Rights Years (1954–1965)*, Washington University Libraries, Film and Media Archive, Henry Hampton Collection.

160 *"near sacred moment":* Visser-Maessen, *Robert Parris Moses*, 206.

160 *"If for any reason you're hesitant":* Visser-Maessen, *Robert Parris Moses*, 206.

160 *"most profound experiences of leadership":* Visser-Maessen, *Robert Parris Moses*, 206–207.

161 *"articulate a 'transcendent' goal"*: Robert J. House, "A 1976 Theory of Charismatic Leadership," paper presented at the Southern Illinois University Fourth Biennial Leadership Symposium, Carbondale, Illinois, October 26–28, 1976, 16.

161 *"You have a job to do"*: Visser-Maessen, *Robert Parris Moses*, 196–97.

162 *explicitly alert people to direct connections*: Andrew M. Carton and Brian J. Lucas, "How Can Leaders Overcome the Blurry Vision Bias? Identifying an Antidote to the Paradox of Vision Communication," *Academy of Management Journal* 61, no. 6 (2018): 2106–129; Andrew M. Carton, "'I'm Not Mopping the Floors, I'm Putting a Man on the Moon': How NASA Leaders Enhanced the Meaningfulness of Work by Changing the Meaning of Work," *Administrative Science Quarterly* 63, no. 2 (2018): 323–69.

162 *"as great a man as any generation could produce"*: Letter from Joseph and Nancy Ellin to Diane and Susan, June 26, 1964, digital collections at the University of Southern Mississippi, https://usm.access.preservica.com/uncategorized/IO_16c20f2f-f8c5-455f-8cb4-f23e4da0be48.

162 *voice, hand movements, and the like:* John Antonakis et al., "Can Charisma Be Taught? Tests of Two Interventions," 374–96.

163 *"as if the situation was normal"*: Visser-Maessen, *Robert Parris Moses*, 72, 126.

163 *"an instrument of outright oppression"*: Visser-Maessen, *Robert Parris Moses*, 69.

164 *"more guts than any one man I've ever known"*: Visser-Maessen, *Robert Parris Moses*, 72.

164 *"engaged in self-sacrificing behaviors"*: House, "A 1976 Theory of Charismatic Leadership," 9.

164 *self-sacrificial style of leadership:* David De Cremer, "Charismatic Leadership and Cooperation in Social Dilemmas: A Matter of Transforming Motives?," *Journal of Applied Social Psychology* 32, no. 5 (2002): 997–1016; David De Cremer, "Affective and Motivational Consequences of Leader Self-Sacrifice: The Moderating Effect of Autocratic Leadership," *Leadership Quarterly* 17, no. 1 (2006): 79–93.

164 *"a visceral feeling of oneness"*: Swann Jr. et al., "When Group Membership Gets Personal," 442.

165 *"I'm taking risks myself"*: Visser-Maessen, *Robert Parris Moses*, 206.

166 *"freedom within a framework"*: Ranjay Gulati, "Structure That's Not Stifling," *Harvard Business Review*, May–June 2018, https://hbr.org/2018/05/structure-thats-not-stifling.

166 *"slowly" and "gently," but nonetheless decisively:* Visser-Maessen, *Robert Parris Moses*, 201.

167 *"organizer should aspire to a state of near invisibility"*: Benjamin Hedin, "Remembering Robert Moses," *American Scholar*, July 31, 2021, https://theamericanscholar.org/remembering-robert-moses/.

167 *"overseer of change and progress"*: Robert Kelley, "In Praise of Followers," *Harvard Business Review*, November 1988, https://hbr.org/1988/11/in-praise-of-followers.

See also Ira Chaleff, *The Courageous Follower: Standing Up To & For Our Leaders*, 3rd ed. (San Francisco: Barrett-Koehler Publishers, Inc., 2009). On followership in general, see Mary Uhl-Bien, Ronald E. Riggio, Kevin B. Lowe, and Melissa K. Carsten, "Followership Theory: A Review and Research Agenda," *Leadership Quarterly* 25, no. 1 (2014): 83–104.

167 *intrinsic motivation:* Richard Martin, "A Review of the Literature of the Followership Since 2008: The Importance of Relationships and Emotional Intelligence," *SAGE Open* 5, no. 4 (2015): 1–9.

167 *"they might face":* Interview with Robert Moses, conducted by Blackside Inc. on May 19, 1986, for *Eyes on the Prize: America's Civil Rights Years (1954–1965)*.

168 *"his voice was very gentle":* Montgomery—Mississippi volunteers (Lucile Montgomery papers, 1963–1967; Historical Society Library Microforms Room, Micro 44, Reel 2, Segment 26), 4, Wisconsin Historical Society, Freedom Summer Digital Collection, https://content.wisconsinhistory.org/digital/collection/p15932coll2/id/33931.

168 *"the more his legend grows":* Visser-Maessen, *Robert Parris Moses*, 2.

168 *"risking life and limb with them":* Visser-Maessen, *Robert Parris Moses*, 8.

169 *a foremost advocate*: See, for example, Brené Brown, *Daring Greatly: How the Courage to Be Vulnerable Transforms the Way We Live, Love, Parent, and Lead* (New York: Avery, 2015).

169 *"vulnerability, not bravado":* Amy C. Edmondson and Tomas Chamorro-Premuzic, "Today's Leaders Need Vulnerability, Not Bravado," *Harvard Business Review,* October 19, 2020, https://hbr.org/2020/10/todays-leaders-need-vulnerability-not-bravado.

169 *calmness and confidence:* Edmondson and Chamorro-Premuzic, "Today's Leaders Need Vulnerability, Not Bravado."

169 *"deliberate cultivation of calm":* Monica C. Worline, "Courage in Organizations: An Integrative Review of the Difficult Virtue," in *The Oxford Handbook of Positive Organizational Scholarship*, ed. Kim S. Cameron and Gretchen M. Spreitzer (Oxford: Oxford University Press, 2012), 304–315, esp. 311.

170 *emotions are contagious in social situations:* Carolina Herrando and Efthymios Constantinides, "Emotional Contagion: A Brief Overview and Future Directions," *Frontiers in Psychology* 12 (2021): 712606.

170 *"rarely revealed his doubts and fears":* Nancy Koehn, "Why Lincoln Hid His Strongest Feelings from the Public," *Harvard Business Review*, October 10, 2016, https://hbr.org/2016/10/why-lincoln-hid-his-strongest-feelings-from-the-public.

171 *"people need a sense of direction":* Bill George and Andrew N. McLean, "Anne Mulcahy: Leading Xerox through the Perfect Storm (A)," Harvard Business School Case Study 9-405-050, January 2005, revised July 22, 2010, 8–9.

171 *"all I needed to just drive home":* George and McLean, "Anne Mulcahy," 9.

171 *"question of personal fear":* Visser-Maessen, *Robert Parris Moses*, 73.

171	*"absolutely haunted" by them:* Visser-Maessen, *Robert Parris Moses*, 203.
172	*as much as you might:* There is, of course, no single model of leadership that works in all situations. Perhaps only a selective or partial approach to these behaviors is best given your own specific goals, organizational context, and constraints.
173	*only 1,600 new Black voters:* "Freedom Summer," Martin Luther King, Jr. Research and Education Institute, Stanford University, https://kinginstitute.stanford.edu/freedom-summer.
173	*political pressure it created:* "Freedom Summer," *History*, last updated April 16, 2021, https://www.history.com/topics/black-history/freedom-summer.
173	*advocacy on behalf of Black political empowerment:* Deborah Barfield Berry, "Freedom Summer Changed the Nation 60 Years Ago: How the Effort Still Inspires Voters Today," *USA Today*, July 17, 2024, https://www.usatoday.com/story/news/nation/2024/07/17/1964-freedom-summer-changed-nation/74235558007/.
173	*"courageous follower":* Chaleff, *The Courageous Follower*.

CHAPTER 9: CULTURE

175	*grand old hotel:* This opening story draws on detail from a number of sources, most notably an interview I conducted with Mallika Jagad on February 25, 2019, an interview with Taj Mahal Palace general manager Karambir Kang on February 15, 2019, and the following Harvard Business School videos created about the Bombay attacks of November 26–29, 2008: Rohit Deshpandé, "Terror at the Taj Bombay: Customer-Centric Leadership," HBS Multimedia Video Case No. 511-703, March 2011. I also draw on Rohit Deshpandé and Anjali Raina, "The Ordinary Heroes of the Taj," *Harvard Business Review*, December 2011, https://hbr.org/2011/12/the-ordinary-heroes-of-the-taj.
176	*four terrorists:* Federation of American Scientists, *The Mumbai Terrorist Attacks (November 26–29, 2008)*, https://irp.fas.org/eprint/mumbai.pdf.
177	*All of them had to stick together:* Mallika Jagad, interview with the author, February 25, 2019.
178	*"no time for melodrama":* Mallika Jagad, interview with the author, February 25, 2019.
179	*"Not one did that. Not one":* Deshpandé, "Terror at the Taj Bombay," 6:45, tape 2.
179	*chefs who had formed a human shield:* Deshpandé, "Terror at the Taj Bombay," 9:05, tape 2.
179	*telephone operators:* Deshpandé, "Terror at the Taj Bombay," 5:50, tape 2.
179	*he felt responsible*: Karambir Kang, interview with the author, February 15, 2019.
179	*like a sea captain:* Deshpandé, "Terror at the Taj Bombay," 8:25, tape 2.
180	*"goal of 'let's get the guests to safety'":* Deshpandé, "Terror at the Taj Bombay," 7:05 tape 2.

NOTES

180   *"level of calm and composure the staff displayed":* Deshpandé, "Terror at the Taj Bombay," 1:25 and 3:15, tape 3.

180   *"traditional Indian values":* Deshpandé and Raina, "The Ordinary Heroes of the Taj."

180   *"something more important to be done":* Deshpandé, "Terror at the Taj Bombay," 2:15, tape 3.

181   *nonfinancial incentives:* For a more complete discussion of the economic and moral/symbolic conceptions of organizations, see my previous book, *Deep Purpose: The Heart and Soul of High-Performance Companies* (New York: Harper Business, 2022), 14–18.

181   *systems of meaning, bringing people together:* The psychologist Edgar Schein defined organizational culture as "a pattern of shared basic assumptions that was learned by a group as it solved its problems of external adaptation and internal integration, that has worked well enough to be considered valid and, therefore, to be taught to new members as the correct way to perceive, think, and feel in relation to those problems." Schein also famously distinguished three levels to culture: tangible artifacts like the way an office is designed or dress codes; the values, beliefs, and behavioral norms the organization adopts; and unspoken assumptions. See Edgar H. Schein, *Organizational Culture and Leadership*, 3rd ed. (San Francisco: Jossey-Bass, 2004), 17.

181   *attempt to make their people bolder:* "Who We Are: The Coca-Cola Company," *The Coca-Cola Company*, https://www.coca-colacompany.com/content/dam/company/us/en/about-us/purpose-vision/coca-cola-company-purpose-summary.pdf; "Netflix Culture—The Best Work of Our Lives," Netflix, https://jobs.netflix.com/culture.

183   *"playing to win" mindset:* Heidi Grant and E. Tory Higgins, "Do You Play to Win—Or Not to Lose?," *Harvard Business Review*, March 2013, https://hbr.org/2013/03/do-you-play-to-win-or-to-not-lose.

183   *"do them right all of the time":* Vince Lombardi, "What It Takes to Be Number One," Vince Lombardi Official Site, https://vincelombardi.com/.

183   *outperform their peers in both revenue and profit growth:* In particular, they relied less on layoffs, as a reduced workforce can leave companies struggling to grow once good times return. Instead, they tried to cut costs by making their businesses operate more efficiently. See Ranjay Gulati, Nitin Nohria, and Franz Wohlgezogen, "Roaring out of Recession," *Harvard Business Review*, March 2010, https://hbr.org/2010/03/roaring-out-of-recession.

184   *viability as an independent phone manufacturer was in question:* This account of BlackBerry draws heavily on Ranjay Gulati and Nicole Tempest Keller, "Transforming BlackBerry: from Smartphones to Software," Harvard Business School Case Study 9-421-052, April 2021.

184   *ailing software company Sybase:* Julia Pitta, "The Rescue of Sybase," *Forbes*, May 17, 1999, https://www.forbes.com/forbes/1999/0517/6310313a.html.

184   *"re-architect the whole company":* Gulati and Keller, "Transforming BlackBerry," 6.

185 *"walking away from what we knew best":* Gulati and Keller, "Transforming BlackBerry," 1.

185 *"turnaround culture must be positive":* John Chen, "Here's How You Win: 5 Lessons from BlackBerry CEO John Chen," *Firstpost*, October 29, 2014, https://www.firstpost.com/business/biztech/heres-how-you-win-5-lessons-from-blackberry-ceo-john-chen-1994899.html.

185 *"he was here to fight":* Gulati and Keller, "Transforming BlackBerry," 11.

185 *past successes:* Gulati and Keller, "Transforming Blackberry," 9.

186 *"right attitudes":* Gulati and Keller, "Transforming BlackBerry," 9.

186 *$1 billion in software-related revenues:* BlackBerry Limited, *Fiscal Fourth Quarter and Fiscal Year 2020 Results*, March 31, 2020, https://www.blackberry.com/content/dam/blackberry-com/Documents/pdf/financial-reports/2020/q4y2020/Q4-Transcript.pdf.

186 *extraordinary accomplishment:* Adriano Marchese and Robb M. Stewart, "BlackBerry Sees Rising Profitability Through Focus on Growth Opportunities," *Wall Street Journal*, October 16, 2024, https://www.wsj.com/business/retail/blackberry-sees-return-to-profit-into-fiscal-2027-f5e620a1?mod=business_lead_story.

187 *$2.6 trillion each year:* Gary Hamel and Michele Zanini, *Humanocracy: Creating Organizations As Amazing As the People Inside Them* (Boston: Harvard Business Review Press, 2020).

187 *"indifference, skepticism, or outright resistance":* Hamel and Zanini, *Humanocracy*, 54, 58.

187 *"iron cage":* "Max Weber," *Stanford Encyclopedia of Philosophy*, revised September 21, 2022, https://plato.stanford.edu/entries/weber/.

188 *encourage employees to speak up and to exercise discretion:* See my articles "The Soul of a Startup," *Harvard Business Review,* July–August 2019; and "Structure That's Not Stifling," *Harvard Business Review*, May–June 2018.

188 *refrain from punishing employees:* Scholars of workplace courage have advocated for such steps, among others. See, for example, Karin Hurt and David Dye, *Courageous Cultures: How to Build Teams of Micro-Innovators, Problem Solvers, and Customer Advocates* (HarperCollins Leadership, 2020); James R. Detert and Ethan R. Burris, "Leadership Behavior and Employee Voice: Is the Door Really Open?," *Academy of Management Journal* 50, no. 4 (2007): 869–84.

189 *"support any employee decision that puts guests":* Deshpandé and Raina, "The Ordinary Heroes of the Taj," 5.

190 *"extraordinary candor helps us improve faster":* "Netflix Culture," Netflix.

190 *rules intended to "prevent irrevocable disaster":* My account of Netflix draws heavily on Ranjay Gulati, Allison Ciechanover, and Jeff Huizinga, "Netflix: A Creative Approach to Culture and Agility," Harvard Business School Case Study N1-420-055, September 2019, 9.

190 *"(almost) no rules rule":* The company's culture memo traditionally included this

phrase, although leaders have removed it from the 2024 version. See "Netflix Culture," Netflix. Also, Jessica Toonkel, "Netflix Is Rethinking Employee Freedom, a Core Tenet of Its Vaunted Culture," *Wall Street Journal*, March 15, 2024, https://www.wsj.com/business/media/netflix-is-rethinking-employee-freedom-a-core-tenet-of-its-vaunted-culture-a33f78e5.

191 *"far superior recipe for long-term success"*: "Netflix Culture," Netflix.

191 *autonomy that the organization formally grants them*: Amy C. Edmondson, *The Fearless Organization: Creating Psychological Safety in the Workplace for Learning, Innovation, and Growth* (Hoboken, NJ: John Wiley & Sons, Inc., 2019), 181–82.

192 *"thoughts, motivations, and behaviors"*: Lakshmi Ramarajan, Nancy P. Rothbard, and Steffanie L. Wilk, "Discordant vs. Harmonious Selves: The Effects of Identity Conflict and Enhancement on Sales Performance in Employee-Customer Interactions," *Academy of Management Journal* 60, no. 6 (2017): 2208–238, 2208. Some have observed that identity penetrates into "the deepest level of our sensemaking and understanding." Dennis A. Gioia, "Organizational Identity as an Emerging Perennial Domain," in *The SAGE Handbook of New Approaches in Management and Organization*, ed. Daved Barry and Hans Hansen (London: SAGE Publications Ltd, 2008), 63–65, esp. 64. Quoted in Dennis A. Gioia, Shubha D. Patvardhan, Aimee L. Hamilton, and Kevin G. Corley, "Organizational Identity Formation and Change," *Academy of Management Annals* 7, no. 1 (2013): 123–93, esp. 125.

192 *might reflect beliefs about the group*: Scholars differ in how they think about organizational identity. Some see such identity as residing in "institutional claims, available to members, about central, enduring and distinctive properties of their organization." Others see organizational identity as more diffuse, something that the group collectively creates via "shared beliefs and understandings about central and relatively permanent features of an organization." Davide Ravasi and Majken Schultz, "Responding to Organizational Identity Threats: Exploring the Role of Organizational Culture," *Academy of Management Journal* 49, no. 3 (2006): 433–58, esp. 434.

192 *"enduring commitment to excellence"*: "The Taj Mahal Palace, Mumbai," Taj Hotels, https://www.tajhotels.com/en-in/hotels/taj-mahal-palace-mumbai.

192 *"a mantra that we hold ourselves to"*: "Why Courage Counts," Pfizer Newsroom, July 25, 2020, https://www.pfizer.com/news/announcements/why-courage-counts.

193 *"Courage at Our Core"*: Mike Uth, "Showing Courage at Work Can Shift Your Company Culture," Progressive Careers, May 2021, https://www.progressive.com/careers/life/courage-at-work/.

193 *a "food revolution"*: Gulati, *Deep Purpose*, 104 and chapter 5 generally.

193 *motivation and performance at work*: Ramarajan et al., "Discordant Vs. Harmonious Selves." For more on multiple identities, see Ramarajan, "Past, Present and Future Research on Multiple Identities."

NOTES [273

- 194 *"extreme, pro-group behavior":* Swann Jr. et al., "When Group Membership Gets Personal."
- 194 *"everyone on our staff were deeply committed":* Karambir Kang, interview with the author, February 15, 2019.
- 194 *"just like in a war zone":* Mallika Jagad, interview with the author, February 25, 2019.
- 194 *"sense of belonging is very strong at the Taj":* Mallika Jagad, interview with the author, February 25, 2019.
- 195 *"The Few. The Proud":* Jeff Schogol, "Marine Corps May Replace 'The Few, The Proud' as Its Recruiting Slogan," *Marine Corps Times*, September 26, 2016, https://www.marinecorpstimes.com/news/your-marine-corps/2016/09/26/marine-corps-may-replace-the-few-the-proud-as-its-recruiting-slogan/. See also Victor H. Krulak, *First to Fight: An Inside View of the U.S. Marine Corps* (Annapolis, MD: Naval Institute Press, 1984).
- 195 *"Corps emphasizes what we call the intangibles":* Major General William J. Bowers, interview with the author, July 29, 2024.
- 195 *inculcates shared values that define the Marine Corps:* Major General William J. Bowers, interview with the author, July 29, 2024.
- 195 *"embark on a fresh start":* Major General William J. Bowers, interview with the author, July 29, 2024.
- 196 *"connect the present to the past":* Major General William J. Bowers, interview with the author, July 29, 2024.
- 196 *"reinjected with our core values":* Major General William J. Bowers, interview with the author, July 29, 2024.
- 196 *"go through thick and thin together":* Mallika Jagad, interview with the author, February 25, 2019.
- 197 *"differentiate it from the competition":* Deshpandé and Raina, "The Ordinary Heroes of the Taj," 6.

EPILOGUE

- 201 *"fine striped silk shirt":* John Williams, "In Search of Gandhi's London," https://www.mkgandhi.org/articles/in-search-of-Gandhis-london.php.
- 202 *sitting back down:* M. K. Gandhi, *An Autobiography: Or The Story of My Experiments with Truth*, trans. Mahadev Desai, introduced with notes by Tridip Suhrud, foreword by Ashis Nandy (New Haven: Yale University Press, 2018), 138–39.
- 202 *wouldn't come out:* Chester Bowles, "What Negroes Can Learn from Ghandi?," https://www.mkgandhi.org/articles/negroes&g.php.
- 202 *so fearful was he:* Charles R. Disalvo, "How the Law Changed Gandi," Thinking of Gandhi, https://www.india-seminar.com/2014/662/662_charles_r_disalvo.htm.

202 *"colonization" of the mind:* For more on Frantz Fanon's thought, see his book *The Wretched of the Earth*, trans. Richard Philcox (1961; reprint, New York: Grove Press).

202 *"British Empire":* Joe Bubar, "The Legacy of Gandhi," *Upfront*, Scholastic, September 2, 2019, https://upfront.scholastic.com/issues/2019-20/090219/the-legacy-of-gandhi.html?language=english#1240L.

203 *Cesar Chavez*: Nishi Malhotra, "20 Greatest World Leaders and Thinkers Who Were Inspired by Mahatma Gandhi," *Better India*, October 2, 2015, https://thebetterindia.com/35422/20-greatest-world-leaders-and-thinkers-who-were-inspired-by-mahatma-gandhi/.

203 *"not to shed a single tear":* Neera Chandhoke, "Gandhi Taught Masses How to Conquer Fear," *Tribune*, January 16, 2025, https://www.tribuneindia.com/news/comment/gandhi-taught-masses-how-to-conquer-fear-474747/.

203 *lead the ongoing resistance:* Padmini Sengupta Rao, *Sarojini Naidu: A Biography* (New York: Asia Publishing House, 1966).

203 *"neither jail nor death":* "Indian Army Is Prepared for Assault at Dharsana," *Bakersfield Californian* (Bakersfield, California), May 14, 1930, 2, as cited in Ranjay Gulati and Malini Sen, "Sarojini Naidu: Ahead of Her Time," Harvard Business School Case Study N9-423-003, August 9, 2024.

203 *"full moral responsibility":* "Mrs Naidu's Statement," *Times of India*, May 24, 1930, as cited in Gulati and Sen, "Sarojini Naidu."

204 *"how much he changed":* Glynis Board, "Gandhi's Life as a Lawyer Revealed," West Virgina Public Broadcasting, January 17, 2014, https://wvpublic.org/gandhis-life-as-a-lawyer-revealed/. See also Charles DiSalvo, *The Man Before the Mahatma: M.K. Gandhi, Attorney at Law* (New Delhi: Random House India, 2012).

205 *panic attacks:* "Simone Biles, an Unexpected Advocate for Mental Health," Pennsylvania Psychiatric Institute, https://ppimhs.org/newspost/simone-biles-an-unexpected-advocate-for-mental-health/.

205 *as of 2023:* Jo Gunston, "Simone Biles: All Titles, Records and Medals—Complete List," Olympics, October 8, 2023, https://www.olympics.com/en/news/simone-biles-all-titles-records-medals-complete-list.

205 *online course:* Simone Biles, "Overcoming Fear," MasterClass, https://www.masterclass.com/classes/simone-biles-teaches-gymnastics-fundamentals/chapters/overcoming-fear.

205 *downright terrified:* Elle Reeve, "Simone Biles and 'the Twisties': How Fear Affects the Mental Health and Physical Safety of Gymnasts," CNN Sports, July 29, 2021, https://www.cnn.com/2021/07/28/us/simone-biles-olympics-gymnastics-physical-mental-health/index.html; Olympic Talk, "Simone Biles Overcame Tears, Fears for a No-Regrets Gymnastics Comeback," NBC Sports, May 16, 2024, https://www.nbcsports.com/olympics/news/simone-biles-gymnastics-comeback-olympics.

205 *"national embarrassment":* Maia Niguel Hoskin, "2021 Was the Year Simone Biles Stood Up for Herself and the Mental Health of Black Women," *Forbes*, January 3, 2022, https://www.forbes.com/sites/maiahoskin/2022/01/01/the-good-the-bad-the-odd-stories-that-impacted-people-of-color-in-2021/.

205 *"an Olympic game":* Lindsay Kimble, "Simone Biles Ends Her 2024 Olympic Games with Four Medals: 'I've Accomplished Way More Than My Wildest Dreams,'" *People*, August 5, 2024, https://people.com/simone-biles-wins-four-medals-2024-olympics-8690143.

206 *as first lady:* "Anna Eleanor Roosevelt," White House, https://georgewbush-whitehouse.archives.gov/history/firstladies/ar32.html.

206 *lack of confidence:* Louise Gannon, "Jessica Alba: 'I'd Definitely Go for the Shy, Nerdy Type of Guy,'" *Daily Mail*, October 27, 2007, https://www.dailymail.co.uk/home/moslive/article-489884/Jessica-Alba-Id-definitely-shy-nerdy-type-guy.html; Maria Yagoda, "Shawn Mendes, Lady Gaga & More Stars Who've Opened Up About the Bullying They Faced as Kids," *People*, November 11, 2022, https://people.com/celebrity/celebrities-who-were-bullied-as-kids/.

207 *"not do otherwise":* Nelson Mandela, *Long Walk to Freedom: The Autobiography of Nelson Mandela* (Boston: Little, Brown and Company, 1995), 95.

INDEX

active inertia, 94
Adams, Nancy E., 29
Adele, 117
adversity, shared, 141–144
The Aeneid (Virgil), 125–126, 169
agency, 8–10, 12, 31–33, 83–84, 120, 138, 144, 151, 187–191, 214–215
Alba, Jessica, 206
Algebra Project, 158
algorithms, quantifying risk with, 19–20
Amundsen, Roald, 70
amygdala, xxxiv
anger, xxxiii
appraisal support, 80–81
Aristotle, xxi, xxxiv
Asch, Solomon E., xxxvi–xxxvii
Ashesi University, 52–55, 66, 133, 161
Atran, Scott, 136–137
attentional deployment, 119–121, 220
Awuah, Patrick, 50–55, 56, 62, 66, 161, 206

Baldwin, Doug, 146
Bandura, Albert, 29, 31, 32, 38, 44, 48

The Beatles, 66
beginner's mind, 108–110, 220
belonging, sense of, 134–140, 152–153, 194–195
Bennis, Warren, xxvii
Biden, Joe, 131
Biles, Simone, 204–205
Binder, Lon, 150–151
bin Laden, Osama, 6, 7
BlackBerry, 184–186
BlackRock, 19
Blumenthal, Neil, 150
bold; boldness. *See* courage
Bondarenko, Yulia, 45
Borschberg, André, 77
Boston Marathon bombing, xxxi–xxxii
bounded rationality, 21
Bowers, William (Bill), 143, 195–196
Bridgestone, 95
British Airways, 122–123
Brown, Brené, xxxiii, 169
Bryant, Bear, 155
Bundelkhandi, Kavita, 75–76
Burdette, Robert J., xli
Bush, George W., xxxi
bystander effect, xxxviii, 90, 214

calm. *See* emotional regulation
capability, perception of, 33–37, 48–49
career goals, 108
Carroll, Pete, 145–147
certainty, sense of, 8–9, 17
Chaney, James, 159
character, xxi, xxv
charisma
    crafting and communicating heroic quests, 158–162, 222
    creating aura of approachability, 165–166
    cultivating, 157–158, 222–223
    encouraging deep personal devotion to heroic quests, 163–168, 222
    evoking strength amid hardship, 168–174, 222–223
    in leaders, 155–157
    problems with notion of, 156–157, 174
Chaudhary, Aisha, 123–124
Chavez, Cesar, 203
Chen, John, 184–185
Chernobyl nuclear disaster, 96, 107
choice, 187–188, 189
Churchill, Winston, 154–155, 157, 172
Civil Rights Act (1964), 158, 173
civil rights movement, 135–136, 158–168, 173
clan, 134, 138, 140, 153
Clausewitz, Carl von, xi
climate cafes, 115
Clinton, Hillary, xxxi
Colbert, Stephen, 119–120
collective courage, xxvii, 62–65, 126, 133–134, 152–153, 169
collective identity, xxv, 132–140, 144–147, 221–222
Collins, Jim, 60

comedy, 112–114, 119
community, 132–140
comprehension
    acting and thinking as you go, 95–98
    beginner's mind, 108–110, 220
    sensemaking, 98–108, 219
confidence. *See* self-confidence; self-efficacy
control, 8–9, 12–13, 42
coping mechanisms
    humor, 112–114
    magical thinking, 11–15, 214–215
    risk-hunting, 16–27, 215
    uncertainty mitigated by, 214–215
Costa Concordia (ship), xxxii
courage
    as an action, xxiii
    acts of, xxii
    defined, xxii–xxiii, 213
    forms of, xlii
    historic examples of, xxi
    as a learned behavior, xix
    morality and, 55–56
    as a personality trait, xix–xxii
    playbook, 213–224
    as a virtue, xvii, xxiii
courageous followers, 173–174
courageous mindset, xix, xxvii, 32–33
Couric, Katie, 34
COVID pandemic, xxiv–xxv, 86, 205
cowardice
    character and, xxv
    cultures of, xxxviii–xl, 197–198, 214
    defined, xxxi–xxxii, 213–214
    examples of, xxxi–xxxii
    good cowards, xl–xliii
    peer pressure and, xxxvi–xxxvii, 214
    timidity, xxxiv–xxxvi

Crean, Thomas, 69–70
crisis management, xvi–xvii
Culp, Larry, 47

Danaher, 46–47
Danone, 193
decision-making, 166
deep purpose, 148
de-fusion, 147–148
detachment from emotions, 169–170
Devi, Meera, 74–76
Dion, Celine, 117
disaster syndrome, 93
Discovery expedition, 71
disruptive innovation, 94
Djokovic, Novak, 81
Dudley Docker (lifeboat), 67
Durkheim, Émile, 12
Dvorak, Dudley, 118

earthquakes, 95–96, 100–101
Edison, Thomas, 26
Edmondson, Amy, xxxix, 191
emotional regulation
    attentional deployment, 119–121, 220
    collective courage and, 126
    detachment, 169–170
    evoking strength amid hardship, 168–174
    reframing, 121–124, 220–221
    rituals, 116–119, 220
    in times of fear, xxvii, 116
Endurance expedition, 68–71
environmental cues, 102–105

Faber, Emmanuel, 193
Facebook, 85–87
faith, uncertainty mitigated by, 9–15
Fanon, Frantz, 202

fear(s)
    absence of, xix
    Aristotle on, xxxiv
    courage and, xix–xx
    culture of, xl
    easing with rituals, 116–119
    fear equation, 8
    as instinctual, xxxv–xxxvi
    limiting with attentional deployment, 119–121
    minimizing with humor, 112–114, 119–120
    outwitting, 115–124
    reframing, 121–124
    of snakes, 29
    social pressures and, xxxvii–xxxviii
    triggers, xxiii, xxxi–xxxii, xxxix, 91–93
feedback, 79–81, 188, 190
felt responsibility, 56
fight, flight, or freeze reactions, xxxiv–xxxv, 90–95, 218–219
Fink, Larry, 19
Firestone, 94–95, 109
Fitch, Dennis, 118–119
flight anxiety courses, 122–123
football, 42–44, 120, 145–147
foot-in-the-door approach, 41–42
Freedom Summer, 135–136, 159–162, 165, 166, 168, 173
freedom within a framework, 166
freeze response, 90–95, 218–219
Fugitive Slave Act (1850), 3
Fukushima nuclear disaster, xxii, 95–107, 206
future-proofing, 13, 21

Gaines, Joanna, 206
Gandhi, Mahatma, 164, 201–204, 206
Garrett, Thomas, 14–15
general competency, 39–40

Gervais, Michael, 120
Ghana, 50–55
Gilboa, Dave, 150
Goffman, Erving, 118
Goodman, Andrew, 159
Grant, Adam, xxvi
Green, Logan, 63–65
Gross, James J., 116, 119
Gu, Eileen, 13

Hael, Gary, 187
Harvard Business School, xxii
Haugen, Frances, 85–87, 206
Haynes, Al, 118
Henderson, John, 13
heroic quest(s)
    courageous self-narratives of, 65–66, 217
    crafting and communicating, 158–162
    encouraging deep personal devotion to, 163–168
    evoking strength amid hardship, 168–174
    moral framing of, 55–57, 217
    role-modeling devotion to, 164–165
hero's journey narrative arc, 57–62, 70, 218
Herszenhorn, David M., 60
heuristics, 24–25
Hitler, Adolf, 174
Horowitz, Jeff, 86
Horwitz, Allan, xxxv
Höss, Rudolf, xxxiv
House, Robert, 161, 164
Hudson, Hubert, 71
humor, 112–114, 119
Hurley, Frank, 69
Hurricane Katrina, xxiv
Hurricane Maria, xxiv
hurricanes, xxv, 93

identity
    collective, xxvii, 132–140, 144–147, 221–222
    conflicts, 82–83
    levels of, 132
    organizational, 192–197
    personal, 132, 137, 144–147
    relational, 132, 133
    sense of, xxiii, 132
    social, 81–84
identity fusion
    collective courage and, 152–153
    de-fusion, 147–148
    experience of, 137–140
    extended fusion, 194–197
    leaders fusing to groups, 164–165
    in organizations, 193–194
    power of, 140–141
    shared adversity, 141–144, 221
    spacious collective identity, 144–147, 221–222
    sustaining, 148–151, 222
India, xiii–xv, 74–76, 175–180, 201–204
institutional cowardice, xxxviii–xxxix
instrumental support, 76–78
interaction ritual, 118
International Space Station, 23
Iroquois, 145
Iyer, Akhil, 142

Jagad, Mallika, 175–180, 189, 194–195, 196
Jain, Suma, xxiv–xxv
James Caird (lifeboat), 67–68
Japan, xxii, 95–107
Jim Crow South, 134–136, 159–168
Johnson, Derrick, 158

Kan, Naoto, 107
Kang, Karambir, 178, 179, 180, 194

Kennedy, John F., 155
Khabar Lahariya (newspaper), 74–76, 84
Khomeini, Ayatollah, 89
King, Martin Luther, Jr., 157, 158, 203
Klotz, Adam, xxxvii–xxxviii
knowledge resources, 78–79
Koehn, Nancy, 170

Lai Lai Ballroom & Studio, 129–133, 139–140, 152–153
leaders
    charismatic, 155–156, 161–162, 222–223
    culture of fear, xl
    encouraging voice and choice, 187–189
    inspirational, xxvii, 172–174, 223
    myth of heroic, 156–157
    "playing to win" mindset, 183, 186, 198
    self-sacrificial, 164–165
    taking action in crises, 105–106
    vulnerability, 169
Lessig, Larry, 87
Letterman, David, 112
Lewis, John, 159
Lincoln, Abraham, 157, 170
Lombardi, Vince, 183
loneliness epidemic, 153
"long body" concept, 145
The Lord of the Rings (Tolkien), 206
Lyft, 62–65
Lynch, Marshawn, 146

Ma, Ming Wei, 130
Macron, Emmanuel, 111
magical thinking, 11–15, 214–215

Mandela, Nelson, 207
Marini, Nina, 52–55
Marjory Stoneman Douglas High School, xxxii, 35–37
Martin, George R. R., 65–66
mass shootings, xxxii, 35–37, 130–133
Masuda, Naohiro, 96–107
McAdam, Doug, 135, 137
McCain, John, 155
meal sharing, 125–126
meaning-making, xxv–xxvi
Meizhong, Fan, xxix–xxxi, xxxii, xxxiv, xli–xlii
mental habits, xxiv
mentors, 83–84
Milgram, Stanley, xxxvii
military
    cowardly conduct in, xxxi
    training, 39–40
Miller, William Ian, xli
morality
    courage and, 55–56
    in heroic quest narratives, 55–57, 217
moral potency, 56
Moses, Robert (Bob), 158–168, 171, 172, 173
Mukherji, Abhijit, 179
Mulcahy, Anne, 78–79, 84, 170–171
The Mystery of Courage (Miller), xli

Naidu, Sarojini, 203
narratives
    heroic quests, 55–57, 65–66, 217
    hero's journey structure, 57–62, 70, 218
    individual, xxi–xxii
    inspirational, 62–65
    magical thinking, 11, 14–15

narratives (*continued*)
  power of, 53–55
  risk mitigation, 22
National Aeronautics and Space
    Administration (NASA), 23, 39
NATO, 112–113
Navalny, Alexei, 58–61, 62
Nazi regime, xxxix
Netflix, 189–191, 198
Nimrod expedition, 71
9/11 terror attacks, xxxi
Nobles, Ernest, 164
Nohria, Nitin, xx
nuclear plants, xxiii, 95–107

Obama, Barack, 6
Olympics, 205
ophidiophobia, 29–31
optimal distinctiveness, 146
organizational culture
  building courage into
      organization identity, 192–
      197, 223–224
  collective courage in, 175–180,
      188–189
  courage established as behavioral
      norm, 182–186, 223
  courageous, 181–182
  cowardice in, xxxvii–xl, 197–198
  creating space for brave conduct,
      187–191, 223
  defined, 181
organizations, 180–181, 182
O'Shannessy, Craig, 81
overconfidence, 48–49, 217
ownership, sense of, xxxvii–xxxviii
oxytocin, 53

Paulson, Ronnelle, 135, 137
peer pressure, xxxvi–xxxviii, 214
performance feedback, 79–81

Peterson, Scot, 35–37, 38
Petit, Philippe, 17–18, 19, 20
Pfizer, 192
Piccard, Bertrand, 77
Plato, 168–169
process-focused approach, 42–44
Progressive, 192–193
psychological safety, xxxiv
public speaking, 120–121
Putin, Vladimir, 59–61, 112–113

Ramarajan, Lakshmi, 144
realistic optimism, 183
Reardon, Kathleen K., 6
Records, William Roy, 118
Reese, Henry, 90
Reese, Linda, 29
reframing, 121–124, 220–221
representativeness heuristic, 24–25
resources
  intangible, 78–79, 86–87
  for self-efficacy, 46–47
  tangible, 76–78, 86
ridesharing, 62–65
risk-hunting
  everyday, 20–22
  improvising better to handle
      unforeseen threats, 24–27,
      215
  limiting scope of risk mitigation,
      22, 215
  reducing scope of planned action,
      22–23, 215
  as an uncertainty mitigator,
      16–27
risk(s)
  fear-triggering, xxxiv–xxxvi,
      xliii
  mitigating, 4–5, 20–27
  organizational culture and,
      xxxvii–xl

"playing not to lose" mindset, 183
"playing to win" mindset, 183
quantifying, 19–20
risk-benefit analysis, 6
uncertainty vs., 7–9
See also risk-hunting
rituals, 116–119, 220
Robb Elementary School, xxii
Roosevelt, Eleanor, 206
Rumsfeld, Donald, 7
Rushdie, Salman, 89–92, 95, 110
Russia, 58–61, 111–114

Saban, Nick, xxii, 42–44, 120
satisficing, 21
Schilpzand, Pauline, 41
school shootings, xxxii, 35–37
Schwerner, Michael, 159
Scott, Robert, 69
self-confidence
   cultivating, xxvii, 31–33, 215, 217
   going small to go big, 41–44, 216
   securing tools needed to perform, 46–47, 216
   seeing strengths through others' eyes, 44–46, 216
self-efficacy
   benefits of, 49
   cultivating, 31–33, 215
   foot-in-the-door approach, 41–42
   perception of capability, 33–37, 48–49
   process-focused approach, 41–42
   securing tools for, 46–47, 76–78
   skill-building, 32–33, 37–40, 215–216
   social persuasion and, 44–46
self-esteem, 83–84
self-narratives. *See* narratives
self-worth, 83–84
sensemaking
   beginner's mind, 108–110, 220
   in everyday life, 107–108
   noticing and interpreting cues, 102–105, 219
   process of, 99
   taking action, 105–106, 219
   trigger alertness, 100–102, 219
Sensemaking in Organizations (Weick), 99
sense of being, 132
Servant of the People (TV show), 113
Shackleton, Ernest, 67–71, 84
Simmel, Georg, 81–82
Simon, Herbert, 20–21
skill-building, 32–33, 37–40, 215–216
The Sky Is Pink (film), 123
snake phobias, 29–31
social identity, 81–84
social persuasion, 44–46
social relationships
   community, 132–140
   conformity within, xxxvi–xxxvii
   encouragement from, 44–46
   identity and, 81–84
   importance of, 72–73
   and sense of self as courageous, 82–83
   support squads, 72–81, 218
Solar Impulse 2 (airplane), 77
speaking up, xxxv–xxxvi
Stancomb Wills (lifeboat), 67–71
Star Ballroom Dance Studio, 129–130
startups, 149–151, 187–188
status quo bias, 93
Student Nonviolent Coordinating Committee (SNCC), 163–164

INDEX

Sullenberger, C. B. "Sully," 34–35, 36
Sun Tzu, 168–169
support squads
   benefits of, 72–73, 171, 218
   building, 84–88
   emotional lift from, 73–76
   feedback from, 79–81
   intangible resources offered by, 78–79, 86–87
   and sense of self as courageous, 82–83
   Shackleton's, 69–72
   tangible resources offered by, 76–78, 86
Swann, William B., Jr., 137, 139, 148

Taj Mahal Palace, 175–180, 182, 188–189, 192, 194, 196–197, 198, 206
Talking to the Enemy (Arran), 136–137
Tata, Ratan, 179–180
team-building, 134, 141–151
temperament, xxi–xxv, xxxv
tennis, 80–81
terrorism, xxxi–xxxii, 175–180
thought patterns, xxvi, 60–61
timidity, xxxiv–xxxvi
tires, 94–95
T-Mobile, 185
training, 32–33, 37–40
Tran, Huu Can, 129–131
Tsay, Brandon, 130–133, 136, 139–140, 152–153, 206
tsunamis, 95–96, 100–101
Tubman, Harriet, 3–5, 7–8, 14–15, 28, 206
"turtling up," 72

Uber, 62–64
Ukraine, xxii, 13, 45, 96, 107, 111–114, 119, 206

uncertainty
   certainty of, 27–28
   faith as a mitigator for, 9–15
   as a fear trigger, xxiv, 91–93
   in a recession, xx–xxi
   risk-hunting as a mitigator for, 16–27
   risk vs., 6, 7–9
   sensemaking in times of, 101–102
Underground Railroad, 3–5
United Airlines Flight 232, 117–118
University of Alabama, xxii, 43
US Air Force (USAF), 23
US Airways Flight 1549, 34–35
US Marine Corps (USMC), 39–40, 141–143, 195–196, 198

valor, xxi
values, xxxii, 55–56, 195–196
Virgil, 125–126
Virts, Terry, 23, 39, 40
voice, 187–188, 189
Voting Rights Act (1965), 173
vulnerability, xxxiii, 169

Wallace, Anthony F. C., 93
On War (Clausewitz), xxi
Warby Parker, 150–151
Weber, Max, 156, 187
Weick, Karl, 99, 102–104, 106, 207
"What Makes a Group Worth Dying For" (Swann), 139
whistleblowing, 85–87
Why Courage Matters (McCain), 155
Wild, Frank, 71
Williams, Serena, 13
Wilson, Mark, 185
The Wizard of Oz (film), 207

Wolgezogen, Franz, xx
World War II, 154–155
Worline, Monica C., 169
Worsley, Frank, 70–71

Xerox, 78–79, 170–171

Ybarra, Joe, 9–11

Zak, Paul, 53
Zanini, Michele, 187
Zelenskyy, Volodymyr, 111–114
Zimmer, John, 62–65

ABOUT THE AUTHOR

RANJAY GULATI is the Paul R. Lawrence MBA Class of 1942 Professor of Business Administration at Harvard Business School. His pioneering work focuses on unlocking organizational and individual potential—embracing courage, nurturing purpose-driven leaders, driving growth, and transforming businesses. He is the recipient of the 2024 CK Prahalad Award for Scholarly Impact on Practice and is frequently ranked as one of the most-cited scholars in economics and business. *The Economist*, the *Financial Times*, and the *Economist Intelligence Unit* have listed him as among the top handful of business school scholars whose work is most relevant to management practice. He is a Thinkers50 top management scholar, speaks regularly to executive audiences, and serves on the board of several entrepreneurial ventures. He holds a PhD from Harvard University and a master's degree from MIT. He is the author of *Deep Purpose*, and lives in Newton, Massachusetts, with his wife and two children.